MW01031271

Miss America's God

Miss America's God

Faith and Identity in America's Oldest Pageant

Mandy McMichael

BAYLOR UNIVERSITY PRESS

Cover design by Will Brown
Cover image based on a photograph by Omar Tursić, Unsplash
Book design by Savanah N. Landerholm

Figures in the book are included under fair use or courtesy of Wikimedia (1.1, 3.2, 4.2, 4.3); Atlantic City Heritage Collections, Atlantic City Free Public Library (1.2, 2.2); Duke University Special Collections, Alix Kates Shulman Papers, David M. Rubenstein Rare Book & Manuscript Library, Duke University, photograph copyright Alix Kates Shulman, used with permission (1.3); Alamy (2.1); ImageCollect, ©ImageCollect.com/Admedia (3.1); AP Images, Associated Press/AP Photo/Al Chang (4.1); and AP Images, Associated Press/AP Photo/Tom Patrick (5.2).

The Library of Congress has cataloged this book under
ISBN 978-1-4813-1197-7.

Printed in the United States of America on acid-free paper with a minimum of thirty percent recycled content.

For Chad, Cady, and Davis

Contents

Acknowledgments

This book, like most, started with simple questions: Why did the Miss America Pageant seem to have such cultural staying power, and why did participants seem to invoke their religious convictions so often? To the extent that this book offers some answers to these deceptively simple inquiries, it is due to the fact that I have had many conversation partners who have assisted me in providing them. Any project that takes over a decade to complete inevitably incurs a lot of these debts, and I have been especially lucky to have many wonderful teachers, friends, and colleagues alongside me in this work.

Since this project began as a dissertation at Duke, my doctoral advisor, mentor, and, yes, friend Grant Wacker deserves special mention. Grant, I tried to avoid the passive voice and write in a way that honors your charity as a historian. I learned to be sympathetic to my subjects from you, and I hope that shines through here. Thomas Tweed introduced me to religious theory, and encouraged me as I (timidly and sparingly) applied it to my work. The mistakes I have made are mine alone, but any theoretical insights are because of his patient guidance. Tim Tyson, Mark Chaves, and Randy Maddox also provided ample feedback and kindnesses along the way, and I am grateful for the opportunity to learn from such fine scholars.

Among Grant's many gifts was the sense of community he created for his graduate students, one that fostered a spirit of cooperation rather than competition. Kate Bowler, Elesha Coffman, Seth Dowland, Elizabeth Flowers, Jennifer Graber, Brendan Pietsch, Wen Reagan, Sarah Ruble, Angela Tarango,

Heather Vacek, and many others watched pageants, donned tiaras, read drafts, offered loving but firm critiques, and endured innumerable coffee or lunch conversations that should have been casual but turned out to be professional. Sorry, friends. I am especially grateful to Heather for hosting me when I was in Pittsburgh for the Miss Pennsylvania pageant, to Elesha for helping me finish strong, and to Kate whose title idea was far better than any of mine.

I have received tremendous institutional and personal support, both from my graduate school alma mater and the two institutions I have served as a faculty member: Huntingdon College and Baylor University. Duke's graduate school awarded both a summer grant and a Kearns Summer Research Fellowship during my time as a student. A dissertation fellowship from the Louisville Institute also afforded material support for this project, thus enabling me to conduct research and travel that would have proved difficult otherwise. Huntingdon and Baylor provided hospitable academic communities in which to develop as a teacher and scholar, and I could not be more grateful for the long-suffering librarians and colleagues who endured my collegiality during these years. Baylor University funded two years of travel to the Miss America Pageant in Atlantic City. You can imagine the funding request to the dean's office. Special thanks to my department chair, Bill Bellinger, and to Baylor's Associate Dean for Humanities and Social Science, Kimberly Kellison, who both believed in the importance of my work and ensured that I received the necessary funds to complete it.

Of course, institutions are made up of people, and a few deserve special mention here. Deirdre Fulton, Beverly Gaventa, Dennis Horton, Mikeal Parsons, Doug Weaver, Lauren Weber, and David Whitford read drafts, provided strategic counsel as to how best to secure funding for research, protected my time, endured inane pageant trivia, or bought coffee. Your friendship is a gift I do not take for granted. Conversations with other colleagues beyond Baylor also enriched my work: Carol Ann Vaughn Cross, Lynn Disbrow, Elizabeth Hutcheon, David King, Samira Mehta, Maureen Murphy, and Sarah Sours are the very best kind of scholar-friends. And, to my emoji-loving Wabash cohort and my Baylor Summer Faculty Institute cohort, I am forever in your debt for challenging me to become a more creative thinker, teacher, and scholar. To my students, both at Huntingdon and at Baylor, my thanks for sharing your pageant experiences, sending me articles about pageants, and asking probing questions that fueled my research.

Librarians in all of these institutions, my undergraduate alma mater Judson College, and the Atlantic City Free Public Library assisted in the exciting work of archival research, and without them I would have been lost. I am especially indebted to Jackie Morillo at the Atlantic City Free Public Library for helping me sort through their Miss America collection, pulling microfilm and making copies. The delightful conversation was an added bonus.

To all of the pageant participants and parents who welcomed me into your world, thank you. This project would not be nearly as rich without your contributions. Beth Hennings Hutchens, Laura Dutton Guffin, and the late Kimberley Butterworth were extraordinarily hospitable pageant buddies. These "pageant moms" adopted me for life. More importantly, their enthusiasm and friendliness often yielded critical insights into the psychology and sociology of pageants that I would not have garnered on my own.

My life is full of family and friends who have gone out of their way to support me in this project. That they have attended pageants, after-parties, and autograph signings; sent me local pageant news; and even played the Miss America board game all in the name of helping me with my "research" is a testament to their love. My Judson sisters, GA's Gone Bad, and Banana-Crown lunch bunch have kept me sane. My parents, grandparents, and extended family have understood time and time again when I needed to miss family events or be semi-present when they visited. My mother in particular went above and beyond from the Miss America Pageant in Las Vegas to keeping my children so that I could write—no task or ask was too big or too small.

The staff at Baylor University Press has been unfailingly patient and generous with their expertise and time. I could not have asked for a better editor than Carey Newman, without whose encouragement I could not have completed this project. He pushed me to think bigger and dig deeper than I imagined possible. My enthusiasm waned, but his never did. The book is better for it. Indeed, the entire staff of BUP—Cade, David, Jenny, Savanah, and Steffi—provided excellent support throughout the process of bringing this book to fruition.

Finally, this book is dedicated to my family. I have been working on this project in some form for the entirety of my children's lives. Their patience—and Chad's—with my many early mornings, late nights, and weekends of writing has been such a gift to me. Davis, you are a delight, funny and sweet and smart. You have given the best snuggles after long days of writing. Cady, you amaze me with your strong, confident spirit. You are curious, caring, and fiercely loyal. I could not be prouder of you both, and I hope that this book makes you proud. Chad, you are my rock. In our fifteen years of marriage, you have pushed me to be a better wife, mother, teacher, and scholar. This book would not have been possible without your steadfast love and partnership. Thank you for the many sacrifices you made to see me across the finish line. Now, bring on the board games!

Introduction

Miss America has captivated Americans for nearly one hundred years because she gives them everything they want—sex, entertainment, competition, religion, and self-discovery. Perfection poured into a ball gown, she whisks viewers away for an evening of enchantment. Transported out of the messiness and imperfection of their own lives into a world of glitz and glamour, fans and critics alike welcome the escape from reality. Through times of stability and uncertainty, tradition and innovation, virtue and scandal, the Miss America Pageant has carried American aspirations like an oversized bouquet of red roses.

The term "pageant" conjures up a variety of images for Americans.[1] Some imagine crying winners receiving a crown while humbly thanking the judges. Others hear Bert Parks singing "There She Is" as the newly crowned Miss America takes her first walk down the runway. Still others recall ballerinas en pointe, opera singers, or marimba players. Some even claim a favorite Miss America: Bess Myerson, Lee Meriwether, or Heather Whitestone, and almost everyone knows someone or knows someone who knows someone who competed in the Miss America Pageant system. Indeed, one would be hard-pressed to find an American with no recollection of a beauty contest.[2] In many places pageants have been, it seems, as American as apple pie.

To be sure, not everyone has liked these competitions. Tension, controversy, and the struggle to survive amidst critiques and protests define American pageant history. For example, after a promising start in the 1920s, the Miss America Pageant ceased temporarily owing in part to objections from religious groups. Through the years, it received complaints from women's rights groups, Civil Rights organizations, and Christian denominations.[3] And still the pageant survived. In the words of sportswriter Frank Deford,

1

"Maligned by one segment of America, adored by another, misunderstood by about all of it, Miss America still flows like the Mississippi, drifts like amber waves of grain, sounds like the crack of a bat on a baseball, tastes like Mom's apple pie, and smells like dollar bills."[4] Americans felt strongly about pageants.

Miss America reinvented itself on numerous occasions to remain not only acceptable but also relevant to potential contestants and society at large. The pageant persisted in part because of this willingness and ability to adapt. And because of the pervasiveness of pageants in American culture, their presence and influence largely have been considered axiomatic.[5] But a long-lived cultural icon like Miss America demands interpretation.[6] The competition offers a little explored window onto American culture that reveals a complicated cocktail of all Americans hold most dear. Perhaps most unexpected, the Miss America Pageant functioned as a site for religious expression and self-discovery for many Christian contestants.[7] And, equally surprising, their churches validated their pageant participation.

Far more obvious, pageants reflected the beauty-obsessed culture in which they emerged. As Miss America evolved from a bathing revue in Atlantic City to a nationally televised competition with talent, interviews, and community service requirements, it consistently privileged those whom society deemed most beautiful.[8] As Albert Marks Jr., a former pageant chairman, remarked regarding the pageant, "The greatest spectator sport in America is not football or baseball. It's watching pretty girls, and that won't change."[9] Gender roles and standards of decency did change, however. Thus organizers occupied a thin space in which they heralded expanding women's roles in a program that benefited from women's continued objectification, and, some might argue, exploitation.[10] The appreciation of beauty celebrated by the pageant flirted with the boundaries of respectable society, but never crossed them. These bathing beauties, they claimed, were virtuous women who were paragons to be admired and emulated.

According to contestants, sponsors, pageant organizers, and other supporters, there was far more going on in the Miss America Pageant than sex appeal. In fact, for many of the individuals involved, the "sexiness" of it was an afterthought if it was a thought at all. Instead, pageants offered opportunities to gain professional experience through interviews, appearances, and performances. They encouraged civic engagement through required community service platforms. They allowed individuals to grow in, and live out, Christian faith.[11] The contests sponsored the chance to compete on a national stage against others embodying those ideals deemed "most American." And, most important for some, the Miss America Organization provided much-needed scholarship money for college.[12] In short, it was not all in the hips.

To be sure, an individual's physical attributes often contributed to her success or failure in the Miss America system. Contestants noted the rigorous training schedules involved to get their bodies competition-ready. A regimented diet and exercise schedule set by a personal trainer was not uncommon. Responses to the physical portion of the competition were as varied as any other sporting event. Miss America 1973, Terry Meeuwsen, said that she felt like a racehorse groomed and ready for a race.[13] Miss America 1980, Cheryl Prewitt, confessed that her exercise team targeted a few fat places on her thighs. She gladly stuck to the schedule because she wanted her legs to be the best on stage as a testament to God's healing touch on her life.[14] A few lamented this portion of the competition, with one Miss Alabama contestant citing it as "unnecessary" and claiming "they show us off like cattle. There are other ways to see if we are physically fit." When asked to recount her least favorite thing about the pageant, another Miss Alabama Pageant participant declared, "Probably walking in a swimsuit in front of about 2,000 people!"[15] Still others saw this portion of the competition as something they had to endure in order to get what they saw as the benefits of the program as a whole. Many, however, perhaps even the majority, found no need to explain anything. Disciplining their bodies was simply one of the many steps they took to participate in this life-enhancing organization.

And yet contestants were quick to note that the swimsuit competition was not why they entered. Most were not female bodybuilders or figure competitors. They were athletes, musicians, and dancers. They were typical college students who saw in pageants an opportunity to make friends, have fun, and achieve their goals. They were aspiring doctors, lawyers, teachers, news anchors, and ministers.[16] In other words, for its more than ninety-five years of history the Miss America Pageant served as a vehicle through which many young women ages seventeen through twenty-five sought to make sense of themselves and the world around them. It offered them access to a stage and a microphone they did not believe was available to them in other venues. Thus, while much changed in the nation and in the pageant over its history, one thing stayed the same: the consistency with which pageant winners discussed their purpose in seeking the title. As part of their narratives, these pageant participants provided explanations of the merits of beauty competitions.[17] Some even employed the language of vocation, with Miss America 1997, Tara Holland, declaring, "As some people are called to be missionaries, some are called to be pastors. And then some are called to do pageants. And

I was one of those that was called to do pageants."[18] For Holland and many others, the contests offered more than the hope for a crown.

The Miss America Organization (MAO), for its part, claimed a distinction as a program that benefited young women. In fact, it billed itself as the largest provider of scholarships to young women in the world.[19] The MAO promised more than scholarships and some bedazzled headgear, however. At various times, they promoted the girl-next-door, the well-rounded woman, the scholar, and the modern woman. Always they strived to promote a form of womanhood acceptable to American society, "your ideal" as Bernie Wayne's famous song put it.[20] In the twenty-first century, the MAO solidified its "ideal" by naming the four "points" of the crown. Scholarship represented one point on the Miss America crown, but Miss America hopefuls were also expected to demonstrate style, service, and success.

The four points—the S's—of the crown played out in the various phases of competition. Contestants at every level in the MAO participated in interview, talent, lifestyle and fitness in swimsuit, evening wear, and onstage question.[21] In addition, each young woman adopted a community service "platform" to which she dedicated her time. Many, if not most, young women chose an organization or cause to which they had a personal connection. For example, Miss America 1999, Nicole Johnson, who suffered from diabetes, championed Diabetes Awareness.[22] Some women like Caitlin Brunell, Miss Alabama 2014, started their own nonprofits.[23] Others raised money for existing charities from the American Heart Association to the Children's Miracle Network. Almost all volunteered time, talent, and money to promote their cause.[24] Competing, for many women, was more than just a hobby. It was a lifestyle that involved traveling every weekend, time-consuming preparations, and expending resources financial and otherwise.

But even though the Miss America Pageant was the oldest and perhaps the best known among such competitions in the United States, it was not alone. Some pageants mimicked the Miss America competition; others defined themselves against it. From the Miss USA pageant to Miss American Teenager and Distinguished Young Women, numerous organizations claimed to celebrate and reward various aspects of femininity, and by extension, "womanhood." In fact, the Miss America Organization even started a companion program—Miss America's Outstanding Teen—for thirteen- to seventeen-year-olds.[25] But the demand for pageants did not begin at adolescence. Countless competitions targeted elementary-aged girls, toddlers, and even infants.[26] And, at each rung of the ladder, there was a demand for sponsors, coaches, hair, makeup, spray tans, and wardrobe—not to mention more questionable practices like eyelash extensions, pageant flippers (false teeth), and breast enhancements.[27] Retailers marketed pageant gowns, shoes, hair extensions, and even a spray adhesive, casually referred to as butt glue, to keep swimsuits from riding up. Pageants were not just exercises in self-discovery; they were big business.

At one time, state and local Miss America pageants were sponsored by organizations like the Rotary Club, Jaycees, and Elks.[28] Local businesses provided jewelry, dresses, and makeup to winners in addition to free services like tanning, dentistry, and haircuts. Far more placed ads in the program book to wish their contestant luck. Schools, banks, and churches crafted loving messages of support that accompanied contestant headshots. In many places, pageants were community events. A longtime Miss America sponsor likened pageantry to "an evangelical movement. People in towns all across the country are caught up in show business. It's more exciting than their own lives, more fun than golf. In every little town they're pulling for their girl, hoping she gets to the top."[29] The expansiveness of pageant culture is the reality that allows the Miss America Pageant to flourish almost one hundred years after its humble beginnings on the beach of Atlantic City.

Nowhere was this more the case than in the American South and Midwest. There, beauty pageants dotted the landscape.[30] Small towns boasted Labor Day queens, peach festival queens, and peanut festival queens—not to mention the countless high school and county fair competitions hungry to crown their own girl-next-door. In some places, citizens heralded the local pageant winner's achievements like they discussed the high school football star. In states like Alabama, Mississippi, and South Carolina, pageant winners starred in local television commercials, attended ribbon cuttings, and donned billboards on the side of the interstate. In essence, they were local celebrities.[31] Many little girls looked up to pageant winners and dreamed of the crown they might one day wear. As a former executive director of Miss Mississippi recounted, "In Mississippi, it's tradition for the best girls to come out for the Pageant. In Mississippi, the best girls just *want* to be Miss Mississippi."[32] Girls attended events at churches, youth retreats, and schools to hear Miss Pageant Winner share her pageant story. They took baton or ballet or learned to play an instrument so they had a "performable" talent. And parents, mothers especially, did everything they could to help their little girl's dreams come true.[33] The grooming, the conditioning if you will, began early with three-year-olds in makeup learning to walk in heels and flash the judges a curtsy and a smile.

Many of these girls wanted nothing more than to be pretty, beautiful, or sexy, entering pageants to see these aspirations validated. Yet this sexualization of young girls in pageants merely mimicked that of the wider culture, or, perhaps more aptly, imbibed it. That is, Miss America, and the host of Miss America preliminary pageants it represents, reflects American culture. American girls were taught at a young age to give and desire praise for their beauty, learning early the value of a pretty face and a flirtatious gaze.[34] While child beauty pageants offered one way through which adults encouraged young girls to use their bodies to please others rather than using them to achieve something, young women learned to value their looks over their abilities in a myriad of ways. The media bombarded young girls with messages that their looks were of primary importance. From the Disney princess craze to Barbie dolls to Bratz dolls, marketers (along with parents) provided young girls countless opportunities to focus on the importance of achieving the right look. Even *Sesame Street* struggled with female characters, noting that "audiences seem to judge them by different standards than the males."[35] Some might believe that the gendering of a puppet is of little consequence, but a beauty-obsessed culture that demanded physical perfection even from its foam-and-felt children's characters speaks volumes.[36] Such conditioning through media and marketing failed to result in the empowered young women that one would expect in the twentieth and twenty-first centuries. In fact, "by age twelve, girls place greater emphasis on attractiveness than competence."[37] Miss America, then, represents just one space among many that rewards that which American culture has deemed valuable. And yet an exploration of Miss America reveals it to be more than a celebration of beauty and sex.

Examining the Miss America competition offers entry into a complex pageant culture that has pervaded much of American culture. To take it one step further, Miss America *is* American culture, and southern culture at that.[38] Investigating the pageant proves key to understanding America qua America. Equally important, studying pageants provides an opportunity to analyze women's experience, including women's religious experience.[39] In peeking behind the rhinestone curtain to the women at center stage, one discovers both obvious and surprising reasons for its sustained success. The Miss America Pageant reflected America's obsessions with beauty, entertainment, and competition. It also represented a site of civil religion and operated for many participants as a vehicle for their religious expression and self-discovery.

In many respects, the role of religion in the pageant defies explanation. Or, rather, evidence does not suggest one all-encompassing answer. Church and contestant used the pageant to form faith and identity, and the pageant used church and contestant to remain relevant in a society increasingly suspicious of pageants. This proved a mutually beneficial relationship for church and pageant even when the two were seemingly at odds with one another. In other words, like most instances where sacred and secular meet, the relationship between faith and pageant is not a simple one. While the runway seems an unlikely place to encounter God, and an even stranger place to preach, God has been no stranger to the stage.[40]

A variety of women participate in pageants and many declared they were not the "stereotypical pageant type," going to great lengths to demonstrate how they broke the mold. Women claimed that pageants empowered them, but pageants utilize a system whose very premise is—arguably—the objectification of women. Understanding this paradox is key to understanding the impact of American culture on the lived experience of women, both those who participate in pageants and those well outside the pageant arena. In short, pageants are complicated sites of cultural ritual that deserve sustained scholarly attention. They project American values with a grin and a wave.

A Note on Methodology

To capture the complexity of the story, I found it necessary to employ both historical and ethnographic research. Two courses shaped my ethnographic research profoundly: "Approaches to the Study of Religion in the United States" with Professor Thomas Tweed and "The Art of Ethnography" with Professor Glenn Hinson, both at the University of North Carolina, Chapel Hill. In the first, I wrote a first draft of how I planned to conduct field research at the Miss Alabama Pageant, including an initial survey. In the second, I immersed myself in North Carolina pageant culture for a semester. The assignments for this class gave me the first taste of what actually *doing* and *writing* ethnography was like, and Hinson's emphasis on collaborative ethnography remained the ideal, even though I found it was not always possible. Luke Eric Lassiter's work *The Chicago Guide to Collaborative Ethnography* (Chicago: University of Chicago Press, 2005), especially ch. 6, "Ethnographic Honesty," informed my approach to ethnographic research and pushed me to include my own experience at some points in the narrative. In addition, ch. 1 of Ruth Behar's book *The Vulnerable Observer: Anthropology That Breaks Your Heart* (Boston: Beacon Press, 1996) offered further reflection on the value and danger of including a personal narrative in one's printed research and a reminder that one's personal narrative necessarily affects her field research.

Most notably, my ethnographic work entailed pageant attendance. I frequented numerous beauty pageants at the local, state, and national level for over a decade. Combined, I visited more than thirty-five pageants and watched many others on television. Local pageants were one-day affairs, but state and national contests often lasted three or four nights. All of the local pageants I observed were in either Alabama or North Carolina. The decision to focus on Alabama and North Carolina was largely one of convenience; these were the two states in which I resided during the majority of my research. In addition, it offered me a comparison between two southern states. Most, though not all, were affiliated with the Miss America Organization. Beyond local pageants, I observed state pageants in eight different states and the District of Columbia: Alabama (2006, 2007, 2009, 2010, 2011, 2012, 2014, and 2015), Nevada (2015), North Carolina (2007 and 2008), Ohio (2015), Pennsylvania (2015), Rhode Island (2015), Texas (2016), Utah (2016), and Washington, D.C. (2015). I also traveled to the national pageant on four separate occasions, seeing one Miss America Pageant in Las Vegas, Nevada (2011) and three in Atlantic City, New Jersey (2015, 2017, and 2018). While at the national pageants, I attended some of the auxiliary events, including the "Show Me Your Shoes Parade" (2015, 2017, and 2018), the Miss America 9/11 Military Tribute Concert and Luncheon (2015), the Miracle Mile and Steel Pier Celebration (2015), the Miss America State Title-holder Association's cocktail reception (2017), and the Official Miss America After-Party (2015 and 2017). In 2015 and 2018, I was able to secure a guest pass through connections to Miss Montana (2015) and Miss Texas (2018) to attend the friends and family visitation after the preliminary competition.

Other ethnographic work was more sporadic. I surveyed the Miss Alabama contestants for four years from 2006 to 2009 (see appendix A). Response rates ranged from a low of 14.6 percent in 2007 to a high of 37.5 percent in 2006. Though I spoke with many individuals informally about their (or their daughter's) pageant participation, I conducted formal interviews with only three contestants. Still, I found that all of these encounters, especially friendships forged with a couple of "pageant moms," informed my work far beyond what the word "informal" might suggest. Thanks in part to one of those pageant moms, in 2007 I attended Work Weekend for the Miss North Carolina Pageant in Raleigh, North Carolina. As part of that event, I attended the training session for individuals seeking to be certified as preliminary pageant judges in the Miss North Carolina pageant system. Finally, in 2013, I made a joint appearance with Ali Rogers, Miss South Carolina 2012 and first runner-up to Miss America 2013. Park Road Baptist Church in Charlotte, North Carolina, hosted Rogers and me to discuss "Faith and Beauty in America: The Church's Ongoing Relationship with the Pageant" for their Summer Sunday School series. All of these experiences added depth to my understanding of pageant culture and enriched my narrative with first-hand observations.

To decipher pageant narratives and situate them within American religious history, I looked to a broad range of fields including psychology, sociology, feminist studies, and women's history, especially women's religious history. These interlocutors feature prominently at different moments of the book, moving in and out of the spotlight, but all influenced my thinking even when not directly cited. Women's studies, in particular, offered a wealth of publications about pageants as well as the beauty culture that it reflected. These explorations of the Miss America Pageant offered a helpful starting point. Often, they provided a counter-narrative to the one told by Christians in the competition. The story shared by Christian Miss Americas was a largely positive one. The presence of alternative, often contradicting, viewpoints of the same event enriched my work.[41]

1

Miss America as Sex

"Beauty may be only skin deep, but that is deep enough to confer an unsettling array of advantages."[1]

Introduction

As the music started pumping, Chris Harrison announced the first semi-finalist to compete in the lifestyle and fitness competition (better known as the swimsuit competition to outsiders) of the 2011 Miss America finals. Each of the fifteen women took to the stage in a familiar gait. After flashing a smile at the camera, they turned to own the catwalk. They descended the stairs effortlessly, gliding toward center stage with their black bikinis firmly in place. They twirled. They smiled. Some placed their hands on their hips to draw further emphasis to both their tiny waists and their swaying hips. Others allowed their arms to swing naturally at their sides. After the initial grin and spin, they pranced down the runway where they paused for a tad more action. The emphasis this year was hip movement. Almost all of the contestants stopped at the end of the runway, planted a foot, extended the other foot to open the pelvis, and hit the beats with each hip before seductively pulling one leg back into the traditional pageant stance (one foot slightly behind the other, angled out in a modified fourth position). Admittedly, it was quite catching.[2] And it looked better than the old stop, pivot, hold, and the walk-around-in-a-circle-without-stopping of yesteryear. But this emphasis on the hips and the movement of them in this way signaled a new level of sexuality in the pageant. Sex appeal has always bubbled just below the surface of the pageant, but with lyrics that proclaimed,

> So come on, let's go,
> Let's lose control,
> Let's do it all night,
> Til we can't do it no mo

playing in the background while women in bikinis bounced across the stage there was really no denying the sex.[3] Sex rocked the runway. Sex accompanied the advertisements. Sex pervaded the pageant.

Sex dictated seemingly trivial contestant decisions.[4] Very few women chose to wear one-piece swimsuits at any level of competition, but it was especially rare at the national level. Of the fifty-three contestants in Miss America 2011, only one—Kylie Kofoed, a Mormon representing Idaho—wore a one-piece swimsuit. The remaining fifty-two women donned heels and a bikini (there was too little material to call it a "two-piece") that showcased their perfectly toned, evenly tanned bodies. The suits left little to the imagination. Tiny scraps of black fabric highlighted long, strong legs, protruding pelvic bones, round backsides, and flat stomachs. Bikini tops accentuated cleavage, collarbones, and ripped shoulders and arms.[5] Raw sexual energy flooded the stage in the competition. Women winked and smiled playfully, letting both judge and viewer know of her availability.

The lifestyle and fitness portion of the competition boasted more than an assessment of a young woman's health. As host Chris Harrison confirmed on the final night of the 2011 competition, "Here we celebrate health, fitness, self-confidence, and okay—can I just say it—looking amazing in a really tiny swimsuit."[6] Apparently, the more skin one showed, the more confidence she exuded. The goal was a bikini-ready body that men found attractive. Following the competition, admirers could purchase merchandise that featured their favorite bathing beauty. Sex quite literally sold. Consumers could flip through a series of photographs to decide which one best captured their attention. The shots offered an up-close and personal play-by-play of a woman's waltz down the runway.[7] Official DVDs joined with clips uploaded to YouTube and personal recordings to ensure that viewers could enjoy these moments again and again. Sex drove the pageant.

Eschewing one-piece swimwear for a two-piece represented merely one obvious way that pageant competitors flaunted their sex appeal. Hair, makeup, gown choice, and onstage walk all offered opportunities for participants to entice viewers and to own their sexuality. Contestants learned to perform not only their talents but also all of the aspects—physical, mental, and emotional—expected of a Miss America. More importantly, the pageant as ritual was predicated on the perfection and performance (embodiment) of prescribed gender ideals, chief among them beauty.[8] For participants, this involved everything from skin-toning exercises and firming creams to create a swimsuit-ready body to breast enhancement surgeries to make their bodies more sexually desirable.[9] Teresa Scanlan, Miss America 2011, wore a wig for the swimsuit competition to give her the long blonde locks she and America desired.[10] At every turn, sex loomed large.

Miss America provided a socially acceptable place for women to bare their bodies in public. The pageant succeeded because it packaged sex in tidy, respectable wrappers and named it something else. Beauty. Confidence. Style. Poise. Physical Fitness. But sex by any other name is still sex. The contest oozed sensuality. Ugly women did not win; desirable women did. Because beauty reigned supreme, contestants cultivated it diligently.[11] They perfected each glance, turn, and hip movement. Contestants' efforts to lure in both judge and viewer alike betrayed the notion that the pageant was merely about developing strong, confident women. To win, women must prove pleasing to others. The competition thus created a culture that encouraged the public consumption of women's bodies while convincing onlookers that they were doing the women a service by supporting them.[12] It was, in a word, about sex. Sex explains the popularity of Miss America, why women participated, and why the pageant has had cultural staying power. Examining the competition through the lens of sex highlights its appeal. Sex illumines. Sex matters. Sex unveils.

Wholesome Women and the Age of Innocence

But the centrality of sex to the pageant was not always so. For much of its history, the competition sought to bury any hint of salaciousness by heralding a form of female beauty considered safe and innocent. Only females were paraded around and judged for beauty, so sex was always at work. And even in the early years the pageant pushed the envelope simply by putting the female form on display. But there was a time in which sex was not so explicit, not so front and center, and not so exploited for commercial ends. Sex operated instead as a silent, hidden, but undeniable partner in the contest's earliest years.

The Miss America Pageant burst onto the national scene in 1921 in an effort to entice people to stay in Atlantic City past Labor Day. Each participant earned a trip to Atlantic City after winning her local newspaper photo contest. Once in Atlantic City, the women in the "Inter-City Beauty

Contest" were "judged on 50 percent audience applause and 50 percent judges' choice."[13] Contestants donned the one-piece bathing suits made popular by swimmer Annette Kellerman. Though modest by today's standards, these suits were controversial at the time. The one-pieces revealed a woman's bare arms and some exposed their collarbones. In addition, a few of the early contestants—including the first winner—chose to display some or part of their bare legs rather than covering them with stockings. Normal Atlantic City policy banned the display of bare flesh on the beach, sometimes arresting women who rolled down their stockings to expose their knees, but the mayor pronounced the illegal swimwear acceptable for the pageant.[14] The suspension of city ordinances regarding appropriate beach attire suggested the contest was less innocent than male organizers presented it to be. Women in normally prohibited swimwear decorating the boardwalk had the desired effect and the competition grew quickly. The first year the pageant consisted of eight contestants; the second it boasted fifty-seven. People flocked to Atlantic City to get a glimpse of the bathing beauties, bringing their money with them.[15] But bare arms and naked knees were not the only hints of sex in the early years of the pageant.

Pageant organizers also used the pageant to endorse what they considered a threatened ideal of femininity.[16] Early winners of the Miss America contest possessed "long hair, youth, innocence and domesticity," all qualities thought to "promote images of the traditional, wholesome girl with no aspirations for the stage or public life."[17] These women, their choices proclaimed, were not flappers or suffragists with painted faces and bobbed hair. Miss America participants were not Hollywood bound. Miss Americas were potential wives and mothers; they were women one could take home to meet one's parents. Thus, contestants represented a safer, more acceptable form of female sexuality, one owned and controlled by men.

For example, at the end of the 1921 festivities, officials named sixteen-year-old Margaret Gorman from Washington, D.C., as the winner. Gorman looked like Mary Pickford, a well-known star in silent pictures. Both Gorman and Pickford possessed long curly hair, bright eyes, and innocent smiles. They offered the security of today's girl-next-door. The selection of Gorman as the first Miss America suggested that the pageant wished to distinguish itself from the new womanhood emerging in the early twentieth century.[18] Seventy-two-year-old Samuel Gompers, president of the American Federation of Labor, confirmed this idea. Speaking of Gorman, he told the *New York Times*, "She represents the type of womanhood America needs, strong, red-blooded, able to shoulder the responsibilities of homemaking and motherhood. It is in her type that the hope of the country rests."[19] Gorman's potential for marriage and motherhood was the womanhood to be celebrated. This reality, however, does not deny sex. Judging women as potential mates highlighted the attributes men found sexually attractive, emphasizing again that the pageant was laden with sex.[20]

Figure 1.1. The swimsuits worn by contestants in the first "Inter-City Beauty Contest" were banned by normal Atlantic City beach policy, but the mayor pronounced the illegal swimwear acceptable for the pageant. Pictured here is the first Miss America, sixteen-year-old Margaret Gorman from Washington, D.C., who took advantage of the relaxed rules by rolling down her stockings to expose her knees.

Finally, the early years of the pageant attested to the growing acceptance of the public display of women's bodies. Even though pageant organizers sought to distance contest participants from the new womanhood represented by actresses and models, its success depended on the rise of modeling as a respected career for women and the use of female images in advertising. The use of women in advertising was prohibited during most of the nineteenth century, but by the 1890s, the bans were reversed.[21] "Chorus girls" also joined the ranks of those set free from the ridicule of Victorian culture.[22] As women posed for advertising photos and modeled clothing for stores, they ushered in a new era in the beauty industry where the promotion of one's looks became a given. Quite literally, they modeled all things other women aspired to be. A contest such as Miss America, even if it claimed to reward traditional forms of femininity, fit perfectly with this growing emphasis on a woman's outward beauty and the cultivation of it.[23] As long as women remained focused on the pursuit of beauty rather than the vote, they posed no threat.[24]

Miss America became a walking advertisement for ideal beauty and, in time, embraced this role as a chance for more public success. Organizers could not control how women viewed their participation or how women utilized the title once they received it. Eventually women became agents of their sexuality and not mere objects even as their bodies were marketed and objectified.[25] For example, Miss America 1925, Fay Lanphier, used her title to launch a brief career as a model and actress rather than returning home to settle down to a life of domesticity.[26] Miss America 1926, Norma Small-wood, leveraged her title to secure advertising contracts, earning an estimated $100,000 during her reign.[27] Lanphier and Smallwood represent the Miss America winners who saw the contest as an opportunity to advance one's career rather than a chance to win a mere sash and crown.[28] These two, and many who followed them, embraced portions of the new womanhood that proponents of the pageant feared.

Miss America groomed, promoted, and celebrated an ideal femininity in its contestants and, by extension, womanhood more broadly. However, not all approved of this new means of encouraging tourism and the preening it involved. Women's groups and religious groups both complained that the contest was immoral and destructive. With Victorian ideals still regnant, critics claimed that pageantry would corrupt the institution of womanhood, not celebrate it.[29] "The danger lies in taking girls of tender years and robing them in attire that transgresses the limit of morality," a resolution adopted by the Ocean City Camp Meeting Association read.[30] "We are persuaded that the moral effect on the young women entrants and the reaction generally is not a wholesome one," noted a later resolution signed by the Atlantic County Federation of Church Women.[31] Religious groups, Baptists, Quakers, and Methodists among them, called their adherents to steer clear.[32] Their voices joined those of women's groups disgusted that women were being elected as the model of womanhood based on their looks.[33] Religious groups and women's groups worried about issues of modesty and critiqued the contest's exploitation of women. Both foregrounded the sex appeal pageant officials sought to downplay. Eventually these voices of protest contributed to the suspension of the pageant from 1928 to 1932 and 1934. Of course, the sudden disappearance of the pageant also followed several years when pageant winners accepted prizes and economic opportunities.[34] Sex, it appeared, was acceptable only when in the hands of marketers and not those being marketed.

Either way, the early pageant did not deny sex. It merely restrained it. Women were judged on their potential to be wives and mothers. Thus it was about male control of female sexuality. Even this supposed innocent display of female sexuality was cause for concern for some as ambitious women used their crown to open more salacious doors. Even innocence, when paraded in front of men and ranked, failed to be innocent. The pageant needed to make adjustments to its strategy if it was going to survive.

Sanitizing Sex and the Age of Marketing[35]

Atlantic City businessmen rallied to bring the boardwalk sensation back to life, carefully crafting a program immune to public scrutiny.[36] Sex remained a critical component in the revived competition, but reformed language and revised rules made sex less conspicuous. The genius of the pageant organizers lay in their ability to market sex as something else, as something more respectable. If the early years of the pageant restrained sex, then the next several decades renamed it. Sex masqueraded as talent, character, scholarship, and other criteria suitable to those of refined tastes. Sex did not disappear from the pageant. Sex enveloped it.

Key to the pageant's makeover was Lenora Slaughter. Since she was the nation's only female pageant director, Miss America organizers hired her in 1935 to relaunch the pageant. Slaughter's boss allegedly said, "Well, you ought to go up there and show those damn Yankees how to do a *real* job with a pageant!"[37] Thus Slaughter arrived in Atlantic City determined to shape the pageant into something of which the nation could be proud. Her flair for marketing saved the pageant. She sold the pageant to local business owners, community members, religious groups, sponsors, and potential contestants as she guarded against potential scandal. Slaughter established a rule that banned contestants from visiting bars and nightclubs, instituted curfews, and forbade contestants to speak to any man alone. Stricter regulations, Slaughter assured, would attract "finer types" of women.[38] Mayor White later confirmed Slaughter's vision, noting, "We are past the time when beauty parades are in the nature of floor shows. This is a cultural event seeking a high type of beauty."[39] To shield the vulnerable young participants further, Slaughter created a hostess committee that operated as chaperones to America's most beautiful women during the week of the pageant. The hostess committee not only protected contestants from potential suitors, it also kept them from unwanted talent scouts. "We guard the Miss America contestants so well," Slaughter recounted, "that their mothers say that we guard them better than they're guarded at home."[40] But policing women's sexuality by banning participants from bars and boys was not the only evidence that sex still hung over the pageant.

Figure 1.2. Despite Lenora Slaughter's efforts to reform the pageant into a respectable enterprise, the pageant still traded on the objectification of women's bodies. This 1935 Miss America Pageant flier and "Official Souvenir Program" highlight the ongoing sensuality of the contest.

Pageant rules forbid contestants from acting on their sexual desires, but the competition counted on women's willingness to market and display their bodies as potential sex objects. Sex sold. And, since the contest's success relied on the support of its sponsors, participants were expected to represent them during their year of service. Winners routinely posed with beauty products, cleaning products, and, of course, in a swimsuit.[41] The market usurped contestants' bodies as a vehicle for endorsing products. Sex and beauty drove the pageant's revival despite a shift in language. Even the promotional materials advertising the 1935 relaunch of the pageant objectified women's bodies.

One advertisement featured a female form from behind. The woman, marked "Miss America 1935," was clearly topless. The "Official Souvenir Program" sported sketches of six bathing beauties posing in their pageant sashes as well as two mermaids and two nude women riding seahorses. The "American Beauty Event," its images proclaimed, had enough beauty, sensuality, and entertainment value for one and all. "You looking for pleasure? Come to the 'Playground of the World,'" these images seemed to suggest.

In her attempts to make the pageant more palatable to the public, Slaughter decided to begin awarding college scholarships to Miss America winners. The first year she raised $5,000 in sponsorships; the second that number grew to $25,000. Companies jumped at the chance to have Miss America as a spokeswoman. The first woman who benefited from the new scholarship aspect of the pageant was Miss America 1945, Bess Myerson of New York. Myerson was the first Jewish winner and the first college graduate to serve as Miss America. She entered the pageant because of the scholarship money available, later using the $5,000 she won to study music at Columbia.[42] Slaughter had made Miss America acceptable, desirable even for a young woman with a college education. She created an American icon, but that icon was still judged primarily on beauty. More to the point, Miss America contestants received financial compensation for their sexiness. Perhaps even more absurd was the implication that a woman's ability to pursue a college degree was determined by how attractive she was in a swimsuit. While it is admirable that Slaughter—and presumably the sponsors she garnered—wanted to support college education for women, the decision to tie scholarships to the competition further highlighted the role of sex in the pageant. Now women were not merely displaying their bodies in sexually suggestive ways; they were being paid for it.

The scholarships muddied the waters by offering financial compensation not unlike that given to exotic dancers or prostitutes.[43] One could not deny that women were being paid for the use of their bodies. The pageant capitalized on contestants' sexual availability. Winners discovered that the scholarships came at a cost. Marketing the pageant as an exercise in educational advancement for women was dishonest at best and harmful at worst. And yet marketing women's bodies to fund their education proved Slaughter's idea with the most staying power. In 2019, the pageant billed itself the "nation's largest provider of scholarship assistance for young women."[44] Slaughter's vision for creating the impression of a "respectable" enterprise that elevated classy young women worked.

Most obviously, the competition continued to thrive on the assessment of women's bodies to determine the winner. Pageant organizers attempted to nullify the importance of beauty by adding other phases of competition such as the talent contest, but pretty girls still took the crown. Slaughter made other subtle changes in her attempts to recognize and celebrate well-rounded women. She shunned the word "bathing suit" in favor of the term "swimsuit" in an effort to play up the athleticism rather than the sensuality of the event. Slaughter reorganized the scoring system to deemphasize the swimsuit portion. And she declared that the winners would no longer be crowned in their swimsuits. Beginning in 1948, winners were crowned in their evening gowns instead.[45] But with Catalina Swimsuits as one of the chief sponsors and the Atlantic City beach as its location, there was no denying that the swimsuit portion of the competition persisted as the main attraction.

The first Miss Alabama crowned Miss America, Yolande Betbeze, tested the centrality of the swimsuit competition to the pageant. After being crowned Miss America 1951, Betbeze refused to pose in her swimsuit, famously saying, "I'm an opera singer, not a pin-up!"[46] Betbeze failed to fulfill her obligation to model Catalina swimwear in malls around the country, a decision that ultimately cost the pageant Catalina's sponsorship. Slaughter stood by Betbeze's decision.[47] Betbeze's refusal to pose in a swimsuit set the stage for Miss America to become more than a pretty face, boosting Slaughter's campaign toward a professional organization. Slaughter secured new sponsorship for the pageant when Catalina Swimsuits dropped them, but even she did not dare suggest cutting this portion of the competition altogether. The display of women's bodies had become a central part of the pageant's identity. If the competition had been about scholarship or talent or personality, the swimsuit competition would have posed no dilemma. But, at its core, the contest knew it relied on sex for its survival.

The commodification of women's bodies in beauty culture, and in pageantry, remained the ugly elephant in the room.[48] Pageants served as an arena in which the baring of women's bodies in exchange for goods was socially acceptable, unlike other professions involving the showcasing of women's bodies such as stripping, pornography, and prostitution.[49] Still, even in pageants, there was money to be made in showing a little skin. Participants' attractiveness acted as cultural capital, and women even earned actual capital in salary and scholarships for their adherence to feminine ideals.[50] More money was made at the winner's expense. Pageant coaches, dress designers, beauty experts, advertisers, and more benefited from the display of women's bodies in these competitions. Still, the pageant drew distinct boundaries between what it deemed the celebration of beauty and more tawdry displays of the female form.

But admitting the harsh reality that the pageant succeeded because of sex would not sell. Thus pageant organizers in the 1930s scrambled to make the competition less threatening to potential constituents. Miss America officials became consumed with making the contest respectable, marketing it as America's ideal. They created an icon that celebrated women as both beautiful and useful. Under Slaughter's able leadership, the pageant grew from a stumbling sideshow to a freestanding enterprise. She successfully gentrified the contest, branding it to the masses as innocuous—beneficial even. That said, Slaughter's efforts also normalized the public exhibition of women's bodies and the objectification such display entailed. Sex remained foundational to the pageant as its success rested on the evaluation of women's bodies by a panel of judges. Slaughter sanitized sex in the pageant, but she failed to remove it.

Resisting Revolution and the Age of Tradition

Turbulent years followed the pageant's golden age of the 1950s. The nation reeled from the Vietnam War, antiwar protesters, hippies, the Civil Rights Movement, the sexual revolution, and the women's rights movement.[51] As the pageant sought to redefine itself in light of the shifting times, sex remained crucial to its success. Faced with criticism of sexism from feminists and racism from the National Association for the Advancement of Colored People (NAACP), Miss America's desire to stay relevant remained. This time the protests did not shut the pageant down. If anything, they revived it. Feminist protestors dragged the pageant's latent emphasis on sex into the spotlight, causing pageant contestants, supporters, and organizers to react, to reinterpret—once again—what the pageant was really about. The pageant, they argued, was not about sex. No! The women who participated did not feel oppressed; they enjoyed competing. Miss America remained committed to preserving ideals of womanhood, including beauty, in the face of threats such as feminism.[52] But sex stayed.

Feminists picketed the pageant for the first time in 1968. Led by the New York Radical Women, the protestors carried placards down the boardwalk that read "Welcome to the Cattle Auction" and "Can Make-Up Cover the Wounds of Our Oppression?" They crowned a live sheep and threw bras and other items of putative female oppression such as copies of the *Ladies' Home Journal*, high heels, and girdles into the "freedom trash can." Contrary to popular belief, the women did not actually burn their bras. They failed to secure a fire permit, so they symbolically disposed of them. As their grand finale, a few feminists snuck into the balcony of the pageant and dropped a banner that read "Women's Liberation" at the end of the broadcast when the winner was crowned. They did not succeed in getting the banner on television, but other media, including radio and newspapers, provided publicity.[53]

Figure 1.3. Carol Giardino and other protestors with signs (left) and "Freedom Trash Can" (right), Miss America protest, Atlantic City, 1968. As part of the 1968 protest of the Miss America Pageant, women carried placards down the Atlantic City boardwalk and threw items of female oppression into the "freedom trashcan." Duke University Special Collections, Alix Kates Shulman Papers, David M. Rubenstein Rare Book & Manuscript Library, Duke University, photograph copyright Alix Kates Shulman, used with permission.

Protestors claimed that the pageant not only put women on display but also hurt women's rights.[54] They argued that pageants paraded women around the stage like cattle, featuring their bodies and breeding over their minds. Miss America resulted from a patriarchal culture that viewed women's bodies as objects of consumption. Equally harmful, it pitted women against one another as competitors striving to meet near-impossible beauty standards. In considering some of the failures of the Miss America protests, Carol Hanisch noted, "We didn't say clearly enough that we women are FORCED to play the Miss America role—not by beautiful women, but by men we have to act that way for and by a system that has so well institutionalized male supremacy for its own ends."[55] She, along with other protestors, lamented that their critiques were seen as lobbied against the participants rather than the oppressive system that affected all women and made pageants like Miss America not just possible, but successful.

Albert Marks, appointed pageant chairman in 1965, faced the criticism that the pageant was "exploitative and degrading to women."[56] He retorted, "We were picketed by a number of wild-eyed females out of New York. They needed a publicity vehicle to climb aboard that dealt with women—and believe me, they got it!"[57] Of course, much of the press described the protestors as unattractive and chalked up the protest to jealousy. The bus company canceled on protestors in 1969 when the women gave Atlantic City law enforcement their bus information. Consequently, the 1969 protest proved smaller.[58] But feminists had succeeded in raising public consciousness about sex in the pageant. Sex, they contended, drove the pageant's success.[59] More specifically, the objectification of women's bodies through exhibition and display kept the focus on women as commodities of desire rather than autonomous agents.

Many of the feminists' critiques concerned unrealistic standards of beauty and the objectification and commodification of women. The Miss America competition, in many ways, was a reflection of everyday realities for American women. One of the biggest issues raised by feminists was what they dubbed "The Unbeatable Madonna-Whore Combination."[60] Contestants in the Miss America competition, feminists argued, were forced to be simultaneously wholesome and sexy. Competitors were held up as paragons of virtue even as their bodies were offered up for the pleasure of the viewers. Stated differently, "Miss America must be provocative but wholesome—a pretty but pure vestal virgin, like Cinderella. Her message is, 'Look but don't touch.'"[61] "Every day in a woman's life," lamented feminist Rosalyn (Ros) Baxandall, "is a walking Miss America contest."[62] It was time, protestors pressed, to resist these oppressive systems.

Not all women felt oppressed by the pageant, however.[63] Indeed, pageant organizers and pageant contenders alike offered testimony to the contrary. To be the model of American femininity, contestants claimed, was not a burden imposed upon them, it was a goal they set themselves. Many wanted to be wives and mothers. Miss America 1975, Shirley Cothran, noted "that when she does get married, she plans to use her husband's name rather than her maiden name. And for the time being, she prefers 'Miss' Cothran rather than 'Ms.'" When asked about the women's movement, Cothran responded, "That is their thing, and this is my thing. I respect what they're doing, and I hope they can respect me for what I'm doing."[64] Other pageant winners saw the women's movement as the enemy limiting their choices. For example, Debra Dene Barnes, Miss America 1968, confessed, "Just the fact that this group of women would say to us who were in the pageant competing that we were selling ourselves. And it was almost verging on prostitution. It did really hurt my feelings because I felt that my femininity was something to be respected and to be celebrated."[65] Miss America contestants were willing participants in beauty culture, admitting implicitly, and, at times, explicitly that they enjoyed being admired and desired. Miss New York 1971, Elizabeth May Condon, claimed, "I don't feel like a sex object."[66] Miss America 1974, Rebecca King, confessed, "Sex objects? I'm not sure I even understand what that is. I don't feel I'm exploited. I got involved for the scholarship money ($15,000), which I plan to use this fall at law school. I would never have gotten involved if I thought it was a body-beautiful contest. And after Atlantic City, you never again have to appear in a swimsuit."[67] And Miss America 1983, Debra Sue Maffett, declared, "If this is being exploited, I hope every woman can be exploited like this."[68] To these women, the pageant was a celebration of who they were that helped prepare them for who they wanted to become; it was not an oppressive system. Far from it. They felt it empowered them.

Pageant supporters also worked to prove that the contest empowered women. They lauded winners' professional accomplishments, noting that the women used the scholarship money to earn graduate degrees. In particular, pageant officials liked to recount the accomplishments of two Miss Americas crowned during the height of the feminist movement. Miss America 1974, Rebecca King, used her scholarships to pay for law school and Miss America 1975, Shirley Cothran, earned a doctorate with the help of pageant funds. Pageant supporters cited these two women and others like them as evidence against the feminists' allegations of oppression.[69] This new accomplished woman celebrated by the competition signaled the coming of a new era in pageantry: one in which women could aspire to more than marrying well. These independent thinkers struggled to embrace a new do-it-all model of womanhood, one that demanded that they look great in a swimsuit and be able to walk down stairs in heels and a ball gown in order to afford an education and be able to speak their minds. The feminist critique still carried weight. Sex still dominated the pageant.[70]

In some ways, feminism and the sexual revolution were just the boost the pageant needed. As rebels and revolutionaries touted free love and fashion included ever tinier skirts, the pageant became a source of tradition and stability. It defined itself against the uncertainty of the times. Miss America, now over forty years old, had reached middle age; she symbolized American values. Here was a woman who could be counted on, a responsible woman who would not shirk her responsibility to be the face of the nation or her family for selfish pursuits and the allure of pleasure. She owned her beauty and delighted in it as a source of feminine strength and power.

Feminists brought the objectification of women in Miss America to center stage, forcing the pageant to respond. While still denying the presence of sex in the competition, pageant supporters simultaneously sought to contain it. Miss America defined itself against more tawdry displays, seeing itself as a defender of traditional values. Sex still reigned supreme in the pageant, but this was a safe version. Despite efforts to downplay its importance, sex took an increasingly more public role in the pageant from this point forward.

Winking at Sex and the Age of Accommodation

The emphasis on sex remained most obvious in the swimsuit competition. On one occasion, the organization flirted with the idea of eliminating this portion of the pageant, but swimsuits proved too valuable to Miss America's success. In 1995, organizers polled the American television audience. Seventy-nine percent of the nearly one million callers voted to keep the swimsuit segment of the contest.[71] In addition, forty-two of that year's participants indicated that "they did not have a problem with waltzing around in public in swimwear."[72] One dissenting contestant, meanwhile, called it a "veiled strip show."[73] Shawntel Smith, a Pentecostal from Oklahoma who went on to win the pageant that year, stated, "Personally, I feel the suit is modest enough that I don't think I'm compromising any of my beliefs or values." Like many voters, she longed to keep this Miss America tradition and believed the swimsuit competition useful in determining a contestant's physical fitness.[74] The swimsuit portion remained, and the pageant succeeded in its attempt to hold onto its television viewers.[75] The display of women's bodies had become an established part of the pageant's identity and they could not afford to drop it.

As swimsuits shrunk, the need to perfect every inch of skin grew. In 1997, the national competition moved to the two-piece swimsuit as an option. By the early 2000s, women in bikinis flooded the stage. In 2017, none of the participants at the national pageant chose to wear a one-piece swimsuit to compete for the title of Miss America 2018.[76] With stockings and skirts a thing of the past, blemishes were harder to hide. Contestants hired personal trainers and image consultants in their quest to achieve a competition-ready body. Some pageant participants, however, went beyond diet, exercise, and choosing a swimsuit for their body type. Some dyed their hair. Some wore wigs. And, as rules regarding cosmetic surgery loosened, some resorted to more drastic—and permanent—measures including breast enhancement surgery.[77] Miss America 1980, Cheryl Prewitt, confessed that her exercise team targeted a few fat places on her thighs. As she recounted, "As demanding as such a schedule was it occurred to me that never again would I have the opportunity to so single-mindedly indulge in getting myself in near-perfect shape—not only physically, but mentally and spiritually, too."[78] Prewitt was just one pageant hopeful who endured a strict diet and daily workouts in the months leading up to the competition. Hair spray, butt glue, and duct tape provided last-minute security and lift, boosting bosoms as well as confidence.[79] In short, contestants knew that their physical attributes contributed to their success or failure in the Miss America system, and they were willing to go to extreme measures to showcase their best selves.

This emphasis on beauty reflected wider ideals in American culture. Despite shifts in what constituted the preferred weight, hairstyle, or body type, the underlying pressure to conform to external criteria of beauty remained constant. As women flocked to the workforce in the 1980s, they noted the importance of appearance not only for marriage prospects but also for career advancement, self-esteem, and social success. Indeed, "beauty was no longer just a symbolic form of currency; it literally *became* money. The informal currency system of the marriage market, formalized in the workplace, was enshrined in the law."[80] Women's looks proved a commodity not just for those in "beauty-driven" trades like acting or modeling or pageantry. Rather, what was termed the "professional beauty qualification" subjected all working women to beauty standards not applied to men in similar fields.[81] Thus, despite the notion that women advanced beyond looks to abilities, what changed for many women was how their attractiveness (or lack thereof) paid off: from marriage to jobs (though marriage prospects remained important). For women in the late twentieth century and early twenty-first century, beauty mattered. Its achievement offered real cultural capital. In the pageant world, as in the wider culture, women's bodies were projects to be perfected.[82] From makeup and fashion choices to liposuction and breast enhancement surgeries, women found their bodies the source of much discussion.

Appearance-based discrimination in the workplace reinforced double standards for men and women. For example, while men gained respect and distinction as they aged, women found themselves bombarded with products to help them prevent or stall the aging process. Old age robbed women of one of their most marketable assets, youth.[83] Even female senators were not immune to accepting beauty standards.[84] Women succumbed to beauty treatments for various reasons from seeing it as a form of empowerment to the need to fulfill a job requirement knowing "they face greater pressure to be attractive and greater penalties for falling short" than do men.[85] Studies even found that teachers believed attractive students to be more intelligent.[86] The presence or absence of culturally decided good looks determined more than just who embarked in a career on the runway. Attractive individuals received rewards that were not always commensurate with their work. Women sought the rewards that accepting beauty guidelines provided. Even women who considered themselves feminists participated in various beauty practices when they found America's beauty culture inescapable.[87] Pageantry represented just one extreme example of what took place across American culture. Attractive women were viewed as objects of sexual desire despite their other qualities and they were rewarded accordingly. Viewed in this light, pageant contestants were merely capitalizing on their most valuable assets, beauty and youth.

In the Miss America competition, sex remained the silent partner. The smaller the swimsuits, the harder pageant organizers worked to say that the contest was not about sex. In 2001, the swimsuit segment received a new name: lifestyle and fitness in swimsuit.[88] This phase of competition purportedly measured a contestant's poise, confidence, mental and emotional health, and physical fitness, but it raised the question of why so little material was required to make that assessment.[89] Miss America's Outstanding Teen Pageant (held in Orlando for the first time in 2005) acted as a feeder system for the Miss America Pageant and did not require a swimsuit competition to gauge physical fitness.[90] Instead, teens competed in a lifestyle and fitness routine that possessed both group and individual components.[91] This method for determining physical fitness mirrored that used in the Distinguished Young Women program (formerly Junior Miss) and suggests that on some level Miss America Pageant organizers recognized the hypocrisy of their claim that the swimsuit phase of the Miss America competition featured athleticism rather than sexuality.

The performance of the swimsuit competition belied the notion that Miss America was about anything other than sex. Women walked the runway in swimsuits and heels not unlike models in a Victoria's Secret fashion show. At times they teasingly removed a sarong in a way that mimicked women at a strip club before beginning their strut across the stage. Announcers joked about the men who tuned in just for this portion of the contest, peppering the event with more than a few suggestive remarks about women "in high heels and not much else."[92] Yes, pageant organizers knew the appeal of women in swimsuits smaller than some lingerie, and they capitalized on it despite the official rhetoric about measuring fitness and confidence.

Indeed, by 2016, sex pervaded every aspect of the competition. Sex had moved out of the background and had stolen center stage even if pageant organizers and contestants still hesitated to admit it. There was a growing awareness of, and even playfulness about, the sex appeal of pageant participants and the necessity of such attraction to the contest's success. For example, at the 2016 Miss Texas Pageant, choreographers had non-finalist contestants parade across stage in their bikinis purely as entertainment. The eliminated young women strutted and pranced and smiled as they ushered in the lifestyle and fitness in swimsuit portion of the finals. These forty-three women were no longer being judged on their confidence, style, and physical health; they were purely decoration—a sort of prelude to the main event featuring the top twelve contestants still vying for the title. This focus on the tanned, toned flesh of participants even after they were no longer competing signaled a new level of sexuality in the pageant.[93]

Evening gowns, like swimsuits, grew sexier by the year. When Deidre Downs won Miss America in 2005, she wore a two-piece white gown that showcased her flat stomach. Rhinestones covered the white crop top that stopped several inches above her belly button. A basic white skirt with a high slit and a large chiffon bow sat snuggly on her hips, leaving her navel exposed. Over time, contestants learned to take risks by displaying more of their body: higher slits, lower necklines, cut-out backs (or no backs), flesh-colored material. Where once elegant ball gowns graced the stage, one now saw contestants poured into dresses that fit like a glove. For example, Ali Rogers, Miss South Carolina and first runner-up to Miss America 2013, described her gown as "unexpected." "I never expected to fall SO in love with a gown," she stated. "And let's be honest. I'm extremely conservative. This gown is very . . . well, not."[94] A white cap-sleeved gown with a slit that rested at her upper right thigh, Rogers' gown was as glamorous as it was revealing. The swirling waves of silver and white provided ample coverage, but strategically placed pockets of sheer material left just enough to the imagination. The rhinestone embellishments that dotted the sheer back and sides of her gown glimmered in the lights as she descended the stairs and glided down the runway, drawing attention to that which could not be seen. In evening wear—as in swimsuit—contestants knew that the audience wanted to see skin.

One cannot deny the implicit, and, at times, explicit, sexiness embodied by contestants in the Miss America Organization. A mere flip through the program book made the point. Beauty and glamour bombarded the onlooker on page after page. Photographs of the winner's year, contestants' headshots, and supportive ads appeared alongside scholarship listings, the pageant's history, and an order of competition. Photographers captured well-coiffed women glancing wistfully into the distance, lips pouty, eyes smoldering. Other photographs depicted confident women with bright eyes, wide smiles, and crowns in place. Contestants posed purposefully, professionally, playfully even. They wore interview suits, evening gowns, and dance costumes. A perusal of the numerous photos revealed a range of roles the women were expected to fulfill: teacher, entertainer, community organizer, model, and more.[95] These women, the photographs proclaimed, had it all and could do it all. Most importantly, they were beautiful and available.

Pageants promoted perfection. Young women who experienced success in the pageant world gained confidence that they could meet the rigid demands placed on women's bodies in the workforce. And yet Miss America winners noted consistently that their win was not just about their looks even though thus far no one has succeeded in becoming Miss America without good looks. Overall, the Miss America Pageant has not valued diversity in size, shape, and "look." More often, it defined true womanhood by modeling cultural norms for the feminine form, claiming the winner to all Americans as "your ideal."[96]

This ideal, not surprisingly, encompassed those characteristics deemed beautiful by the culture. Hairstyles, dress designs, and swimwear changed with the fashion tides, but consistently winners possessed the four standard characteristics of beauty: facial and body symmetry, a clear complexion, and youth. They also embodied thinness.[97] With the pageant's emphasis on physical fitness, contestants routinely spoke of diet and exercise as a primary form of preparation, but that was just the beginning. Winners went far beyond taking up jogging and buying a gown currently in vogue. They hired personal trainers, bought wigs, used enhancements, and had plastic surgery. Pageantry was a serious business.

Exposing Sex and the Age of #metoo

Leaked emails pushed the issue of sex and the pageant into the spotlight. News of Miss America CEO Sam Haskell's inappropriate comments to and about former Miss Americas surfaced in late 2017. Haskell, who is married to Mary Donnelly-Haskell, Miss Mississippi 1977, joined the Miss America board in 2005. His memoir, *Promises I Made My Mother*, revealed lessons ingested as a boy from Mississippi determined to live an honest, faith-filled life that would please his mother.[98] Haskell routinely represented these homegrown values when he traveled the country on behalf of the Miss America

Organization and each year when he presented at the national pageant, speaking in an almost folksy way about the pageant and the young women involved. For example, at the 2018 Miss America Pageant, Haskell quoted Martin Luther King Jr. noting that everyone can serve and from the biblical book of Esther about being prepared for such a time as this. He spoke of scholarships and winning in life and even worked in a comeback to John Oliver's claims that Miss America was dishonest about the amount of scholarships they awarded, proudly proclaiming that Miss America remained the "top provider of scholarships in the nation" and that they had awarded 1.2 million dollars that year before arriving in Atlantic City. Indeed, Haskell threw in a "Thank you, John Oliver. You've helped make us better!" for good measure.[99] At times, his words seemed to drip with paternalism for these young women placed in his care. Often credited with saving the pageant, Haskell took over the reins of the pageant when it was in bad shape. And yet his actions outside the spotlight did not match the image he portrayed to America. "But Haskell's behavior behind closed doors shows he regularly maligned, fat-shamed and slut-shamed the former Miss Americas, calling them shocking names and in one case laughing at the suggestion that one of the women should die."[100] Despite public rhetoric to the contrary, Haskell wanted a Miss America he could control, not empower. And, when one dared dissent from his leadership, he had ways of making her life difficult.[101]

As the sex and sexism in the pageant was exposed for the harmful patriarchy it was once and for all, former Miss America contestants joined forces to tell their stories and to hold the leadership accountable for behavior that failed to match up with the stated purpose of the program. Forty-nine former Miss Americas signed a letter noting, "we are deeply disturbed and saddened to learn of the sickening and egregious words used by Miss America leadership in reference both to our group and to specific members of our sisterhood."[102] They urged for the resignation of Haskell and other offending parties. Thanks in part to their action, a whole new board was instated, one consisting of mostly women. From the moment that Gretchen Carlson, Miss America 1989, took the helm as board chair, she spoke of big changes that would be coming to the pageant. There was speculation that the swimsuit component would be removed, but it is unclear how many people believed that pageant officials would actually take this bold step. Yet the 2018 decision to eliminate the swimsuit competition is in keeping with what the Miss America Pageant has shown itself to be: a surprisingly consistent barometer of the culture in which it exists.[103]

The competition has evolved numerous times in its almost one-hundred-year history, always responding to cultural demands. Now, with the #metoo movement providing cover, the Miss America Pageant did not ask, as it did in 1995, whether they should remove the swimsuit competition. Rather, they simply acted, doubling down on the language of empowerment and using the momentum of the movement to redefine themselves as something other than an event predicated on the objectification of women. "Miss America will represent a new generation of female leaders focused on scholarship, social impact, talent, and empowerment," Gretchen Carlson proclaimed.[104] Miss America leaders even jettisoned the language of "pageant" in favor of the designation "competition." Participants were no longer "contestants" but "candidates" vying for the job of Miss America. It also got an updated tagline: "To prepare great women for the world, and to prepare the world for great women."[105] And yet removing the swimsuit competition did not remove sex. Rather, it exposed it.

Unraveling Sex and the Claim of Empowerment

Some women passively accepted their role as models of ideal beauty, but others actively embraced it. They relished the opportunities that pageants provided to put their bodies on display. In short, they saw the pageant as empowering. Thus, after a rocky start, the pageant rose to take its place as a reputable enterprise for young women. It filled a prominent spot in a culture consumed with the display of female bodies. This exhibition of beauty flirted with the boundaries of respectable society. Thus the commodification of women's bodies in beauty culture, and in pageantry, was undeniable.[106]

Until 2018, the pageant never explicitly owned the sex appeal present. It worked hard to emphasize beauty, not sex, and stamped out any hint of scandal or suggestion that the Miss America Organization promoted loose morals. Perhaps the most obvious example is the way pageant officials handled the Vanessa Williams controversy. Vanessa Williams, Miss America 1984, was the first African American to win the pageant. Unfortunately for Williams, she was also the first individual asked to give up the crown. Near the end of her year of service, *Penthouse* magazine announced that they possessed sexually explicit photographs of Williams with another woman. They planned to run the pictures to coincide with the end of her reign. The pageant received an onslaught of negative media coverage, and pageant officials asked Williams to resign.[107]

The pageant defined itself against pornography; they could not support a winner who openly flaunted her sexuality in such an explicit way. The Miss

America Organization promoted the highest moral standards and an idealized form of womanhood. According to pageant supporters, the contest existed to encourage women, not exploit them. Miss America winners were to be chaste moral exemplars. By presenting herself as a sexual actor, Williams became a fallen idol, a temptation to be scorned and shunned.

The Miss America Pageant did not just define itself against pornography. It also crowned itself queen of all the pageants. In particular, it understood itself as morally superior to the Miss USA pageant within the Miss Universe pageant system. The Miss USA pageant emerged in the 1950s (1952) after a dispute between the Miss America board and their swimsuit sponsor. When Miss America 1951, Yolande Betbeze, refused to pose in her swimsuit, they lost their swimsuit sponsor. Catalina started a competing pageant that became known as Miss Universe.[108] While some women participate in both systems, most find a home in one or the other. There is no talent competition in Miss USA. Contestants are judged on three phases of competition: swimsuit, gown, and interview. Miss USA is connected to the Miss Universe pageant. Whoever wins Miss USA competes in Miss Universe.

Miss USA was owned by Donald Trump from 1996 to 2015. Women win modeling contracts. Traditionally Miss USA lives in New York City during her reign. She embarks upon a media tour, though it appears that Miss USA has attempted to remake itself in recent years too, adopting the motto "confidently beautiful" and emphasizing community service like its rival pageant Miss America. But it remains the more liberal of the two pageants. For example, whereas Miss America rules demanded that participants be born female, Miss USA began allowing transgender contestants in 2012.[109]

Still, in both Miss USA and Miss America, women were expected to be single. That is, they could not be married or pregnant. Indeed, they must never have been married or given birth to a child. They were to be available women.[110] No man must own them so that they can be displayed and ogled by all. They were women for the world who were available for the taking. They can be wooed. They want to be wooed. These rules, too, betrayed the idea that Miss America existed to empower women. If it was about supporting women and helping them grow, it would not matter if they were married or not. Nor would it matter if the women were mothers. Something else was at play. And one of those things was the undercurrent of sex that pervaded the pageant.

Miss America was a "safe space" in which women could bare their bodies because it did not celebrate sexuality; it controlled it. The assumption was that contestants were virgins to be admired, but not acted upon. They represented innocent beauty. It was also permissible because the end goal was different. With pornography, prostitution, and stripping, the goal was sex or at least sexual arousal. That is understood. The Miss America Pageant claimed a different goal—that of female empowerment—and that matters. So, you cannot explain Miss America by sex alone even if sex is deeply woven into its fabric. When the new board changed the language used for the program, referring to the annual September event as a competition rather than a pageant, it reinforced what organizers had claimed about the pageant for some time: it was not just another beauty pageant. Miss America was tradition. The shift toward "empowerment" seems to be all around, and it needed to have come sooner than it has. But that does not change the fact that this is a bold move for an organization that started as a bathing revue on the Atlantic City beach. Pageant officials have chosen to ditch the one thing that has been part of the competition from the beginning. Whether it will have the payoff they hope in terms of recruiting more participants and keeping the organization afloat for another century remains to be seen as does whether the pageant can escape the sex factor that has always bubbled below the surface.

Conclusion

Pageants reflected the beauty-obsessed culture in which they emerged. In the nineteenth century, developments in the world of modeling and entertainment opened a new realm of possibilities for the modern woman, one in which pleasure could be sought and experienced outside the home with less fear of being ostracized. As models, actresses, and chorus girls gained respectability, they paved the way for the acceptance of pageants into the wider American culture. Pageants provided a space for women to parade their good looks and be rewarded for it. To varying degrees, women found their experiences empowering. With the acceptance of the public display of women's bodies, the time was ripe for pageants to take off.

The Miss America competition evolved from a bathing revue in Atlantic City to a nationally televised contest with talent, interviews, and community service requirements, but at its heart, it still privileged those society deemed most beautiful. Miss America provided a socially acceptable place for women to bare their bodies in public, in part because of how they chose to talk about those bodies and how they positioned themselves against other societal displays of the female form. According to contestants, sponsors, pageant organizers, and other supporters, there was far more going on in the Miss America Pageant than sex appeal. In fact, for many of the individuals involved, the "sexiness" of it was an afterthought if it was a thought at all. And yet an individual's physical attributes contributed to her success or failure in the Miss America system. Equally important, the pageant depended upon the latent sexiness of the competition and its participants for its national success. At its roots, it was a contest that rewarded beauty. But if sex were all the pageant was about, it would not have yielded such a widespread influence on mainstream American culture. Sex needed to stay buried, lurking in the shadows of the competition, in order for Americans to accept Miss America as a respectable organization.

In the end, the Miss America Pageant and its participants were suggestive, not seductive. Indeed, any time sex exploded in the pageant, it necessitated immediate action whether by the resignation of the reigning queen in the case of Vanessa Williams or the ousting of the board chair in the case of Sam Haskell. Sex could not inhabit center stage. The competition thrived on society's obsession with sex and beauty, but the Miss America contest succeeded because it offered more than a cheap thrill. Far more racy displays of female bodies were available with the swipe of a screen. Miss America relabeled sex appeal, both for the commodity and the consumer, as empowering. If Miss America were only about sex, it would have died out. And, if it was not at least a little about sex, well, "how many people do they think want to *see* a scholarship?"[111]

2

Miss America as Entertainment

"Pageantry is like an evangelical movement. People in towns all across the country are caught up in show business. It's more exciting than their own lives, more fun than golf. In every little town they're pulling for their girl, hoping she gets to the top." [1]

Introduction

As the lights dimmed, cheers flooded the theater. Women and men alike sported buttons and ribbons proudly proclaiming their chosen contestant. Signs featuring participant photos bobbed up and down, plastic clapping light-up hands emerged as if on cue, and even an occasional cowbell could be heard echoing through the auditorium. The excitement was palpable. In less than three hours, a new winner would be crowned. Women performing talents, strutting in swimsuits, and waltzing through the evening gown competition had been carefully crafted into a staged affair intended to dazzle and delight the onlooker. Program books in hand, audience members rushed in, sank into their seats, and prepared to be entertained. The show was about to start.

Before there was *America's Got Talent*, *America's Next Top Model*, *American Idol*, or *Dancing with the Stars*, there was the Miss America Pageant. From its inception on the beaches of Atlantic City to the radio to television, the contest rode the waves of the entertainment industry as contestants sought to wow the crowds with their winning personalities and infectious smiles. Singers, baton twirlers, dancers, instrumentalists, and, yes, ventriloquists, delighted live—and eventually television—audiences in their quest for the crown. The Miss America competition harnessed the spectacle of the circus and presented it as culture, a kind of theater for the middle class. The pageant as performance involved an implicit invitation for the viewer to consume and critique the contest's components. Over time, the pageant adapted to fit its changing venue as it sought to keep up with the entertainment needs of both participant and viewer.

Figure 2.1. Spectators line the beach in Atlantic City to be entertained by the bathing beauties at one of the early pageants in the 1920s.

Potential entertainment value drove production decisions. For example, when the pageant moved to television in 1954, timing and framing became more important as television changed the format and scope of the pageant.[2] Camera angles were considered, walks had to be perfectly timed, talents had to be shortened to a regulated time, and flashy production numbers replaced Miss America's coronation speech.[3] In addition, the live audience gained a new level of importance as a participant in the event. Perhaps the most important thing that came from broadcasting the Miss America Pageant into living rooms around the country is that, at least for a time, it became a must-see event. Everyone from presidents to housewives tuned in to cheer on "their" representative in hopes that their state would take home the crown. Families hosted parties, made top ten lists, and scored contestants right alongside the judges. It became a national pastime as America's sweethearts performed their way into the hearts and televisions of Americans from California to Maine.

As television became central to American monoculture, the pageant stole center stage as an entertaining presentation of idealized American womanhood. Later on, as television became decentralized with the advent of cable, the pageant lost some ground as a common feature of our culture.[4] It remained, however, committed to principles of entertainment, crafting an experience for contestants and viewers meant to attract and hold their attention. Pageant organizers inserted new phases of competition, game-show-mimicking quizzes, and reality television gimmicks in attempts to catch the next wave of entertainment.

In time, Miss America's influence as entertainment reached beyond one night a year. The new winner's face was plastered on advertisements and her appearance (and, eventually, talent) sought at community events. Websites devoted to pageantry crept up as predictions were made, tips for winning were given, and winners were profiled and celebrated.[5] Pageants also permeated American pop culture in the late twentieth and early twenty-first centuries. From television series to movies to newspapers to books, Americans found themselves bombarded with images of women (or girls) in crowns or in search of one. Movies such as *Drop Dead Gorgeous* (1999) and *Miss Congeniality* (2000) satirized contestants as shallow, spiteful individuals with win-at-all-costs attitudes. These movies also suggested that pageants and their participants, while somewhat frivolous, posed no real threat to the culture at large. At times, they suggested, they might even do some good for a segment of the population. These women were harmless objects of amusement. These fictionalized accounts provided an escape to viewers, offering a source of recreation as well as an initiation into one side of pageant life. Like the actual pageant, movies provided entertainment—a sense of pleasure—rooted in the female form and its display.[6]

Women have long been seen as a source of entertainment. From sitting rooms and parlors where daughters were called upon to sing and play the piano before dinner to dance halls and barrooms, women existed to please others (namely, men and those who appropriated the male gaze). The settings, obviously, were quite different, but a woman's purpose was not. She performed a role to garner the attention of men, to win the affection of friends, or to acquire the power such recognition offered. Moreover, many women craved and even enjoyed this attention. They took pleasure in their work as entertainers, even if they did not name their participation using this vocabulary. As parlors faded from view, other arenas took their place. One was the pageant. Pageants provided a literal stage on which women were allowed to showcase their talents, seek after fame, and enjoy the thrill of performance.[7]

In other words, pageants existed to entertain and thrived because they adapted to remain pleasing to their constituents. As America's oldest pageant, the Miss America Pageant has served as a source of enjoyment for almost one hundred years. It has adapted to a variety of media platforms to engage its intended audience on multiple levels. Americans obsessed with beauty and pleasure find in pageantry a sense of intrigue and delight. With television, Hollywood, and theater as the background, the pageant emerges as yet another example of America's preoccupation with the stage. In a culture consumed with leisure and entertainment, it is not surprising that an enterprise like Miss America has met with success.[8] Miss America amazed audiences from the beach to the boardwalk to the comfort of one's living room. In a word, Miss America was fun.

Parlors, Pedestals, and Pictures: Women as Entertainment

American women found pleasure in the pursuit of, display of, and cultivation of beauty and talent long before the Miss America Pageant elbowed her way to center stage as the undisputed queen. Women practiced instruments, studied voice, and perfected recipes. They prepared for a life of entertaining as daughters, eligible maidens, and then as wives. They developed beauty remedies and marketed makeup. Women performed in barrooms, burlesque shows, and theaters. They flooded amusement parks, beaches, and, eventually, pageant stages.[9] Women entertained. They used their bodies, their brains, and their beauty as sources of, and keys to, pleasure. Pageants offer a window through which to view America's fascination with show business in all its myriad forms. Miss America contestants acted as both consumers and producers, demonstrating women's centrality to the entertainment industry.[10]

May Day celebrations represented some of the earliest celebrations of pulchritude in America. May Day festivities, once festivals of fertility rites, celebrated other feminine ideals in nineteenth- and twentieth-century America. More specifically, Southern May Day Queens represented the quintessential southern belle.[11] At Judson College, for example, May Day included field day festivities, crowning the Queen of May, and dancing around the May Pole. It resembled the medieval tournament with dancers and other entertainers performing for the queen and her court of honor.[12] These much anticipated events involved elaborate productions intended to amuse both audience and participants. These activities celebrated "society's definition of femininity, whereby men offered women protection in return for deference."[13] Women took their place on the pedestal, delighting in a rare opportunity for personal display.[14] The queen and her court embodied southern womanhood: the perfect mixture of humility, grace, and beauty. Some took pleasure in fulfilling culturally expected roles, the performance of which perpetuated existing ideals of womanhood.[15]

Americans' fascination with royalty, rule, and women as sources of entertainment did not end with crowning college women queen for a day. The first modern beauty contest can be traced to Phineas T. Barnum in 1854. Barnum (inadvertently) discovered a solution to the problem of displaying middle- and upper-class women while increasing the emphasis on beauty.[16] Barnum proposed a contest to determine the most beautiful woman in America. The new challenge resembled the competitions he already held for babies, dogs, and flowers. However, Barnum's plan crossed the lines of decency for the majority of Americans in the mid-nineteenth century.[17] Having successfully navigated many other issues of morality surrounding the acceptability of women in public entertainment spaces, he did not anticipate the many negative reactions he received, many of which prefigured ongoing critiques of the pageant for its entire existence. Indeed, Barnum marketed his museum to families as moral education, creating a space that even single women could attend without fear of tarnishing their reputations.[18]

Thus Barnum was no stranger to repackaging entertainment as something noble and not base, a pattern that would adhere to the pageant up into the modern era. With a few tweaks, he resurrected his quest to discover America's beauty. His contest became a daguerreotype competition where contestants (or someone else) submitted a picture as their entry. In effect, Barnum instituted the "Miss Photogenic" contest. He intended to turn the photographs into paintings to be hung in a "Congress of Beauty" so that the public could vote on their favorites. Barnum appealed to Americans' sense of national pride, claiming that the top ten beauties would be placed in a book of world beauties. He encouraged Americans to help him prove once and for all that American women were the prettiest in the world.[19] This was not about objectifying women or demeaning them in some way. Quite the opposite, Barnum argued. His contest elevated America's women as far superior to other women around the world. Like its modern descendent, Barnum's proposed "Congress of Beauty" offered a possibility of escape from the mundane of the everyday through its carefully scripted celebration of the ideal.

Following Barnum's daguerreotype contest, photo contests grew in popularity. Newspapers hosted these competitions as a way to increase readership, offering prizes to females and emphasizing the importance of beauty as central to women's role in society. Photo contests ensured that women could maintain their sense of demureness and decorum since women could be nominated without their knowledge or consent. The newspaper competitions proved widely successful as young women and their admirers alike relished this new form of amusement and the awards it offered. One of the most popular of these contests occurred in 1905, when "Promoters of the St. Louis Exposition" invited newspapers "to select a representative young woman from their city to compete for a beauty title at the Exposition . . . according to one report, [there were] forty thousand photo entries."[20] Barnum, and those who copied his genius idea, had struck gold. Americans enjoyed celebrating beauty.

Several factors suggest that toward the turn of the century beauty contests experienced an even greater level of acceptance as sources of entertainment. First, one of the first resort pageants from which the Miss America Pageant evolved took place at Rehoboth Beach, Delaware, in 1880.[21] Second, carnivals as a site for beauty contests gained prominence at the end of the nineteenth century.[22] Finally, while as late as 1907 the *Ladies' Home Journal* (*LHJ*) denounced pageants, by 1911 it hosted its own beauty contest.[23] The *LHJ* found an ally in the halls of pageantry; together they sold more products. These contests increased the pageant's influence beyond the lower classes as they incorporated and modified middle-class values. This move by the *LHJ* signaled a mainstreaming of beauty contests, in a sense granting middle-class Americans permission to enjoy them.

The rise and acceptance of beauty pageants as an acceptable form of amusement mirrored the growing cultural acceptance of other forms of entertainment involving the female form. For example, burlesque had recently found a home in American culture as working-class men found pleasure in the live performances of women. Indeed, the opposition faced by pageants also mimics that experienced by burlesque.[24] Women appeared in print ads, in theaters, and on the big screen. And, though the question of how much to display was up for debate, few disputed that women's bodies were intended for enjoyment in one venue or another.[25] It was, as in all things, a matter of degree.

Pageants, festivals, carnivals, and other contests of beauty—as with most of life in the nineteenth century—were highly divided by class. But all classes encouraged the cultivation of beauty among women in some form and, increasingly, such activities were packaged as entertainment. Whether in local barrooms or ballrooms, a woman's attractiveness served as a source of pleasure for anyone willing to pay the cost of admission. Women embodied beauty, increasingly performing cultural expectations or parodies of them on the public stage to the delight of their many admirers. Their bodies provided the entertainment. In the case of the early years of burlesque, women also utilized their voices, their talents, and their wit to hold the attention of the audience.[26] In this way, burlesque as entertainment provides an early example of the tension experienced by pageant contestants. In both cases, participants were both actors and acted upon.[27]

Miss America becomes central to the culture in part because it manages to close the class divide—it makes it respectable for women to step out of the house, into a swimsuit, and onto a stage to use her body for the enjoyment of others.[28] It presents such action as an extension of her duty as a woman. She understands her role—and it has been dictated to her—as one in which she must provide pleasure to others. Her body, her mind, and her talents are primarily viewed as objects to be consumed and enjoyed by someone else. She actively participates in this performance meant to amuse and entertain. Even before the pageant found its way to the airwaves, it was billed as entertainment and a source of pleasure as it was embedded in "a week-long elaborate festival that included staged spectaculars, sports events, automobile races, orchestra and dance competitions, nightly balls on the boardwalk, and the opening parade."[29] It was everyday amusement at its finest.

Figure 2.2. A pamphlet advertising the 1935 Miss America Pageant highlighted the many activities of pageant week. From its earliest days, the pageant capitalized on its entertainment value.

To be sure, women were agents of pleasure and not just passive bodies consumed by others. At the turn of the twentieth century, women sought pleasure more explicitly with some fighting for access to birth control and others shortening their hemlines and smoking in public. This "new woman" fought for the vote, went to the movies, and was otherwise concerned about consuming amusement, not just producing and providing it. As she stepped onto the stage, behind the camera, and onto the runway, she declared it her choice and she reported pleasure in performing. In short, she was both actor and acted upon as she performed roles meant to entertain. Thus this is a story of increasing, but never total, agency. Performing always existed within a range of constraints. Cultural norms and decency laws continued to police female behavior in attempts to protect women from defaming their character. Some might argue that a fear of women's increasing agency drove the regulations.[30] The pageant arose in the midst of these debates, eventually earning a spot on the side of respectable entertainment both for participants and viewers.

Live from Atlantic City! Miss America Takes on Television

Looking back from the twenty-first century, it seems impossible to imagine not being able to watch the Miss America Pageant on television. For over half of its existence, television has defined the Miss America Pageant. The contest has entertained countless Americans, serving as a great equalizer of sorts as school teachers, bus drivers, and presidents alike gathered with their families (at least for a time) to tune in to the live broadcast. As the pageant evolved to fit a television audience rather than the Atlantic City tourists it had been created to keep occupied with revenue-enhancing activities, it entered a new era of entertainment that deemphasized the need to see things live. Now one could simply turn a television dial.

The Miss America Pageant took to television slowly. In keeping with its beginnings as a moneymaking scheme, the pageant's primary concerns were financial. Would allowing the pageant to be televised cause the organization to lose money? More specifically, organizers worried that loyal pageant attenders would elect to watch the free broadcast of the pageant rather than forking over the money for a seat in Atlantic City's Convention Hall. Thus pageant officials sought a deal with television affiliates to ensure that entering into this new entertainment medium would not cut too far into their bottom line. This involved decisions like not broadcasting the entire show, not allowing local stations to carry the broadcast, and prohibiting television cameras from blocking audience views.[31] Yet if Miss America wished to contend in the entertainment industry, perhaps it could not afford *not* to venture into television and, eventually, to succumb to its formatting. Ultimately Miss America did opt to adapt its program to fit a television screen and to reach a television audience, and in so doing it rode the entertainment wave from live theater to live television, making a big splash along the way.

Prior to 1954, the Miss America Pageant could only be viewed in person. Atlantic City was an entertainment venue, and Miss America was the main attraction the weekend after Labor Day. Days of preliminary competitions, interviews, and a parade culminated in the main event held in Atlantic City's Convention Hall (later renamed Boardwalk Hall) on Saturday night.[32] Fans lined up hours before the show was to start, clamoring for a place inside the theater. This was variety show entertainment at its finest. Jugglers, trampoline acts, singers, magicians, and ventriloquists all delighted the audience with their carefully scripted talent presentations. The final night of competition routinely lasted three hours or more. The move to television changed that. Pageant format evolved slowly, but from its television debut cameras and time slots shaped the content of the pageant even as organizers insisted that television not interfere with the integrity of the event.

Miss America first hit the television airwaves in September 1954 when Evelyn Ay, Miss America 1954, crowned Lee Meriwether Miss America 1955. Organizers tried to have the pageant proceed as always, allowing the television to cover the pageant largely as a news event with as little interference as possible. The live pageant began at 8:30 p.m., but the televised broadcast picked up at 10:30 p.m. It covered the last three talent performances and continued through the announcement of the top five finalists, the onstage questions, and the announcement of the winners. Backstage announcers narrated the events to the at-home audience. Much to the dismay of the live audience, the crowning took place backstage where a television camera reported the action to viewers at home.[33] A faceless mass replaced the countless volunteers, family members, and local supporters as the intended audience, so decisions were made with them in mind. By playing to the masses, producers increased their reach, their profit, and, potentially, their influence. Another change that television brought despite efforts to keep it from intruding was the elimination of the outgoing Miss America's farewell speech. The telecast cut away this portion of the pageant. Thus Miss America literally lost part of her voice when the shift to television occurred.[34] Her reflections on the year failed to offer the same kind of amusement as that of the talent competition. This is but one example of how television began to dictate how Miss America would entertain its at-home audience.

As Miss America grew more at home posing for the camera, more changes ensued. Choreographers were hired to script production numbers for professional dancers to fill the time between phases of the competition. Expensive sets were crafted. Professional entertainers were hired to produce a professional-quality product. Which colors would appear best on camera were considered. Blocking was done not to the audience, but to the cameras. In other words, Miss America became a production and not just a pageant.[35] The preliminary competitions, while still important for determining the top ten finalists, also served as practice runs for the final night. Contestants timed their walks, their turns, and their glances to ensure they played not only to the judges but also to the cameras. Miss America 1965, Vonda Kay Van Dyke, was one who "played to the judges to win" while still acknowledging the importance of the audience, both live and television, "because win or lose the *public* would build a career in entertainment."[36] She, and many of her pageant sisters, recognized that much was at stake in connecting with the television audience. At the least, it foreshadowed how they might engage audiences during their year as Miss America. At most, it gave contestants a taste of stardom, setting them on a career in Hollywood or on Broadway. For the majority, of course, they walked away with neither a crown nor a contract.

Other evidence that the pageant had become a production was the strict time frame that television forced on it. Gone were the days of long speeches, multiple encores, and untimed talent presentations. Organizers crafted a tightly regimented variety show to be consumed by their television audience in a set amount of time. In 2018, the once three-plus-hour event had been condensed to a mere two hours, and that included commercial breaks.[37] Unlike the live iterations of the pageant, it was the television audience and not those in the auditorium that dictated the pageant's shape. The Miss America Pageant was no made-for-TV movie, but it was theatrical live television that culminated in the crowning of the woman who had bested the rest. It proved mesmerizing, enticing viewers near and far.

Television increased the Miss America Pageant's influence. Expanding the pageant from the boardwalk to the bedroom captivated the imaginations of more people. The Miss America Pageant grew from a local phenomenon centered in Atlantic City to a national event for viewers from Atlantic City to Walla Walla, Washington. In the early decades of television when there were limited programming choices, Miss America quickly became the thing to watch. It offered the audience something to tune into that captured the ideals of the nation.[38] It remained entertainment for the masses for decades, in part because it was a socially acceptable form of family entertainment that offered some titillating aspects. For example, a teenage boy might reasonably expect to watch the Miss America Pageant with his parents, but not Baywatch.

The televised Miss America Pageant created a fan base and a fan culture. It energized hometowns by emphasizing the girl-next-door as it touted her achievements and her dreams on national television. The pageant offered viewers, both at home and in Atlantic City, the chance to escape into a perfectly painted scene for a couple of hours to enjoy a land of beauty, wit, and charm.[39] Observers imagined themselves as the glamorous women sporting fashion-forward trends on the runway (or, alternately, as being with such women). The pageant proved aesthetically pleasing to viewers, but it also gave them something slightly more substantive. Consumers tuned in year after year. The shape of the pageant might have shifted, but its role as entertainment remained a crucial piece of the Miss America Pageant's identity. Its desire to remain competitive in the entertainment industry would prompt further changes as it headed into the new millennium.

Shifting the Spotlight: The Impact of Reality Television

The 2000s brought struggles for the Miss America Organization as they fought plummeting television ratings.[40] In a primetime lineup increasingly crowded with reality television shows from *American Idol* to *America's Next Top Model*, "the original reality competition show" of Miss America found its commitment to tradition and decorum lacking in curb appeal.[41] Faced with the possibility of extinction—or at the least—the loss of its television audience and the television contract that kept it financially viable, Miss America scrambled to demonstrate its continued relevance as an American cultural touchstone. Not willing to feature contestants eating bugs or similar shock-inducing activities, producers looked for other ways to engage viewers. As Kevin McAleese, executive director of the Miss Philadelphia Scholarship Pageant noted, "Television is a very competitive game, we all get that. The question is, how do we adapt to that and bend the rules a little, but not give up all the values that we've stood for 85 years? We've got to be realistic, because we've got to be visible, and if you're not on television, you're not visible."[42] In their attempt to attract viewers, pageant producers gave Miss America repeated facelifts to prove that America's oldest sweetheart still deserved a little love.

In the early 2000s, the contest remained on network television where it tried to spice up the competition with a bit more flare and a nod to other reality shows. Miss America enlisted *The Bachelor* host Chris Harrison to emcee and *American Idol* favorite Clay Aiken to entertain at the 2005

competition held in Atlantic City in September 2004, C-list stars who perhaps only emphasized the pageant's irrelevance or solidified its space as reality television. That year's pageant also showcased a casual wear competition
for the top ten, a multiple-choice civics quiz for the top five, and a head-to-
head talent competition featuring the final two contestants. This move to
heighten the suspense mimicked fan-favorite elimination shows, only here
the elimination took place in one evening rather than over a series of weeks.
Participants competing for the Miss America 2005 crown also wore skimpier
swimsuits than their predecessors. Where once the pageant tried to distance
itself from its origins as a bathing suit competition by emphasizing its focus
on talent and scholarship, in the early 2000s "the challenge [was] not to move
away from female exploitation, but to make it work for the pageant—without
giving up too much of the core values."[43] In other words, pageant producers
recognized that it was the swimsuit competition, not the talent competition
or the onstage questions, that was keeping the competition afloat. Despite
its commitment to scholarship and well-rounded women, it was beauty that
delighted television audiences, not brains. The racier swimwear came a little
too late, however, with a mere 9.8 million viewers tuning in to see Deidre
Downs crowned Miss America 2005.[44] These record low numbers led ABC
to drop Miss America's contract, leaving the organization searching for a
new television home and questioning whether this entertainment staple of
the twentieth century could be successful in the shifting tides of the twenty-
first-century entertainment industry.

The pageant relocated to Las Vegas in 2006 where it was hosted in January instead of the traditional September. The new physical locale coincided
with a move to cable television, which simultaneously cut into its viewing
potential and freed it to reinvent itself. The organization landed a contract
with Country Music Television (CMT), which hosted the pageant for two
years.[45] While some might have imagined that a move from network to cable
would lead the organization further down the runway toward the sexy and
scandalous, CMT instead "determined to restore the contest's luster, turning back the clock to those gauzy days long before it became freighted with
reality-show gimmicks."[46] President and chief executive of the Miss America
Organization, Art McMaster, applauded CMT's efforts to return to tradition, noting, "These last few years, we've been playing games with the show.
We saw all these reality shows that had been out there, that had been very
successful. But that doesn't mean everything needs to become that."[47] In its
quest to return to the Miss America of yesteryear, CMT eliminated the casual
wear competition and multiple-choice civics quiz in favor of showcasing more

talent (the final five instead of the final two), bringing back the formal state sashes, and reinstituting the Miss Congeniality award. The pageant enjoyed a modicum of success, securing 3.1 million viewers, which proved enough for CMT to agree to another year of courting America's sweetheart.[48]

After a two-year run on CMT, Miss America was dumped again.[49] TLC rescued them, partnering with the pageant for the next three years. Again the pageant received a makeover as it worked to remain attractive in a crowded entertainment market. TLC expanded on CMT's behind-the-scenes coverage, airing a four-part series titled *Miss America: Reality Check* in 2008 in the weeks leading up to the main event. The purported aim of this series was to rebrand Miss America as modern and relatable, rather than a holdover from another time.[50] Producers sought to rid pageant contestants of stale pageant tendencies such as overly scripted walks, helmet hair, and thick layers of makeup in favor of a more free-flowing, natural look. Experts on the show consulted with participants and shepherded them through a variety of challenges, some related to pageantry and others simply for potential entertainment value. The series was highly successful. Recasting Miss America as the original reality show where contestants competed to see who was "the best at everything" drew in approximately 19.2 million viewers in 2008, a huge improvement from the 2.4 million of 2007.[51] And, when those viewers tuned in to the final night of competition, many felt as if they "knew" the contestants competing. Rather than simply cheering for their state representative, some had other favorites in mind for the crown. *Miss America: Reality Check* introduced the television audience to a side of the contestants never seen before and the results were not surprising. America liked peeking behind the curtain. TLC continued some form of this behind-the-scenes coverage in their 2009 and 2010 productions of the show as well.

The shift to reality television involved an attempt to close the gap between the contestants and the audience. "We recognized that the difficulty with our show was that people didn't get to know these contestants," Art McMaster commented in 2010.[52] Producers wanted to reemphasize Miss America as the girl-next-door. These were all-American women with hobbies, families, and faiths just like those in the television audience. They were people you could root for. And, with the advent of "America's Choice" in 2008, people at home got the opportunity to vote their favorites into the final round of competition. The pageant also added online contestant biographies, pictures, and videos to increase fan buy-in. By increasing its online presence, the Miss America Organization expanded its footprint from one day to months. It was audience participation at its finest. The live event became a national phenomenon in which the entire nation could participate. No longer sideline judges, Americans could affect the outcome of the competition. Harkening back to the days of the dime museum contests where anyone with money could cast a vote, the modern pageant allowed anyone to vote with a call, a text, or the click of a mouse. And vote they did, to the tune of almost 200,000 votes for "America's Choice" 2013.[53]

The pageant reunited with network television in 2011 when ABC renewed their contract. In its quest to remain a staple of American pop culture, the pageant allowed the television audience to vote on people's choice awards, showed more behind-the-scenes footage, and added more suspense to the results show. This drive to remain entertaining seemed to cloud their claim to be a scholarship program. Perceived audience desires dictated the production in ways like never before. Most prominently, recent pageants featured more eliminations than those of the past. Instead of a television broadcast that featured the top ten competing in each phase of competition, recent years cut contestants after each phase of the competition, adding a bit of drama as contestants were left standing in their swimsuit or sitting in their talent costume when their name was not called to move on to the next round, their rejected bodies still on display. In addition, eliminated contestants remained on stage as a kind of backdrop for the evening's competition rather than being allowed to watch the remainder of the contest from backstage. Hosts asked questions of the non-finalists to pass the time or had them participate in whimsical filler activities in between phases of competition. They remained, despite no longer having a shot at the crown, part of the show. Non-finalists were expected to cheer on their competitors while smiling politely as they performed for both live and television audiences. Their role as entertainers remained central. Mourning and disappointment must wait.

Thus in the pageant, as in show business, the show must go on.

Fame, Fortune, and Fans: Promoting Miss America

Despite its rocky relationship with television and its diminishing role in American society, the pageant survived. Thousands of young women around the nation still competed in local and state pageants, fervently hoping to make it to the national pageant.[54] And like any competition, Miss America hopefuls had their dedicated fans. These fans showed up to cheer with signs, buttons, and glowing batons. They demanded merchandise from signed pictures of their favorites in bikinis to T-shirts and jackets with the signature crown bedazzled on them. They started blogs and websites devoted to all things Miss America. While Miss America never regained the 85 million television viewers it boasted in 1960, the shifts made in the early 2000s landed it securely back on network television, and, in 2013, back on the Atlantic City Boardwalk. Americans, it seemed, still enjoyed a little glitz and glamour coupled with down-home charm. Following the pageant and its contestants remained a source of amusement for many Americans.

Miss America as entertainer stretched beyond the one night a year that she was seen on stage. Early in pageant history Miss America functioned as a spokeswoman for sponsors of the program, touring the country, speaking, or appearing in advertisements.[55] As the program expanded, Miss America's celebrity status grew with it. Program participants routinely accepted speaking engagements in schools, community centers, and churches.[56] Miss America drew a crowd, or, at times, went to the crowd as an entertainer for sporting events, community festivals, or local pageants.[57] While Miss Americas performed much charitable work during her year of service, she also received appearance fees as a valued entertainer.[58] She spoke. She sang. She danced. She signed autographs and posed for pictures. Event organizers relied on Americans' fascination with pageants, some hosting Miss America year after year.

Miss America's fan base demanded access to Miss America not just through attending appearances in their local towns. Fans read Miss America's magazine articles, her dating and beauty advice books, and interviews with her in newspapers.[59] They wrote fan mail and requested autographed pictures or personalized advice. With the advent of social media, fans could get their fix instantly—in real time. With Facebook, Twitter, Instagram, Snapchat, and more, Miss America could blast an image of her latest community service appearance, performance, or a fun makeup tip with just a few clicks. And her appreciative fans liked, commented, and shared her picture, commentary, video, or advice just as easily. Miss America fans enjoyed the play-by-play, finding fellow pageant lovers along the way. The Miss America Organization's Facebook page boasted the largest number of followers of its social media sites with the page sitting at over 500,000 followers and over 525,000 "likes." Miss America's Instagram had 195,000 followers while her Twitter feed sat at just 76,000.[60] Miss America's social media presence boosted its visibility as an organization as fans had a way to share their love of America's beauty with their friends and followers.

Miss America's social media presence also boosted her public visibility as it allowed the organization to quickly and efficiently let fans know about Miss America's public appearances, including additions or changes to her schedule. Miss America's community service activities, performances, and speeches were publicized through her social media accounts, letting her followers know exactly what she had been up to on any given day. This also offered additional advertising for Miss America's sponsors (hair, clothes, gym, car, etc.). Many state pageants followed suit, maintaining a strong social media presence, including Twitter handles and Instagram accounts that were passed down along with the crown.[61] Certainly the image portrayed on both the state and national social media accounts was a whitewashed one. Each individual placed her stamp on her sites, sure, but it was not an anything-goes site. The image(s) being conveyed were the image(s) that the state or national pageant wished to convey. They were carefully monitored. For example, Cara Mund, Miss America 2018, reportedly lost access to official Miss America social media accounts after being told that she was "bad at social media." She, of course, saw this as yet another instance in which Miss America leadership took away her voice and depersonalized her in the name of preserving and promoting the Miss America brand.[62] Mund, like Miss Americas before her, saw her individuality erased. She was to represent something larger than herself and that trumped individual need or desire. This modern-day monitoring mirrored the rules instituted by Slaughter. It was just the latest reminder that though contestants might find enjoyment in their participation they existed for the entertainment and delight of others. Performance trumped authenticity.

The hub for all things Miss America remained the pageant's official website.[63] Here fans could order official Miss America merchandise, read about the history of the pageant, and follow Miss America's fundraising efforts for their national charity, Children's Miracle Network Hospitals. One could learn how to find and enter a preliminary pageant in one's community, read the official press releases of the Miss America Organization, and find volunteer opportunities. The website also featured links to all of the state organizations and to the pageant's national program for teens, Miss America's Outstanding Teen. It pointed to all things Miss America.

The online presence of Miss America extended beyond Miss America's official website and social media accounts. Individual contestants, from the local level to the national level, kept websites or blogs that gained followings. Some even kept a website, or archived a website, long after their year of service was completed.[64] Pageant coaches and self-proclaimed pageant experts developed their own social media presence that invited fans to follow them for the latest in pageant fashion trends and for live-tweeting of state and national pageants.[65] To be sure, it also secured them new clients as their clients made the finals or won the crown. Pageant VoyForums invited discussion and critique of every possible pageant question, problem, or issue imaginable. Here anonymous posters offered play-by-plays of local pageants and, many times, hurtful assessments of pageant participants. However, this, too, became a source of entertainment and amusement for many pageant faithful. They thrived on the drama. Indeed, managing Miss America's fans and giving them the scoop they desired became a thriving business. VoyForums and Facebook comments on pageant pages served as a reminder that some of the entertainment offered by the Miss America Pageant came at the contestants' expense.[66] By choosing to participate, young women subjected themselves to constant scrutiny in the name of fun. They were primarily objects of amusement, not individuals deserving of respect.

Pageant podcasts, contestant interviews, pageant predictions, and more became more than just a hobby for some; it provided a unique business venture that presented itself in the form of fan websites. One of the most popular was a website named Pageant Junkies—Hopelessly Addicted to the Miss America Program.[67] The site, run by Carey Lakey, boasted some 20,000 followers and contained both free and VIP (members only) content. Lakey, a self-proclaimed pageant guru and former pageant contestant, started her blog as a way to communicate her top ten lists for the Miss America Pageant to her friends more easily. Her hobby of providing yearly pageant predictions grew into a moneymaking enterprise. As of 2017, she offered seminars and webinars for pageant contestants looking to increase their chances at winning. She provided consulting for pageants and pageant hopefuls. Lakey also hosted a pageant podcast. She interviewed local, state, and national winners, using her website as the outlet for their message.[68] Gradually, she built up a following, hosting gatherings with other "junkies" throughout the year across the nation. Miss America offered more than one night of entertainment a year for Lakey and her followers. It was a full-time obsession.

The pervasiveness of pageants as entertainment can also be seen in the presence of books, movies, and reality television series featuring pageants. Pageants as entertainment trickled onto the big screen with movies depicting pageant contestants and a reality show (*Toddlers and Tiaras*) following the pageant craze. Even as Americans decried the horrors of doing this to one's children, they turned in weekly for their dose of pageant chaos. Films like *Drop Dead Gorgeous* and *Miss Congeniality* (followed by *Miss Congeniality 2*) poked fun at pageants, even as they captured some of their endearing qualities. The award-winning film *Little Miss Sunshine* unveiled the overly serious nature of pageants as well as the financial, emotional, and physical costs of competition, but it also demonstrated the main character's desire to compete, entertain, and win. TLC's reality series *Toddlers and Tiaras*, like *Little Miss Sunshine*, noted the unrealistic expectations placed on young girls by their parents, trainers, and ultimately themselves.[69] And yet Americans could not look away. They found themselves sucked into *Toddlers and Tiaras*, *America's Next Top Model*, and, enduringly, the Miss America Pageant. Through pop culture and social media, Miss America was once again something to be discussed. It had gone viral.

Conclusion

Miss America fans lived all over the country. Each September they descended on Atlantic City or channeled Atlantic City into their living room to cheer on their favorite contestants. Some hosted watch parties complete with top ten lists, games, prizes, and tiaras. Others decided a Miss America–themed party was the way to go.[70] And still others enjoyed the suspenseful evening alone. They tuned in because they found pageant gazing enjoyable.[71]

Entertainment pervaded the pageant. Hours were spent perfecting staging, lighting, and sound. Pageant officials approved television hosts and planned production numbers. Contestants dedicated years to dance lessons, music lessons, or theater training. Miss America hopefuls chose music and costumes with the judges—and the audience—in mind. They learned to connect with fans via a wink, a smile, or a knowing glance. In other words, contestants enjoyed putting on a show and all that it entailed. They soaked up the spotlight or wilted in it. Fans found both enthralling. Thus, Americans, for their part, tuned in year after year to consume the action of another year's production. The Miss America Pageant entertained. And some of its contenders dedicated their lives to the entertainment industry.

But entertainment alone did not explain the pageant's success. Some components of the pageant defied explanation as entertainment. For example, one would be hard-pressed to think of the interview, required platform, or emphasis on community service as entertaining. Rather, they represented a different facet of the competition, one equally crucial to the pageant's attraction to its participants. Miss America was not just another reality show. It bore significance, for its contenders, and for many of its fans, beyond the staged production.

To be sure, one must understand that pageants existed to entertain. They provided the vehicles through which women placed themselves before an audience to perform and to be admired. And yet to stop there would be to state the obvious. Contestants, viewers, organizers, and sponsors spoke of value far deeper than a well-crafted production. Even if the pageant's capacity to entertain kept it afloat, it alone did not explain the pageant's success. Just as pageants were about more than sex, they were more than entertainment. Neither fully explained its long-standing success as America's oldest pageant.

3

Miss America as Competition

"Former Miss Americas are a unique breed. They are achievers, certainly; even the least type A's among the group are generally pretty driven women. They are competitive—and not just because most have spent years pushing themselves into the position of Miss America, but because after that tremendous accomplishment comes and goes, many find that there is no off switch for their considerable ambition. And so any gathering of former Miss Americas rapidly and invariably turns into its own contest. Who among these women is the most beautiful, most intelligent, most accomplished, most altruistic, most ideal of the "ideal" that Bert Parks used to sing about? It's a never-ending race with no official winner. And yet, for all this internal jockeying for position, it is also a group of women who are generally affectionate—toward one another and toward the program that has provided them with a lasting identity."[1]

Introduction

The singer crooned, "There she is, Miss America, there she is, your ideal," and America's newest sweetheart pointed her finger to the peaked vaults of Planet Hollywood's domed ceiling. In doing so, she expressed her commitment not only to be a saintly beauty, but also an ambassador for God and America. Caressa Cameron, Miss America 2010, struggled to position the crown on the new Miss America, Teresa Scanlan, who rejoiced in her victory by gesturing heavenward. The repeated motion from announcement to crowning to emotional first walk down the winner's runway was difficult

to ignore.[2] Miss Nebraska, newly crowned Miss America, wanted the world
to know that she attributed her victory to God. Indeed, her winning moment
looked a lot like the end of any nationally televised sporting event. In a rush
of adrenaline, many an athlete has thanked God, gestured heavenward, or
knelt for a quick prayer. Scanlan's victory celebration proved no different. She
had vanquished the foe and taken the crown. A little celebrating was in order.

*Figure 3.1. Teresa Scanlan, Miss America 2011, gestures heavenward after her win. A formerly
homeschooled conservative Christian from Nebraska, Scanlan wanted the world to know that
she gave God the glory for her victory.*

Offering thanks to God for one's ability to beat out the other competitors was not the only thing pageants shared with American sports culture or with competition in general. Miss America contenders, like their

counterparts on the athletic fields, committed to strict diets, exercise reg-
imens, and grueling practice schedules. They hired trainers and coaches.
They invested money in "gear." They sacrificed weekends to contests. They
endured criticism and defeat. They dusted themselves off and tried again.
They attracted fans. There were announcers, judges, program books, light-up
noisemakers, pageant merchandise, and, in some states, concession stands
with alcohol. Some contestants shot straight to the top. Some never made it
past the first round. There were one-timers and lifers, novices and experts,
interlopers and naturals. In short, Miss America was the ultimate competition, one in which individual contestants competed against their personal
bests and against one another.[3]

Women have long seen one another as rivals.[4] From baking contests to
needlepoint, women showcased their domestic skills to secure a husband. As
beauty culture grew in America, the pursuit of beauty became another way
that women sought to best one another. Later, as women's goals and possibilities for advancement extended beyond marrying well, the competition
among women continued. Often women knew—instinctively—that there
was not room at the top for multiple women and thus worked against one
another for those few positions of power available be they in politics, health
care, or industry.[5] Pageants moved the contest from the sitting room and the
boardroom to the stage. There were rewards at stake both tangible and intangible, but all desirable. Miss America was their Super Bowl and the crown
was their trophy.

Pageants demanded a particular body type. American ideals of beauty set the
requirements, however, rather than the features needed to achieve specific athletic feats.[6] While styles changed, winners exhibited standard features of beauty:
facial and body symmetry, a clear complexion, youth, and thinness. With the
pageant's emphasis on physical fitness, contestants spoke routinely of diet and
exercise as a primary form of preparation. In this sense, it does not simply mirror
an athletic competition; it is one. Winners discussed doing whatever it took to
win. This went far beyond buying a gown currently en vogue (though there is
much to say there too). For example, many white contestants in the latter part
of the twentieth century achieved a perfectly tanned body through sunbathing,
sunless tanners, or tanning beds. Other participants ensured cleavage by taping
their breasts together. Some competitors even went so far as plastic surgery. To
win, one needed the right body.

Pageant success also required an array of highly specific skills. The many
facets of competition meant participants needed to be adept at everything from
discussing current events to advocating for a community service platform and

walking in high heels.[7] In addition, each contender adopted a talent. Because talent accounted for 35 percent of the overall score, these performances were key. Each skill must be mastered. Even the smallest details held great significance. Pageant coaches helped contestants hone their skills in the same way that political strategists helped political candidates hone their talking points.

This intense training and required physique was akin to that endured by professional athletes. Just as many athletes had strength and conditioning coaches in addition to the coaches calling the shots on the field, the most successful pageant contenders often hired coaches and personal trainers. These individuals did everything from setting contestants up with a meal plan to helping young women perfect their walk for the swimsuit competition. It was not uncommon for a participant to have multiple professionals helping her prepare for a pageant. Interview coaches, walking coaches, talent coaches (of various stripes), fitness trainers, personal stylists, and dress designers all marketed their services to young women in pursuit of a crown.[8] Training for a pageant was a process with many moving parts. Pageant contenders did not seem to mind the long hours of preparation or the finances expended, seeing both as valuable investments to achieving both their immediate goals and to their life beyond the Miss America stage.

Of course, no sporting event would be complete without its adoring fans. At all levels of competition: local, state, and national, supporters arrived ready to cheer their favorite(s) on to the final round. At the state and national levels, in particular, expectations for one's cheering section were quite high. Clapping light-up hands, glowing batons, and buttons and signs with a contestant's face on them dotted the audience.[9] A quick glance would likely also reveal spectators filling out scorecards, compiling a top ten (or fifteen) list, and trying to guess the winner. Some people even placed money on their contestant. Odds were given and bets were taken in Atlantic City casinos just like it was any other sporting event.

A contestant's biggest supporters were often her family. Her entourage accompanied her just like she was playing travel ball. Among the tribe, there was talk of judges' decisions, questions about contestants' wardrobes, and discussion of talents, walks, and onstage answers. Mothers formed alliances with other mothers, and there existed a sort of pecking order based on one's daughter's success. In short, there were as many pageant moms as soccer moms all convinced that their role as a dedicated spectator meant they knew what it took to win. And that it should have been *their* daughter.

In other words, pageants offered the thrill of competition for participant and spectator alike. Like all modes of competitive expression, Miss America offered the hope of prizes, the delight of winning (and the defeat of losing), the prospect of perfection, and the promise of community. The Miss America Pageant has adapted to shifting roles for women, adding and modifying components of the pageant to match with societal expectations. With American sports and politics as the background, the pageant stands as another example of America's obsession with winning, with women's bodies at the center of the competition. Thus it is no surprise that Miss America has met with much success. The pageant tapped into Americans' deeply rooted need to be the best. Except, instead of a medal, a crown was at stake.

Save It for the . . . Stage? The Competitive Nature of Pageants

Pageants, like politics and sports, involved a set of rules and a series of contests that resulted in winners and losers. Competitors in 2017 reached Miss America by winning their state title. To compete at the state level, most states required that a young woman win a smaller, local event known as a preliminary pageant. The local pageants followed all of the rules of the national one. Young women participated in five phases of competition that made up a portion of their total score: lifestyle and fitness in swimsuit (15 percent), evening wear (20 percent), talent (35 percent), private interview (25 percent), and onstage questions (5 percent).[10] Each part of the contest demanded specific uniforms, preparation, and execution. Most obvious to outside observers was the need for talent, be it singing, baton twirling, or playing an instrument. And, of course, the attractiveness of the contestants.

Contestants recounted submitting themselves to harsh criticism and grueling schedules. On approaching the pageant, Terry Meeuwsen, Miss America 1973, said she "felt like a racehorse that had been exercised, fed and groomed for a year. I was ready to go."[11] Kate Shindle, Miss America 1998, also committed to a healthy diet and rigorous exercise regimen. Reflecting on her quest to get into "swimsuit shape," she wrote, "I've worked my ass off to be fit and healthy. I've done push-up pyramids that turn my arms to Jell-O . . . I've learned that two-a-day workouts are my friend and junk food is my enemy." She continued her training the week of the pageant, riding an exercise bike, doing the Abs of Steel video, and squeezing in crunches any chance she got.[12] Bree Boyce, Miss South Carolina 2011, lost over one hundred pounds on her quest to capture the crown. Boyce reported exercising two to three hours a day when she was preparing for a pageant.[13] Each of these young women (and many more) refused to leave anything to chance. They worked as if their life depended on it, taking on the time commitments and lifestyle changes required for athletes, embracing pageant preparation as they would any demanding job.

Judges at the local, state, and national levels all followed the same criteria when evaluating contestants. Indeed, a certain number of judges at local and state pageants had to be Miss America certified. Depending on the state, they might have to fill out an application and submit letters of recommendation or receive specialized training through a seminar or training session. They were then added to the list of qualified panelists in the state. At least one novice judge was required as well.[14] In 2017, women received a numerical score from each of the judges for each of the five categories of competition, much like an athlete competing in gymnastics or figure skating received multiple scores. These scores determined which contestants continued to the final round at state and national competitions. Winners were decided based on overall scores or a process known as Final Ballot.[15] This is a shift from the early days of the pageant when women's measurements were taken and scores assigned to individual features of her body including eyes, legs, and hands. Each contestant's numbers were added up and the woman with the highest score won. The highest possible score was one hundred.[16]

In 1989, the Miss America Organization added a community service requirement. Contestants compiled portfolios, detailing their work on social issues from autism acceptance to advocating adoption. A separate panel evaluated the contestants' records and announced the five finalists for the Quality of Life Award during the competition week of Miss America.[17] It was competitive philanthropy. In addition to the national awards, states presented a contestant with the Miss America Quality of Life Award for community service. Even though a contestant's charity work did not constitute a separate phase of competition, it played into two of the categories: interview and onstage questions. Judges routinely asked contestants to comment on their platform, giving basic statistics about the issue, the need for volunteers, and/or how she grew interested in that particular cause. Panelists also asked contestants to comment on their involvement with their philanthropy. Contestants with a high degree of involvement in her chosen platform often fared well in the competition overall. Just as athletes who participate in extra camps and voluntary practices stand out, so, too, do the Miss America contestants who put in the extra work to excel in community service.[18] Their determination and drive to raise funds, plan events, and organize nonprofits pays huge dividends in the interview room and on stage.

The cutthroat nature of pageants has been well caricatured in movies and media. *Drop Dead Gorgeous* depicts small-town pageant sabotage in a mockumentary of sorts, complete with a missing costume, a falling stage light, and even a dead pageant contestant. While actual contestants tended to focus on camaraderie rather than competition, there was no denying that in each phase of competition, contestants went head-to-head against one another. There were no teams; it was an individual sport. In the end, only one woman could take the crown. And, yes, at times, that resulted in a tensely competitive atmosphere. While true that each individual was in it for herself, the cattiness displayed by some pageant contestants is perhaps no different than the trash talk popular in male locker rooms or the sidelines. Beauty contest participants laughed about one's swimsuit walk or pageant turn just as football players might ridicule the other team's running back consistently forgetting the play.[19] In both cases, there were carefully crafted moves that—to be successful—one must master. They were skills.

Pageant contenders, like their peers in more traditional sporting arenas, proved committed, focused, and strategic.[20] Pageant hopefuls talked about which talent group was the weakest as they awaited their number placement just as runners awaited heat and lane assignments. They anticipated the announcement of judges as some might the referees for a big match. Some might skip out on a particular local pageant because of the number of veteran state pageant contenders registered. Others might choose to participate in a smaller, closed pageant with fewer resources because it was easier to win. Some young women even decided to attend college or graduate school in a state that was viewed as a less competitive pageant state than their home state. Debbye Turner, Miss America 1990, participated in Miss Arkansas for three years before competing in and winning Miss Missouri.[21] Likewise, Mallory Hagan, an Alabama native, earned the Miss New York crown on her way to becoming Miss America 2013.[22] These are but two examples of this competitive pageant tactic in play. It is, of course, similar to political candidates who reestablish residence in a location where they are more likely to win as Hillary Rodham Clinton did in relocating from Arkansas to New York.[23] Or, when lacrosse players choose to attend college in the South where the sport is just now gaining a following. Pageant participants could be just as strategic as their political and athletic counterparts.

The number of participants varied greatly from state to state. Just as football reigned supreme in the South, pageants had a decidedly southern flavor.[24] Southern states like Alabama, South Carolina, and Texas regularly boasted forty-plus competitors in the state pageant (representing the hundreds—at times over a thousand—women who participated at the local level) whereas Vermont, Montana, and Alaska sometimes attracted fewer than a dozen. Thus, while all pageants involved the same elements of competition, the level of competition varied from year to year and place to place. It only took one rock star contestant to launch a state onto the national stage. Competition, though predictable, was not static. Just as Democratic nominee for United States Senate Beto O'Rourke shook up an otherwise Republican race in Texas in 2018, one rookie contestant can become the person to beat at the national level even if she hailed from a "less competitive" pageant state. As with the political climate in our nation, pageant trends in the twenty-first century were shifting too. More progressive answers to onstage questions seemed to be more acceptable, and "blue" states were beginning to fare better on the traditionally conservative pageant stage.[25]

Like basketball introduced the three-point shot, football developed safer equipment, and baseball invented the designated hitter, the Miss America Pageant has adapted over time to ensure that its contest remained relevant. The most recent change occurred in 2018 when pageant officials eliminated the one competition phase that had persisted since Miss America's inception in 1921, the swimsuit competition. None of these changes, whether in sports or in pageants, have been introduced without complaint. Indeed, purists have argued that the proposed or implemented changes fundamentally changed the nature of the competition. In other words, it prompts the question of how much, if anything, must remain the same before a pageant (or a sport) has simply become something else.[26]

Still, the pageant continued, at its heart, to be about awarding a winner, declaring only one woman "the ideal." And it remained competitive.

And the Winner Is . . . : The Promise of Prizes

As in any competition, the thrill of competing was not the only incentive for pageant participation. Pageants offered the promise of prizes, especially for the winners. Indeed, some pageant participants and competitive athletes entered the arena with the rewards in mind. From contests where everyone won participation ribbons to national events where only the elite were allowed to contend for the top award, rewards were an important part of the system. Pageant participants, like competitive athletes, were not competing just for the sake of winning. Prizes were at stake.

The most obvious rewards pageant winners received were crowns. At every level of the Miss America Pageant system, local, state, and national, winners were awarded crowns. The official Miss America preliminary crown, state crown, and national crown held symbolic significance much like the Heisman Trophy. It was distinctive from crowns awarded in other pageant systems, but consistent across the program. For those in the know, it held meaning beyond itself; it pointed to the institution of Miss America. While the size of the national crown exceeded the size of the state crown and the size of the state crown exceeded the size of the preliminary crown, the shape and make of all three crowns were the same. The four points of the rhinestone crown represented the four *S*'s of scholarship, success, style, and service, indicating the kind of winner being sought in competition, the expectations of the person wearing the crown, and the type of leader and example that Miss America should be in the community.[27]

But crowns were not the only jewels chased by pageant contestants. Miss America hopefuls also spoke of competing in order to earn college scholarships.[28] The winner and runners-up earned the most scholarship dollars, but contestants also received scholarships for winning the talent competition and the swimsuit competition. Perhaps more surprising, scholarships were awarded for community service, academic achievement, and interview skills. Indeed, some state pageants held a separate scholarship interview with different judges that doled out scholarships from state institutions and pageant sponsors. Amounts of the scholarships varied significantly. For example, the talent winner at a local preliminary pageant might earn a $50 scholarship whereas a preliminary talent winner at the national competition earned $2,000. But the discrepancy was not merely a local versus national one. Big differences existed between states as well. For example, the winner of Miss California competed for a $22,000 scholarship in 2018 compared to Miss Rhode Island's $5,000.[29] Still, some participants never placed at the state pageant and yet walked away with thousands of dollars in scholarships. Of course, contestants also expended significant financial resources to participate in pageants. The notion that using their gifts to compete might score them a full-tuition scholarship to a particular school or a large sum of scholarship money to be used at any school enticed many young women to compete. Like athletes, however, many more failed to earn large college scholarships despite the large amount of training and resources put toward their goal.[30]

Local, state, and national winners also won a variety of prizes from pageant sponsors. Here, too, one can see a huge difference from state to state. It might be akin to the difference between playing at a Division III school and playing Division I ball. Both afforded perks, but one clearly outstripped the other. Some states provided the state pageant winner a clothing allowance or a clothes sponsor. Winners might receive other awards such as a car, free dry cleaning, personal training, makeup, or housing during their year of service in addition to the scholarship money received.[31] They might be allowed to keep all—or a portion of—their speaking fees. The list is almost endless. These perks added up and resulted in a nice package for many state winners.

On the national level, a Miss America in the twenty-first century could earn a six-figure salary during her year of service in addition to the $50,000 scholarship she won at the pageant.[32]

To state the obvious, winners of the state pageants received a trip to Atlantic City to participate in the Miss America competition. Even here, however, disparity existed between large "pageant states" like Arkansas and Oklahoma and states like Montana and Rhode Island. States with more contestants, volunteers, and sponsors had more resources to prepare "their" candidate for the big show in Atlantic City. For example, the Miss Arkansas website indicated that Miss Arkansas 2018, Claudia Raffo, won a $30,000 scholarship and "more than $75,000 in awards, wardrobe, transportation, and gifts."[33] Having the full monetary backing of the state made a difference when a competition evening gown could easily cost $1,000 with custom gowns by well-known pageant designers costing even more. To be competitive at the highest level could get very expensive. On occasion, the national pageant has had swimsuit or evening wear sponsors to eliminate these costs to the state winners.[34] Likewise, many state pageants secured clothing sponsors to ensure their winners had designer wardrobes for the national competition. Contestants representing states without these resources were, obviously, at a disadvantage.

While many of the prizes sought in pageants were monetary, others were tied to perceived personal, social, or spiritual gains. Winning held intrinsic worth because of the additional opportunities it presented. The crown, the trophy, or the medal opened doors that otherwise would have been closed. Winners received access to forms of power and platforms for change that they would not have had otherwise.[35] In other words, winners gained both cultural capital and symbolic capital in addition to tangible prizes.

Cultural capital refers to "forms of cultural knowledge, competencies or dispositions." This knowledge "equips the social agent with empathy toward, appreciation for or competence in deciphering cultural relations and cultural artefacts."[36] Put differently, cultural capital helped an individual increase his or her social standing. Examples include education, language skills, and physical attractiveness. Most notably, the attractiveness of pageant contestants afforded them cultural capital. Their beauty was a form of currency just as an athlete's height or speed might be. No matter how great a shot a basketball player might be, if she is 5'6," she is not going to play center for the WNBA. Similarly, Miss America contestants can only make it so far on the strength of her talent if that talent is not coupled with a pretty face. That said, when beauty was combined with talent and education, the contestant had even more cultural capital at her disposal.

Another non-tangible reward for pageant participants was the symbolic capital their status as beauty contestants gained them. For pageant winners, their title functioned as their special position or recognition. This celebrity status, though limited, afforded them access and power in particular venues. Their "honour in the sense of reputation and prestige" provided resources that might have remained unavailable to them without the crown.[37] Just as local politicians and star football players sometimes appeared at fundraising events and prayer meetings, pageant winners found themselves the recipient of invitations to store openings, civic club events, and youth retreats.[38]

Pageant participants garnered various amounts of symbolic and cultural capital during and after their tenure on stage. Indeed, some might coast off of their name recognition for decades just like a professional athlete. Think, for example, of Vanessa Williams, Lee Meriwether, or Terry Meeuwsen. While it is true that each of these women went on to do other things, they are all remembered as a former Miss America. For some, the pageant helped launch their careers.[39] While not tangible, the cultural capital and symbolic capital earned by pageant participants like these and others at times proved as enticing as scholarships and clothing allowances.[40] Miss America contestants spoke often of the many rewards that the pageant afforded them. In their quest to be named the nation's ideal, pageant participants took every opportunity for advancement. Winners competed for crowns, clothing, jewelry, and scholarships, but more importantly the title that granted access to other positions of power.

Winning Isn't Everything: The Benefits of Competition

The possibility of winning and the benefits it afforded was not the only thing to be gained from competing in the Miss America system. Like in any competition, individuals entered the pageant knowing that losing was a possibility and believing it a worthwhile endeavor anyway.[41] Indeed, not everyone entered the Miss America Pageant system expecting to become Miss America any more than everyone signed up for soccer imagining themselves competing in the World Cup. That is not to say, of course, that these individuals did not want to win. Nor is it to suggest that no one entered with only winning in mind (or even that most did not).[42] It is simply to acknowledge that people's motivations are always a jumble, and it is thus difficult if not impossible to ascertain with certainty their interests in competing beyond what they said. And contestants offered numerous justifications for their involvement.

They saw value in the act of competing. Their reasons mirrored reasons individuals cite for participating in both individual and team sports, and, yes, even political races. The assumption was that, win or lose, other skills and lessons could, and would, be learned along the way.

Pageant participants claimed that the contests aided in character development, promoted a healthy lifestyle, and taught important life skills much like any competition. Pageants encouraged discipline and time management, goal setting and perseverance, preparation and hard work. Contestants gained confidence, resiliency, and grit. Proponents of the Miss America competition argued that their program developed leaders and trained good citizens even as they endorsed their organization as one that represented the very best a community had to offer.[43] Pageants provided contestants space to take risks, develop camaraderie, and manage conflict. In other words, one learned more than how to walk across a stage in a swimsuit.

And yet, like other forms of competition, not everyone reaped the same—or equal—rewards. There existed tiers of participation in pageantry. As in any activity from learning a language to mastering an instrument, natural talent and abilities, time and effort invested, and desire to win all factored into an individual's potential for success. At the most basic, participatory level were the young women who entered pageants to have something to do, because their friends were participating, or to have fun. These women put little time or energy into preparation outside of scheduled rehearsals and the actual competition—much like recreation league athletes. They did not invest in expensive pageant clothing or create a nonprofit around their chosen community service cause. Pageants, for this group, were one activity among many, a hobby. If they happened to have some success, it was welcome and enjoyed, but part-time pageant participants did not wish to commit every waking moment of their life to chasing a crown.

At the next tier were the young women who saw pageants as a means to an end. Pageants presented them an opportunity for self-discovery and self-improvement. To be sure, these women enjoyed the thrill of competition and many at this level progressed through the ranks. They chose to enter pageants because they wanted to win, but also because they saw the potential benefits of the process. The intangibles mattered to contestants at this level, and they (or their parents) saw beyond the immediacy of pageant participation to how it might prepare them for life. These participants were poster children for the Miss America Organization, heralding its benefits to all who would listen. They spoke of gaining interview experience or building a resume. These women crammed in extra drills and practices because they enjoyed it, perhaps even viewing the contest as another outlet for their true passion, be it singing, dancing, or playing an instrument. Pageants loomed large in their world, but the competitions were not all-consuming. The quest for the crown was kept in perspective. In athletics, these women would be the club team players, simultaneously talented enough to get noticed and committed enough to invest extra time. They competed at a higher level.

At the top were the elite contestants. These women were in it to win it. Some had been competing in pageants their entire life and the pageant world was all they knew.[44] Others happened into it later, but dove in with such intensity that they were soon competing at the highest level. These women invested countless hours to training, at times hiring multiple pageant coaches to assist them with everything from their swimsuit walk to their interview voice. Elite competitors spent money on music lessons, personal trainers, and custom-made evening gowns. They traveled the preliminary pageant circuit weekend after weekend until they won a spot in the state pageant.[45] They partnered with community organizations, hosted fundraisers, made appearances, gave speeches, and started nonprofits to promote their platform. Pageants were their life. They were the Olympic athletes of the pageant world, giving everything to chase their dream.

Just as an athlete could ascend through the ranks from recreation league to elite sports, the boundaries between the groups were not impenetrable. In fact, one might view it more as a continuum than distinct categories. Competitors floated back and forth between the tiers depending on age, giftedness, and life circumstances at any given moment. It should also be noted that all the time, money, and hard work in the world cannot promise a Miss America any more than it can guarantee an Olympic athlete. Some natural ability must be present. Likewise, at times a novice might enter the pageant on a lark and find herself placing—or winning—the state competition.[46] In pageants, as in any athletic event, there is always room for a prodigy, for someone who was naturally gifted to skip levels and soar through the ranks. But even in the case of an exceptional contestant, more time and commitment was required once they reached a certain level if they wanted continued success.

When contestants made it to the national pageant, few, if any, would not be in it to win it. Some might be more realistic than others, but no one would declare that they did not want to walk away the winner. In other words, nobody entered the Miss America Pageant to lose. The national competition was the main event, and, at times, even those who once counted themselves among the recreational league stepped it up if they happened to land themselves a state crown. Such intensity and focus might be driven by the individual, the state pageant board, or both, but the higher one rose in the system, the greater the expectations.[47] There remained various levels of skill, natural beauty, and investments of both time and money, but as the gap between the best contestant and the worst grew smaller, the competition became more fierce. Participants knew that they had one shot at the Miss America title. Do-overs were not allowed.[48] As such, more than one state contender descended onto the runway convinced that she would take home the crown.[49]

The reality remained that most of the women lost. Thus, contestants learned not only how to celebrate victory, but how to handle defeat. Learning to lose well, and to correct one's mistakes, was an important part of the competition. At the preliminary level, little was at stake. Loss was inevitable for almost everyone as winning one's first preliminary pageant was the exception, not the rule. Contestants expected to lose more than they won. And, since states held multiple preliminary pageants, women had numerous chances throughout the year to earn a spot in the state pageant. Even at the state pageant, contestants understood that they would likely compete for several years before they won. Competitors needed experience, to learn the ropes, to be groomed, and to mature if they wanted the best shot at the national crown.[50] There was much to be gained from not winning the state pageant too young or on one's first attempt. Some women competed in the Miss America Pageant system for five, six, or even seven years.[51] Indeed, contestants could compete in the system from ages seventeen to twenty-five. They did not want to peak too soon.

Loss when one was about to "age out" of the system or at the national level was a different ball game. Many contestants found such disappointment and devastation a hard blow from which to recover.[52] The loss of identity and sense of self that came, particularly when they had invested years of their life to achieving this one goal, was hard to overcome. Some lost focus and sank into periods of depression. Elaine Campanelli, Miss Delaware 1975, was one such competitor. Excited by the prospect of being Miss America, Campanelli left Atlantic City without the coveted Miss America title.

For Campanelli and others, post-pageant life was a letdown. They struggled to understand their new reality and, at times, tried to escape. "Like many other competitors or athletes," Campanelli wrote, "I needed my exhilarations. Consequently, and almost every night[,] I began to drown my sorrows in the proverbial bottle, which led to cutting classes and more depression."[53] Campanelli credited God with rescuing her from self-destruction and, like many other Miss America losers, learned to reframe her participation to emphasize the things she had gained in her pursuit of the crown. "If it were not for pageants," she concluded, "I'm not sure I would have pursued a college career."[54] Thus the loss got folded in as life experience that afforded numerous opportunities, including the access to education and the ability to persevere through adversity. Participants needed to convince themselves— and others—that all of that effort had been worth it. They wanted to prove that they were still better off than those who chose not to enter the arena at all and they would not know what they knew now if not for the hardship and loss endured.

To be sure, not all contestants experienced pageant loss so keenly, but varying degrees of grief appeared to be a normal response. For example, Donna Cherry, Miss California 1984, noted, "I hurt so much, I couldn't straighten my body."[55] She reported physical pain that continued for six weeks after the Miss America competition ended. Without the grueling preparation schedule, contestants faced a lot of unstructured time, which made depression all the more likely. Joanne Caruso, Miss Connecticut 1984, "went into a deep funk." "For four months, she laid around a lot, not doing much of anything but re-living the pageant experience."[56] This huge sense of loss was a refrain among the contestants. That they had tried and failed proved debilitating, at least for a time. Reframing the loss as an opportunity for personal growth could help, but the sting of the defeat could run deep.

Just as few football players made it to the Super Bowl, not all pageant contestants walked the Miss America runway and fewer still earned the crown. But as pageant propaganda proved quick to remind, the competition offered something for everyone. It was the journey—the process—as much as the outcome. It fell to competitors who failed to win the top prize to reinterpret their experience, but they had plenty of language for doing so. As the Miss America program advertised, participants could gain life skills whether they progressed to the next level or not. While in some ways this seems like "concession" prizes, learning to sustain loss served former pageant competitors well in their lives beyond the pageant. The competition was valuable in and of itself.

A Place to Belong: Pageant as Community

Competition created community. Competitors, be they in athletics, politics, or pageants, held one another accountable and pushed one another to improve. They sought, and at times found, meaning beyond themselves through their respective activities. Contenders drew strength from engaging with others like them; competing gave them a sense of belonging. They banded together to defend against detractors, explaining their group to disciple and skeptic alike. Thus merely joining the competition, regardless of the outcome, marked participants as part of the community. The chosen community became an essential part of their identity, offering them an extended family built around mutual interests rather than a shared bloodline. Common experiences and insider language also marked each group. Sports, politics, and pageants all reinforced shared values even as they shaped beliefs, and encouraged individual growth even as they rewarded conformity to the ideal. In other words, pageant competition looked and functioned like a community, the good, the bad, and the ugly.

Pageant participants spoke about gaining a pageant family, and the organization adopted family language at times to discuss relationships within the pageant community. For example, fellow competitors referred to one another as sisters and to the group as the Miss America sisterhood. At the national pageant and at some state pageants, the contestants were divided into three competition groups, Mu, Alpha, and Sigma, suggestive of the pageant contenders being one big sorority. "Sister" captured the complicated relationship well. Pageant sisterhood, like both sorority sisterhood and biological sisterhood, entailed encouragement and support in addition to competition and jealousy.[57] At times, contestants borrowed dresses from one another, rode side-by-side in parades, and made appearances together. Other times, they hid their wardrobe choices until it was time for approval or rushed in their paperwork so they could grab a particular song choice first. But, at the end of the day, they knew that few outside the pageant world understood their world and found solace in the ties that bound them one to another. State pageants had organizations that united local titleholders past and present. The Miss America State Titleholders Association offered the same thing for competitors at the national level.[58] Then, of course, there was the most elite group of all, the sisterhood of former Miss Americas. As Kate Shindle, Miss America 1998, wrote, "The Miss Americas are a sorority of sorts; it is not at all rare for them to begin a group e-mail message with 'My dearest sisters' and conclude it with a prayer or a request for prayers. Although some of these women barely know one another, they share a steely bond forged by the Miss America experience, an experience that requires a young woman to take on a mantle that grows both more storied and more burdensome with each passing year . . . that kind of shared crucible makes for some serious camaraderie."[59] The competition, it appeared, never ended, but neither did the community it forged.

Figure 3.2. Competing in the Miss America Pageant initiated women into a select sisterhood. While only one contestant could take the crown, the shared experience bonded them together. Pictured here are two groups of Miss America sisters posing on the boardwalk sixty years apart. The competitors for Miss America 1954 (bottom) and Miss America 2014 (top) are very clearly marked as one unified group.

"Sister" was not the only familial term used in the Miss America Pageant system. There were also pageant moms. "Pageant moms" could refer to biological moms, but the term might also denote a woman who served as a pageant director or traveling companion, someone who filled a maternal role for a contestant in her mother's absence. Dr. Betty Campbell, a music professor at Judson College, served in such a role for Titilayo Adedokun, Miss Ohio 1993. Adedokun, a former student of Campbell's, was born in the United States to Nigerian immigrants. When she went to compete at Miss America (where she finished as second runner-up), it was Campbell who stepped in to accompany her. Finally, some state pageants had dressing-room moms. Actual mothers were not allowed backstage during competition so a dressing-room mom was assigned to each contestant to assist with wardrobe changes during the contest.[60] In farewell speeches, titleholders thanked one's pageant family alongside their own, noting the many contributions from the pageant community that made her year a successful one.[61] Such recognition made sense since winners, especially on the national level, spent more time with their pageant family during their year of service than they did with their actual family.

Thus the community extended beyond those playing sports, running for office, or competing in pageants to include coaches, fans, commentators, sponsors, judges, referees, volunteers, and recruiters. It required an army of volunteers to produce each pageant, host fundraisers, and coordinate public appearances for the contestants and/or the winner.[62] It involved choreographers, photographers, program printers, and more. The hours spent working together led to a deep sense of loyalty to one another and to that year's queen. Like a winning sports team that made it to the state playoffs, if a local pageant winner had some success at state, rounding up sponsors and volunteers for the next year's pageant proved easier. Some local contests were so well established that they ran like a well-oiled machine thanks to the volunteers who returned year after year. This was merely compounded at the state level, with some states buying large blocks of tickets at the national pageant to support "their" girl. The pageant family stretched far and wide, each member playing a different role and each relating to other components of the pageant community in myriad ways. The competition also expanded beyond the participants as awards were given to volunteers at the state and national level for outstanding pageants, directors of the year, years of service, most money raised for the Children's Miracle Network, and more.[63] The competition created and fostered networks of people that functioned as community and competed as one.

Once in the pageant community, one could find it difficult to extricate oneself. This was especially true, of course, for state and national pageant winners. Once a Miss America, always a Miss America—as the saying goes. But even local winners found themselves volunteering year after year after they aged out of the system. Some saw it as a chance to groom the next Miss [State] winner or even Miss America; in a way, volunteering offered the prospect to continue chasing the crown. If they could not win, helping someone else win was the next best thing. Other formers embraced volunteering as an opportunity to pay it forward. For example, Melodie King competed for four years in the Miss Alabama Pageant. An accomplished pianist, she regularly won talent and interview awards, but could never break through to place in the top ten at state. She continued her involvement with the state pageant after she finished competing. The personal rewards she gained through her pageant participation, including the relationships she built with volunteers, pageant directors, and other contestants compelled her to invest in the next generation of pageant contestants. Melodie King directed a preliminary pageant in the Miss Alabama system, serving as the executive director for the Miss Jefferson County contest for fourteen years before moving to North Carolina.[64] Her story represented that of many young women who found a home in the pageant and wanted to provide that same safe place to others. The pageant survived in part because its alumnae believed in the family the competition provided. Without the larger pageant community, it would cease to exist.

Along the way, young women were socialized into this new family. The pageant community possessed its own insider language and promoted a unique set of values. Contestants spoke of formers, closed pageants, and number draws. They borrowed theater language like run-through, staging, and dress rehearsal. There were fashion-forward pieces and butt glue. A learning curve existed, but once one was fully immersed in the pageant world, discussing pageant strategy and odds of winning felt as natural as discussing last year's Yankees stats would for a baseball fan.[65] The pageant community advocated stage presence, competition, and style. This family encouraged confidence, community service, leadership development, and a healthy lifestyle. The group valued poise, femininity, and articulateness. Contestants were groomed with these values in mind. And, for those who found a home in pageantry, they confessed a deep satisfaction to be among those like her. It really was its own tribe.

The pageant family also included—to varying degrees—biological families. Most obvious, of course, were the parents of the competitors. Some parents were all in. They drove their daughters to appearances, invested in professional wardrobes, and even designed T-shirts and buttons to be worn by supporters at the state or national pageant.[66] They attended functions with other pageant parents where they shared competition gossip and, at times, deeper aspects of their lives. These families worked with the pageant to help their daughter take advantage of every perceived opportunity. They were on board with the values promoted by the pageant and wanted to help in any way possible. Some traveled the pageant circuit with their daughters. Others helped her research her platform or find the perfect dress. Mothers who had participated in the Miss America Pageant system themselves could be particularly helpful.[67] Some contestants even had family members who

made parts of their wardrobe. This was true for Caitlin Guffin, a gifted ballerina who competed in the Miss Alabama Pageant for two years and whose
grandmother made her talent costume.[68] Savvy Shields' father helped her
prepare for interviews while her mom "played many roles" as "encourager,
bedazzler, dance cleaner, life coach, practice judge, health food guru, funny
text giver, caption helper, and good light finder to best friend and mom."[69]
Parents could not judge pageants or volunteer on boards while they had a
daughter of competition age, but some leveraged the knowledge they gained
while their daughter was competing to judge or host or direct or coach after
she aged out.[70]

Other families worked alongside the pageant. They wanted to support
their daughter's chosen hobby, but they found full-on immersion a bit daunting. They kept their distance, always attending competitions to cheer for
their daughter, but drew the line at eating, drinking, and sleeping pageants
alongside her. They might value some but not all of the pageant community's
chosen beliefs. Of course, some parents came to this position after an initial
hesitation to support their daughter's quest for a crown. Cheryl Prewitt's dad
did not approve of her initial decision to enter a beauty pageant. "No way
is a daughter of mine going to parade herself around in front of a bunch of
strangers."[71] Since Prewitt was eighteen, he did not forbid her from competing, but he kept his word not to support her, refusing to attend the first
several pageants in which she participated. The week before her first attempt
to capture the crown of Miss Mississippi, her mother mentioned casually
that her father had decided to come. After attending the competition, he
confessed he was glad he came and he supported her efforts after that.[72]

Perhaps some parents worked against the pageant community, but these
parents were more difficult to locate within the pageant system. They could
not understand why their daughter wanted to participate and refused to support her. They searched for other groups or activities that promoted values
they found more compelling, hoping their daughter would lose interest in
pageants. It is far easier to find parents of non-contenders whose parents
disparaged pageant participation and searched for alternative forms of competition.[73] Grandparents, aunts, uncles, cousins, and brothers might fall into
any of the above categories. The point remained the same: the contestants'
families could also enjoy the warmth of the pageant community. And it got
harder to avoid it if their relative made it to the national stage.

Biological sisters presented additional possibilities. Little sisters sometimes followed in their big sisters' footsteps, winning the same crown a sister had once worn.[74] At times, biological sisters even competed against one

another, with the Miss Alabama 1999 contest boasting three sisters, Julie Smith, Jill Smith, and Jennifer Smith, vying for the state crown (spoiler alert: one, but only one, won).[75] Madison Fuller, Miss Texas 2018 and Miss Texas Outstanding Teen 2010, also competed against her two sisters, Morgan and Mallory, for the Miss Texas title, though all three never competed on the state stage in the same year.[76] Two of the three Wineman sisters, Alexis, Miss Montana 2012, and Danielle, Miss Montana 2015, represented the state of Montana at Miss America. When asked when she would be competing for Miss America, the third Wineman sister (Amanda) replied that she would be foregoing pageantry as she was in law school.[77] This, then, demonstrated that even when a family was extremely involved in the pageant community, it did not necessarily mean that all of their daughters would choose to compete.

At the most basic level, however, pageants acted as a community because of a common interest and shared experience. The people involved loved the pageant and all that the main event entailed. Glitz. Glamour. Competition. Camaraderie. And they extended the experience in multiple directions. A little sister pageant, Miss America's Outstanding Teen, provided the opportunity for young girls (ages thirteen to seventeen) to participate until they aged into the Miss America system.[78] The Rising Stars program paired girls ages seven to eleven with a contestant in the state's Miss system (as of 2018, not all states had this program). This mentoring program allowed for early grooming, ensuring the future of the program by hooking the girls young.[79] Finally, Princess Camp, run by the Miss America's Outstanding Teen program, billed itself as a program "designed for girls, ages 5 to 12, who are looking to improve upon skills that promote self-confidence and poise and find mentoring from today's young teen leaders."[80] The pageant community held the potential to exert an enormous influence on its members, both those competing and those serving. This group of people worked toward a common end, with each fulfilling their particular roles toward achieving that goal.

As a particular community, pageant participants, volunteers, and fans were not always understood by those on the outside, and indeed proved an easy target for those who chose to denigrate the contest and all it embodied. Loyal pageant members were undeterred. The community encompassing the Miss America Pageant functioned as a self-perpetuating entity, understanding its appeal even if and when those outside of it did not. While some involved sought to bridge the gap between insiders and outsiders, others were perfectly content to enjoy life inside the pageant bubble. They belonged. They did not need anyone else to understand. Increasingly, however, contestants and pageant officials alike worked both to update and explain the relevance of the competition.[81]

This pageant family exerted an enormous influence on its members, setting the standard for what mattered. While this community could, of course, be an extension of one's biological family, it could also be in addition to or over and against. Competition fed contestants' desire to belong, prompting them to choose pageants over other things. Competition created community and community drove competition.

Pageant Culture: The Spread of a Phenomenon

The culture created by this national competition mimicked those of national sporting leagues. Pageants did not just look like sports or politics. They functioned like other competitive enterprises, creating a particular culture with their own celebrities, advertising, merchandise, and fan base. Pageant culture revolved around two primary things: the annual pageant in September and the woman who won. Miss America was both event and person. There were tickets and judges, programs and sponsors. Competition saturated the whole, driving decisions and increasing interest. Miss America as competition contributed to a unique pageant culture.

Pageant fans anticipated the September event just as football fans looked forward to the Super Bowl. There were parades and watch parties. Odds were given and bets taken. Supporters declared their loyalty to a particular contestant (or contestants) with T-shirts, buttons, or signs. Boardwalk Hall in Atlantic City became a sports arena, though arguably one with far more rhinestones, sequins, and heels than one would find at a NASCAR race. Spectators varied in their participation, but unspoken rules and customs dominated the pageant as they did a ballpark. For example, audience members stood and applauded when the reigning Miss America took the stage at the beginning of the competition and when she offered her final walk before handing over the crown.[82] Decorum dictated that spectators not interrupt contestants' talent competition with insults or employ flash photography during the contest. A general respect for the competitive process dominated the event with play-by-plays of the event carrying into the evening as pageant-goers filed back onto the Atlantic City Boardwalk.[83]

Pageant winners took on an almost celebrity status, making public appearances, signing autographs, and posing for photo ops. Their faces adorned billboards, television talk shows, and program advertisements. Some states even added an additional layer of competition by giving an award to the contestant who sold the most program advertisements or whose photograph received the most votes. Pageant week was a reunion for formers who enjoyed their celebrity status year after year.[84] These women were admired because of the title they held, not necessarily any knowledge they possessed. They had bested the competition. That made them worthy of attention in pageant culture.

The competitive culture of pageants also created a market for pageant merchandise. One could shop through the Miss America website or in Boardwalk Hall the week of the pageant. State and local pageants might also design and sell their own merchandise and memorabilia. One could also purchase videos and pictures from the competition. At the national pageant, one could buy magnets, T-shirts, water bottles, and more—all emblazoned with the official Miss America logo. There was official Miss America jewelry, Christmas ornaments, and even a cookie cutter in the shape of a crown. At the 2019 competition (held in September 2018), one could even preorder high-top tennis shoes with the new crown logo. There was a market for merchandise.

Conclusion

Pageants promised young women experiences akin to those offered by sports and other competitive enterprises, but, arguably, the risks were much greater. They cut to the core of an individual's identity. And, because there were both fewer winners and fewer opportunities to win, the stakes felt higher. Not surprisingly, individuals who failed to capture the illustrious crown were more willing to speak about the drawbacks of participation and its negative impacts on their lives and careers. Their stories, however, were not as ubiquitous since, as with all history, the winners' stories took center stage. And yet there is evidence of eating disorders, obsession with perfection, low self-esteem, constant comparison, anxiety, depression, and a sense of never being good enough among winners and losers alike.[85] The cost of competing, at least for some, outweighed the potential benefits. In some ways, no one is a winner and everyone is a winner in pageants. Or, put differently, there were gains—and losses—for every competitor.

As noted, participants spent numerous hours training for the national competition. When they walked away without the crown, every respondent in one study "grieved." Many of the negative effects isolated involved self-esteem and body image. Kathy Manning, Miss Mississippi 1984, who won one of the three preliminary swimsuit awards, confessed, "My body was my identity and it isn't anymore."[86] Now overweight, Manning's "self-esteem has suffered and . . . she has had to do a lot of searching and redefining of self."[87]

Another common response was to dwell on things one could have done better. Thus, even for those contestants who won a lot of pageants, it seemed that continued winning was the only thing to protect their sense of self. Their self-esteem, perhaps subconsciously, was tied up in what others thought of them, and they craved the constant affirmation of their worth that a pageant win supplied.[88] This, too, may be something pageants shared with other competitions, but since the judging was more subjective than a political race that was won or lost by counting ballots, it proved slightly different.

Miss America's self-description as a scholarship pageant provided another example of how the potential risks did not match the potential benefits. Miss America celebrated its shift from beauty pageant to scholarship pageant to competition. Many supporters showered the organization with accolades for their commitment to women's higher education. It was billed as a competition in which anyone could participate and benefit if they worked hard enough. However, one must hold this "good" in tension with other things. Miss America was still a beauty pageant. It enjoyed, and some may argue exploited, women's bodies even as it funded women's accomplishments. Attractiveness remained a requirement, even if an unstated one. In some ways, this proved more damaging than the pageants that acknowledged that theirs rewarded beauty over brains. For starters, the scholarship pageant lingo might have lured women who would never participate in a beauty pageant per se. It neutralized the activity, making it appear as any other competition. More important, the Miss America Pageant expanded the myth that women must excel at everything. In theory, the pageant celebrated the whole woman. In reality, it added more items to the list. No longer was a pretty face enough. Ideal women possessed talent that could be showcased on stage, spoke articulately about politics and current events, volunteered in the community, walked elegantly in heels, and wore a smile while doing it.[89] It was, in some ways, the ultimate competition for women.

Pageants were fiercely competitive, offering rewards, providing community, and promoting a culture of insiders and outsiders. Contestants prepared for the five phases of Miss America as diligently as a gymnast perfected her four routines. The Miss America program offered a boot camp of sorts to explore and perfect the qualities that society deemed most desirable for women.[90] But the thrill of competition and the benefits that went alongside it, while crucial for understanding the Miss America Pageant, still failed to capture the essence of why young women participated. In the twenty-first century, women were flooded with opportunities to play lacrosse, soccer, and basketball. They could compete in cheerleading, swimming, track, and any number of activities with similar rewards and fewer drawbacks. More women were entering into politics where the potential for effecting actual change was greater. Instead, many chose pageants. Pageants related much with competitive culture; they survived and thrived, in part, because of these shared characteristics. But, in the end, pageants were not, strictly speaking, merely competition. There seemed to be more at play than play and more at stake than a win.

4

Faith *of* the Pageant, Faith *and* the Pageant

"The cult of beauty exemplifies an important tenet of popular religion: all aspects of life can provide religious illumination when believers see them in a sacred perspective."[1]

Pageants provoked controversy. On September 7, 1968, the Atlantic City Boardwalk experienced the best-known protest against the Miss America Pageant. The women's movement was not, however, the first or the last group to criticize the nation's premier beauty contest. The competition faced critics almost from its inception. Religious and women's groups alike admonished participants, sponsors, and casual supporters, believing the competitions detrimental to the young women participating as well as to society at large. Religious leaders argued that their constituents should stay away from these tawdry flesh shows, some even working to shut pageants down altogether.[2] This adversarial relationship did not last. In 2011, the Christian Broadcasting Network presented a story on the ninetieth anniversary of the pageant, highlighting the many Christian winners—and participants—through the years.[3] Gone were the pitchforks and torches of the early years, bedazzled signs and noisemakers having taken their place.

Christians did not give up the fight and join the parade on their own. Someone wooed them. Pageant organizers hired one of their own to remake the contest. Lenora Slaughter, a Southern Baptist from Florida, arrived in Atlantic City in 1935.[4] The changes she instituted prompted an almost genial relationship between Christians and the Miss America program. As time marched on, the harsh religious critiques of the early years seemed a thing of the past. To be sure, the relationship between religion and beauty contestants was never a monolithic one. A general shift, however, from taboo to acceptable did occur among Christians as the competition sought to rebrand itself as a respectable enterprise. The rising social status of contestants, which made exhibition tolerable, allowed Christians' growing acceptance of it. In addition, a watershed moment in 1965 seemingly sealed the fate of the organization and church forever. The Miss America Pageant got religion.[5] From that point on, it became not only accepted, but also common that Miss America would both possess and profess her faith. The broader cultural respectability achieved by the competition made this phenomenon possible.

Miss America 1975, Shirley Cothran (Baptist); Miss America 1980, Cheryl Prewitt (Pentecostal); Miss America 1990, Debbye Turner (Christian); Miss America 2001, Angela Perez Baraquio (Catholic); and Miss America 2016, Betty Cantrell (Greek Orthodox) were just five of the many winners that saw pageantry as a religious opportunity. Pageantry also became increasingly accepted within Christian communities as leaders, laypeople, and the Christian media celebrated Christian winners.[6] When the Miss America Pageant mandated that contestants adopt a platform for their year of service (1989), the link between church and pageant grew even stronger as contestants used the opportunity to live out their faith on the national stage.

Thus the delicate dance between church and pageant continued. Of course, some Christians continued to oppose the spectacle of pageants, but gradually their voices became marginalized as the pageant was seen as a preserver and protector of American womanhood. In the face of threats such as feminism, the Miss America Pageant promoted an ideal of femininity in keeping with Christian values, one that did not threaten to usurp male power.[7] A correlation exists between the institutions of church and pageant, one easily observed, but not easily explained. The relationship proved beneficial to both as each struggled to prove its relevance in an ever evolving world. This manifested itself as faith *of* the pageant and faith *and* the pageant.[8]

Faith *of* the Pageant: Miss America, National Identity, and Civil Religion

On September 12, 2001, the contenders for Miss America 2002 voted on whether to continue with that year's competition. After the acts of terrorism perpetrated against the United States on September 11, 2001, contestants wondered what the pageant had to offer a grieving nation. Reflecting back on those moments of uncertainty, Katie Harman, Miss America 2002, wrote, "Would a telecast of this nature be suitable for a grieving nation? . . . In a two-to-one vote, the contestants resolved that terrorists would not bring down the Miss America Organization—a time-honored program committed to outfitting goal-driven young women with the scholarship dollars and skills necessary to inspire a people in need. Indeed, the American people needed a Miss America."[9] Miss America pointed beyond the individual wearing the crown. The woman chosen reflected the ideals of America, and, particularly in times of stress and transition, she preserved and performed these ideals, offering a sense of security to the nation.[10] In other words, Harman and her Miss America sister class were not the first who felt the call to serve as a beacon of hope to their nation. They stood in a line of Miss America contenders yearning for the opportunity to bring light, courage, and beauty to their fellow Americans.

In war times, Miss America stepped in as a political actor. Much like the 2001 Miss America contestants, she recognized a need as well as her responsibility to act to meet it. America was, quite literally, watching her and she was happy to accept the role of Ideal Patriot. The Miss America Organization cultivated a close relationship to the United States military, with Miss America and some of her sisters being the face of home to troops around the world. The Miss America USO Troupe launched in 1967 when contestants traveled to perform in Vietnam.[11] This relationship with the armed forces remains intact as winners offer visible reminders of all the soldiers were fighting to protect. Indeed, later in the pageant's history, some contestants were in the military themselves.

Figure 4.1. The Miss America Pageant collaborated with the United States military, launching a Miss America USO Troupe in 1967 intended to inspire the troops while they were serving abroad. Pictured above is Jane Jayroe, Miss America 1967, entertaining Marines at Freedom Hill in Da Nang, Vietnam.

Women participated in the Miss America competition to be part of something that was bigger than themselves. They relished the idea that they could make a difference on a grand scale, that they could represent beauty, truth, and goodness to the American people. At times, this meant representing the face of the nation when it was confronted by a foreign threat. In other moments, it meant rallying the nation behind a particular cause, celebrating a national event, or even inspiring civic responsibility. Miss America, as Ideal Citizen, modeled communal pride and sought to cultivate a moral society.

Miss Americas attended ribbon cuttings, rode in Fourth of July parades, sang the national anthem at sporting events, and spoke at Key Clubs. They embodied the American Spirit. In the late 1980s and early 1990s, the pageant made this expectation more explicit. The new leaders emphasized community service, professional development, and public speaking. Miss America officials required contestants to submit written essays on community issues and to answer onstage questions to demonstrate their grasp of current events. Each contestant also selected an official social "platform." The winner worked on behalf of her particular social cause during her year of service. Platforms ranged from specific causes like suicide prevention or breast cancer awareness to general topics like volunteerism. Undoubtedly, pageant organizers thought it would provide them some good publicity, but it also placed pageant hopefuls square within the bounds of U.S. women's reform history. Since at least the nineteenth century, women were expected to act as the moral guardians of society. Pageant contenders stood aligned with the likes of Elizabeth Cady Stanton and Frances Willard who saw the world as a home in need of reform.[12]

Women have long been upheld as paragons of virtue simultaneously to be admired, protected, and emulated.[13] The hopes and dreams of the nation are mapped onto their bodies.[14] Miss America celebrated this reality by rewarding those women who, in their estimation, had absorbed and conformed best to the American expectations of womanhood. Contestants sought to represent America's best in look, word, and deed, tapping into long-standing ideals of patriotism and service. This was American civil religion at its finest as young women shouldered the responsibility of unifying the nation with the gospel message of American exceptionalism.[15] Judges, producers, and viewers all projected their expectations onto these seventeen- to twenty-five-year-old women, viewing them as the best America had to offer: they were the American dream.

Figure 4.2. In the twenty-first century, Miss America hopefuls did not simply offer inspiration to the troops as Ideal Patriots; they might be the troops. Theresa Vail (top), Miss Kansas 2013, shows off her combat boots in the Miss America "Show Me Your Shoes Parade." Vail served as a dental technician in the Kansas Army National Guard. Jill Stevens (bottom), Miss Utah 2007, poses with her sash, gun, and crown. Stevens worked as a combat medic in the Utah Army National Guard and has served multiple tours in Afghanistan. Both Vail and Stevens won the coveted "America's Choice" award at Miss America, with Vail finishing in the top 10 and Stevens finishing in the top 16.

Of course, the pageant is bigger than the person wearing the crown. Each year a new winner earned a position of honor as America's ideal, but the competition itself was also an act, or ritual, of civil religion and Boardwalk Hall a sacred space.[16] For some, it was an act of patriotism simply to watch the pageant. Like the local Fourth of July parade, the Miss America contest celebrated "life, liberty, and the pursuit of happiness." Most competitions opened with the national anthem, the Pledge of Allegiance, and/or a color guard presentation. There was the remembrance for Miss Americas who had died in the last year and a tribute for the Miss America celebrating the fiftieth anniversary of her win. This celebration of national pride continued with a series of rituals as familiar as a church service to most Americans. Women competed in swimsuit, talent, evening wear, and onstage questions as onlookers rated them on their scorecards. God and country weaved fluidly throughout the production as ministers offered prayers, singers belted out "God Bless America," and women spoke in favor of patriotism, volunteerism, and, quite frequently, the importance of religion, namely, some form of Christianity.[17] At times, crowning moments brought tears for both winners and spectators, all overcome with the magnitude of the moment. It was downright spiritual for some.

America's women longed to participate in this national tradition. They welcomed the chance to feel as if their very presence made a difference and appreciated the access to a national stage provided by the pageant. Under the watchful eye of the American public, Miss Americas functioned as Ideal Patriots and Ideal Citizens, but also as Ideal Housewives, Ideal Scholars, and more. Upon the pedestal, they accepted, cultivated, and reflected America's values. At times this meant that certain bodies were discouraged or excluded from the role. It also meant that individuals who managed to win despite not embodying the ideals sometimes faced opposition or more strenuous expectations from the public.[18] Indeed, Miss America was a responsive institution as much, if not more so, than it was a prophetic one. In general, the pageant did not set trends; it reflected them.

Miss America functioned as civil religion for millions of Americans. The women who wore the crown served as a symbol of the collective good that America had to offer. The pageant itself operated as a religious ritual and expression of patriotism. Miss America—the person and the pageant—existed to show the nation and the world what a true American woman should be, look like, and do. Miss America celebrated America's ideals in the face of real or perceived threats, uniting Americans to defend American exceptionalism before enemies real and imagined with wide smiles, perky personalities, and that plucky American spirit.

For example, Jean Bartel, Miss America 1943, inspired national pride during World War II, taking on the mantle of Ideal Patriot. She found herself on the front lines as a wartime Miss America, and was among the many women who used their gifts to support the war and encouraged others to join them. As women everywhere left their homes to enter the factories, Bartel took to the road to sell war bonds to do her part for the troops. During her year of service, she sold $2.5 million in war bonds, earning recognition by the United States Treasury Department for selling more than anyone else that year. Bartel—like Rosie the Riveter—became a symbol of American womanhood, one who was willing to go to any lengths to serve her country. Bartel became a symbol of the women of whom this great nation was made.[19] Women, summed up in Bartel, were the reason to stand strong against the enemy.

Figure 4.3. The ideals of the nation were mapped onto the person of Miss America figuratively, but sometimes winners offered a literal picture of America's supposed exceptionalism. Pictured here is Margaret Gorman, Miss America 1921, enveloped in the ideals of the nation, from the Statue of Liberty crown on her head to the Stars and Stripes around her shoulders.

Year after year the nation's ideals got mapped onto the bodies of the Miss America hopefuls. The pageant and its representative served as a communal reminder of all that America stood for at any given time. Miss America was quite literally a reflection of American ideals.[20] As the nation's understanding of ideal womanhood shifted, so too did the pageant's expectations of a winner and what was celebrated and lifted up for emulation. The one thing that remained the same rang true in the words of the now-famous song, "She took the town by storm with her all-American face and form." Miss America was always beautiful. She was the object of desire. How else could she be something/someone worth inspiring a nation?

Thus the Miss America competition was more than sex, entertainment, or competition; it carried with it a sense of national reverence and sacredness. The pageant was an institution, and Americans looked to its winner as a model of all they held dear. Her presence—at various moments—inspired pride, provided hope, induced courage, and infused meaning. She was a symbol as much as she was a role model, a barometer of the nation's shifting allegiances. Americans looked to Miss America for affirmation of their deeply held sense of America's exceptionalism. She demonstrated what they knew instinctively; Americans were nothing short of amazing. Miss America had it all and she showcased it to the world.

Miss America, the person and the pageant, united her citizens against a common enemy, stirred up a sense of national pride, provided a platform for patriotism, offered connection to a common cause, and stood as a sacred symbol of America. The pageant is America, and it is the religion of Miss America. As such, churches have legitimately seen Miss America through religious lenses.

Faith *and* the Pageant: The Unlikely Partnership between Church and Pageant

Making Pageants Palatable: Miss America and Religion, 1921–1965

In the early years, controversy plagued the pageant and its contestants. The pageant groomed, promoted, and celebrated idealized femininity in its contestants, and, by extension, celebrated that ideal within the culture at large. Yet many disapproved of its mission. Religious leaders complained that the contest was immoral and that it encouraged women to make poor choices. Others questioned the reputation of young women who entered such a contest or concluded that even "good girls" found themselves corrupted by pageantry.[21]

Religious groups published public statements denouncing beauty pageants. For example, Southern Baptists passed a "Resolution on Beauty Contests" in 1926 that stated:

Whereas, The purity and sanctity of the home depends upon a proper respect for and safeguarding of our girls; and

Whereas, "Beauty contests" and so-called "bathing revues" are evil and evil only, and tend to lower true and genuine respect for womanhood, emphasizing and displaying only purely physical charm above spiritual and intellectual attainments,

Therefore, We, the Southern Baptist Convention do deplore and condemn all such contests and revues.[22]

This sentiment was common among religious groups in the early decades of the twentieth century who declared the pageant "damaging to the morals of men, women and children."[23] Religious voices of disapproval joined those of women's groups such as the Atlantic County Federation of Church Women. In a resolution to the City Commission and pageant directors, they wrote, "We are persuaded that the moral effect on the young women entrants and the reaction generally is not a wholesome one."[24] Indeed, "for all its lucrative appeal, the Miss America Pageant of the 1920s became the center of criticism. It was condemned by civic and religious organizations for not only being indecent, but also because the contest exploited women for pecuniary purposes, while at the same time corrupting them through rivalry and competition."[25] These arguments sound similar to those made later in the century by feminists in their attack of the beauty revue. In contrast to the 1968 feminist protest of the pageant, however, these early critiques helped shut the pageant down for five years.[26]

The scandal that seemed to follow the competition and its winners failed to encourage the kind of support pageant organizers desired: "Although Victorian norms and conventions of womanhood and femininity more or less relaxed during the 1920s, other freedoms that women sought . . . led to a general nationwide anxiety over the apparently loose morals that middle-class women were adopting, and this anxiety extended to the Atlantic City beauty pageant."[27] When the Miss America contest took a brief hiatus from 1928 to 1932, it appeared that religious organizations and women's groups (and morality) had won.[28] This victory proved short-lived, though, as in 1933 many businessmen in Atlantic City rallied support to bring the pageant back. The contest continued to struggle amidst criticism that the young women were not of sound character or that the bathing attire was inappropriate.[29] Indeed, Miss America 1933, Marian Bergeron, was "asked to leave her Catholic high school for getting 'entirely too much undue publicity.'"[30]

The year 1935, however, marked a new era in Miss America Pageant history, one in which the pageant organizers sought to remake the contest into a reputable enterprise. Eddie Corcoran hired Lenora Slaughter, a member of the St. Petersburg, Florida, Chamber of Commerce staff (and the nation's only female pageant director) to produce the pageant.[31] And so it was that Slaughter moved to Atlantic City in 1935. Making pageants more palatable to Christians required changes. A Southern Baptist, Slaughter knew the importance of image and worked to create a new, more wholesome Miss America.

Part of Slaughter's genius involved appealing to religious and women's organizations for support. She planned "to out-women's club the women's club," and she did.[32] Slaughter made the Miss America competition the social event with which everyone wanted to be associated. She convinced Mrs. Charles D. White, the mayor of Atlantic City's wife and a Quaker, to lead the new hostess committee that she instituted to "protect" the girls. "The Quakerest of Quakers," according to Slaughter, White worked with Slaughter to sanitize the pageant. As Slaughter stated, "My training had always been working with civic leaders and proper people and I realized that the best way to protect the Pageant was to protect the girls from scandal, and the best way to do that was to get the best people in town on my side."[33] Slaughter made it an honor to serve as a hostess, judge, or board member. The changes she instituted had the added benefit of ensuring few, if any, charges of misconduct.[34]

In addition to securing sponsors for the national competition, Slaughter worked to make the local pageants less commercial and more community-centered. She believed she could increase the respectability of the enterprise. She recalled the mistake of the director prior to her: "The director . . . was running these pageants all over the country in amusement parks, fairs, things like that. In the state contests they had the girls parading around in swimsuits in front of the theater before the pageant. It was awful. I wanted to throw out all the cheap promotions. I said I believe I can get civic organizations to run the pageants and we can get the class of girl that we should have."[35] Slaughter managed to do just that, rallying support in small towns across the country. In fact, she successfully promoted a relationship between the

Jaycees and the local competitions. She quipped, "What better than to have the ideal men of America run a pageant for the ideal women?"[36] While this partnership between the "ideal" men and women did not catch on nation-wide or continue into the twenty-first century, the beauty contest remained extricated from "commercial" ventures such as carnivals and amusement parks.[37] Owing in large part to Lenora Slaughter's vision, the national pageant secured a place within the hearts of rank-and-file Americans, religious constituents included.

Slaughter's reform efforts, however, involved more than procuring new sponsors. She reworked the pageant from the inside out. During her tenure, she established a rule that banned contestants from visiting bars and night-clubs, instituted curfews, and forbade contestants to speak to any man alone. In an effort to emphasize the accomplishments of the contestants, she also added a talent component to the competition.[38] Slaughter swapped the word "bathing suit" in favor of "swimsuit" in an effort to play up athleticism rather than sensuality and instituted scholarships for winners as women fought to gain a place in higher education.[39] Christians felt increasingly at home in the pageant as Slaughter improved it. Many who once opposed the pageants became its strongest allies.[40] Under her leadership, it evolved from a strug-gling sideshow to a freestanding organization attractive to many American women, including Christian women. Slaughter's vision rescued the competi-tion and its participants from many of the earlier critiques of misconduct and salaciousness by providing greater structure. Miss America did not become a household name (or a saintly role model) overnight, but many of Slaughter's "girls," as she called them, worked toward making the role more than a pretty face during this transitional period.

Jean Bartel, Miss America 1943, promoted this new, upright image for the competition and its participants. A Christian Scientist, she encapsulated everything Slaughter hoped for in a pageant winner: moral, talented, civic-minded, a college student, and, of course, beautiful. As Bartel recounted, "There was a very low expectation of the girls in the contest in those years. We weren't automatically respected—that took a long time."[41] During her year of service, Bartel earned the respect she desired. Promoted as "The Girl Back Home," during her tour to promote the war efforts she sold $2.5 mil-lion worth of war bonds, mostly to women. People loved her. During this period of pageant history, specifics of one's religion remained largely a private affair, with the pageant promoting a more general morality instead. Even the press consistently deemed Bartel "wholesome." As Deford recounted, "No matter how many times it happens, the press finds itself surprised every time a beauty pageant winner is something other than a classic dumb blonde. They wrote about and interviewed Jean endlessly."[42] The United States Treasury Department honored her as the individual who sold the most Series E Bonds that year. The new face of Miss America was born.[43]

Bartel's "wholesomeness," though remarkably good publicity, had its drawbacks. Because of her strict adherence to Christian Science teachings about the illusion of the sickness of the body, Bartel refused to see a doctor when she became ill with pneumonia. Slaughter, ever a savvy businesswoman, convinced a doctor to pose as a newspaperman in order to diagnose Bartel and coaxed Bartel to fulfill her duties to the press even though sick. After receiving a prescription from the doctor-turned-journalist, Slaughter gave Bartel penicillin in her orange juice.[44] Not surprisingly, Bartel recovered. It appeared that the respect for Miss America's privacy, even her religious expression, had its limits.

Bartel's work during her year of service helped rebrand the Miss America program. In addition to sanitizing Miss America's image, she helped introduce the college scholarships for which the pageant became famous.[45] In fact, according to the sportswriter and journalist Frank Deford, "she must be, in any ranking of Miss Americas, unquestionably declared the most important one. Everything changed because of her example." Slaughter offered Bartel equal praise, saying: "Every succeeding Miss America owes her the greatest debt."[46] Bartel's service as Miss America helped Slaughter realize that her vision for the pageant as a "rare entertainment venue for 'respectable' girls" was possible.[47] Slaughter's reform efforts curtailed the large number of religious critiques of the pageant and, with the help of "her" winners, she "picked the pageant up by its bathing suit straps and put it in an evening gown."[48] That is not to say that the pageant was free from scandal and controversy for the remainder of its history, of course, but Bartel represented a significant step in the direction of Slaughter's vision.

The first Miss America to benefit from the newly instituted scholarship program was also the first Jewish Miss America, Miss America 1945. Bess Myerson, a New York contestant, entered the pageant because of the $5,000 scholarship. Though not necessarily credited with making the pageant more "wholesome," Myerson played a crucial role in making it more respectable. As the first college graduate to win, she represented a new era in pageant queens, one allured by the promise of education more than the temptation of Hollywood. When Slaughter met her, Myerson was competing in the Miss New York City Pageant. Slaughter liked what she saw, but she knew there might be a problem. She asked Myerson to change her name to something more suitable for show business, like Beth Merrick. As Myerson noted in PBS's *Miss America: A Documentary Film*:

> Lenora Slaughter said my name was not a good name for show business. And I said well, you know I have no intention of going into show business . . . I said . . . the problem is that I'm Jewish, yes? And with that kind of name it'll be quite obvious to everyone else that I'm Jewish. And you don't want to have to deal with a Jewish Miss America. And that really was the bottom line. I said I can't change my name. You have to understand. I cannot change my name. I live in a building with two hundred and fifty Jewish families. The Sholom Aleichem apartment houses. If I should win, I want everybody to know that I'm the daughter of Louie and Bella Myerson.[49]

Myerson kept her name.[50] Anti-Semitism plagued the nation in 1945 and the pageant proved no exception. Many sponsors did not want a Jewish winner, and some judges received anonymous phone calls threatening them if they continued voting for Myerson.[51]

Myerson took home the crown and the scholarship, much to the delight of Jewish citizens across the United States.[52] Not everyone was pleased with Myerson as the face of American womanhood, however. She thought she would spend her year touring the nation and promoting pageant sponsors, as Bartel had done, "but after an obligatory four-week performance tour, where drunks in the audience demanded she play the piano in her bathing suit, there were few requests for her time. None of the sponsors wanted a Jewish girl—even a Jewish Miss America—posing with their products."[53] Myerson experienced exclusion and hatred throughout the year from not being allowed in country clubs to not being allowed to visit war veterans. For example, one mother of a war veteran refused to let Myerson see her son, saying, "I don't want you near him. Because of the Jews, we got into this war. Because of the damn Jews, my boy was maimed. We would have been better off if Hitler had killed every last one of your people."[54] Myerson handled this rejection and others with the poise expected of a Miss America, but her reign proved tumultuous.[55] Nevertheless, Myerson represented an important moment in the pageant's, and the nation's, history. In 2018, she remained the only Jewish Miss America, though others have competed for the title.

And so it was that the contest remained primarily a Christian, or at least culturally Christian, endeavor. Such affiliations went largely unacknowledged, however, until 1965. It is possible, of course, that no one spoke about the Christian identity of contestants because it was presupposed. For example, Barbara Jo Walker, a Methodist Sunday school teacher and

Miss America 1947, sang and spoke at the Southern Baptist Convention in May 1948. However, in a newspaper article where she criticized falsies and called two-piece swimsuits a "matter of morals" her religious affiliation went unnoted by both her and the reporter.[56] But, as the social movements of the 1960s swept the nation, one contestant emerged to testify.

Miss America 1965, Vonda Kay Van Dyke, was the first winner to speak about her faith publicly and the audience responded enthusiastically. When officials suggested that she had broken her contract, Van Dyke reminded them that Parks, the emcee, had broached the topic of religion. She agreed, however, not to talk about religion during her year of service unless someone brought it up. But her religion became the characteristic for which Van Dyke was best known. Everywhere she went individuals asked her about her Christianity.[57] Van Dyke found herself with many religious speaking engagements including church events and Youth for Christ rallies.[58] Eventually pageant officials allowed contestants to speak openly about their faith during the contest and subsequent year of service.[59] Van Dyke paved the way.

From Protestors to Proud Parents

This collaborative (though largely unpublicized) relationship between Christians and pageantry remained past Slaughter's tenure. Religious communities not only tolerated but celebrated Christian participation in pageants.[60] In the latter half of the twentieth century and into the twenty-first, Christians praised pageant participation far more than they condemned it. Names of the women competing were placed on prayer lists, church members attended the pageants to support contestants, and churches sponsored ads in the pageant program books. Articles about the winners appeared in denominational publications, and winners were invited to speak or share their talent at church events. Christian programs, both television and radio, interviewed participants, lauding the young women for standing up for their convictions. Christians pushed past former prejudices to join forces with this most unlikely organization.

At a very basic level, churches supported pageant participants with prayers, cards, and attendance at competitions. Like proud parents, they cheered for their contestants regardless of the outcome. Ads served as one venue for these messages. Stephanie Shelton's church, the congregation at Tuscaloosa, for example, confessed that they were "praying for [her] and wishing [her] the best at Miss Alabama!"[61] Likewise, Heather Hendrickson's church, The Living Word Church of Sylacauga, wrote, "Heather, We have watched you grow and mature into a vessel fit for the Master's use. You are a blessing. We love you."[62] This was not simply a southern phenomenon.[63] An ad in the Miss America 2011 program read, "It takes a village to raise a child, but a congregation to raise the spirit. Best wishes to our Miss New Jersey Ashleigh Udalovas[.] From your family at First United Methodist Church."[64] Ads were not the only means for conveying church support, but they remained one of the most visible. More personal expressions of well wishes also took place. Julie Payne, Miss Oklahoma 1998, prayed with her parents before the Miss America competition. She also received a fax from her home church and a "prayergram" from First Baptist Church in Woodward, Oklahoma, while away at the pageant.[65] Contestants experienced congratulations and support from congregations and school religious groups.

State program books in an evangelical-saturated state such as Alabama surfaced myriad church advertisements. These pages offered scriptural admonitions to pageant supporters in addition to heralding their picks for the state crown. For example, First Baptist Church of Spanish Fort sponsored a one-page ad in the 2000 Miss Alabama program book that featured Christin Kelly, Miss University of Mobile. At the bottom of the page, they included Matthew 5:16, "Let your light so shine before men, that they may see your good works and glorify your Father in Heaven," as well as a message of encouragement for Kelly that read, "We at First Baptist Church of Spanish Fort love you and wish you the very best."[66] A 2003 ad from Bishop Jim Lowe and the Guiding Light Church offered Proverbs 16:3: "Commit to the Lord whatever you do, and your plans will succeed."[67] One 2007 church ad for Lauren Womble, Miss Clay-Chalkville, took the opportunity to list all of its Miss Alabama winners. It included no Scripture passage, choosing instead to write, "North Park Baptist Church salutes all of our Miss Alabamas[,] Julie Coons Williams . . . (1989)[,] Resha Riggins Miles (1990), & Melinda Toole (2006)[.] Congratulations Laurie Womble as you continue the winning tradition."[68] More important than the individual messages presented by church ads, however, was that numerous churches felt impelled to support their daughters in this way. Public praise of Christian participants represented a far cry from the 1926 Southern Baptist resolution condemning pageants.

In addition to the moral support given to contestants, Christians celebrated the crowning of their daughters. For example, Jamie Langley, Miss Alabama 2007, noted that she received a lot of backing from her fellowship at Trinity Baptist Church. "I got so many phone calls and letters and notes from people in my church. It's been incredible, and I have felt very loved."[69] The Baptist Church of the Covenant in Birmingham, where Deidre Downs, Miss America 2005, was a member, hosted a Miss America viewing party attended by fifty to seventy-five church members. Sarah Shelton, Downs' pastor, remarked, "I think we all knew she was really good, but I think even she was surprised she won. We were all sitting on the edges of our seat—lots of cheering and lots of cell phones going. It was a lot of fun!"[70] Nearly one hundred people gathered at Lawton-Centenary United Methodist Church to watch Miss America 2007, Lauren Nelson, compete.[71]

Sometimes church members traveled to the Miss America competition. In 1996, Julie Smith, who would become Miss Alabama 1999, went to support fellow member Alison McCreary, saying, "She's always willing to go the extra mile for people. We just wanted to be there for her."[72] The *Alabama Baptist* reported that "McCreary's public access as Miss Alabama is a great opportunity to share her faith."[73] Even the title of the article, "McCreary's faith shines bright even without top beauty crown," suggested God's hand in McCreary's remaining Miss Alabama instead of becoming Miss America.[74] Churches prized having someone represent them at the local, state, and national levels. They seemed to interpret their success and failure as part of God's perfect plan.

Adherents of other religions rallied to support their contestants too. One Jewish participant, Loren Galler Rabinowitz, Miss Massachusetts 2010, competed at the ninetieth-anniversary Miss America competition in 2011. The granddaughter of Holocaust survivors, Galler Rabinowitz was also a Harvard graduate and a former ice dancer. Like her Christian pageant sisters, she embraced her faith, fielding questions about "keeping kosher and her Conservadox Jewish lifestyle."[75] As with Bess Myerson, Miss America 1945, Galler Rabinowitz's participation elicited comments and well wishes from Jews across the country. As Detroit rabbi Jason Miller noted, "While all of us from Metro Detroit will be hoping for another Miss Michigan to win the Miss America contest, Jewish people across the country will be pulling for Galler Rabinowitz."[76] To be sure, these well wishes did not necessarily represent all Jews any more than Christian supporters of their contestants did. Of importance here, however, is that both groups organized encouragement for their daughters. Galler Rabinowitz failed to reach the finals, but she won the Miracle Maker Award for raising the most money for the Children's Miracle Network, and, it seemed, the hearts of Jewish people across the country.[77]

Sometimes Christians took things a step further than merely supporting their daughters' choice to participate. Some actively encouraged their youth to see the contests as an evangelism opportunity. Among the young women urged to compete by religious mentors was Miss America 2001, Angela Perez Baraquio, who started as Miss Hawaii. Baraquio, a Catholic, recalled that her parish priest convinced her to enter the local preliminaries, which eventually led to Miss America. According to Baraquio, Father Maurice McNeely said, "You can do this. You need to do this. Catholics need to be in the forefront more so they can witness to Christ."[78] She heeded his advice and began competing in local preliminaries at age eighteen, finally winning Miss America at age twenty-four. Baraquio, a member of a large Catholic family and the product of the church's schools, embraced the opportunity to be a public witness for the Roman Catholic Church and her faith.

As Miss America, Baraquio lived out her faith commitments on the national stage as her priest had hoped. She insisted on attending Mass the day after she was crowned before flying to New York for her interviews. She used the year to promote her platform: "Character in the Classroom: Teaching Values, Valuing Teachers." Baraquio also denounced the swimsuit competition, confessing to Diane Sawyer of *Good Morning America* that she wished the pageant would do away with it.[79] Catholic publications rejoiced with their daughter, proudly claiming Baraquio as one of their own.[80] Like any story of faith in action, they hoped her story would encourage other Catholics. More important, they used Baraquio's success to show Catholics' potential in America in the twenty-first century.

Christian participants and their supporters seized beauty contests as a venue for missions.[81] They saw opportunities for evangelism not just when their contestants won, but also in how Christians conducted themselves in various phases of pageant competition. After 1996, one of the most visible ways a contestant testified to the difference that her faith made was in choosing to wear a one-piece swimsuit.[82] For some, donning a one-piece swimsuit represented a theological choice with political implications. On the national stage, Mormon contestants remained the most consistent and vocal about opting out of the bikini and other immodest clothing. Miss Utah 2006, Katie Millar, chose costumes that met her more modest standards. All of her dresses had sleeves, a high neck, a modest neckline, and a slit that came only to her knee. She also competed in a one-piece swimsuit, which many contestants (and judges) considered the kiss of death. Nevertheless, Millar proclaimed, "My message as Miss Utah expands beyond just the pageant world. I hope that I am an example to all young women that you can uphold traditional values and be successful at the same time."[83] The Mormon press praised her for achieving this goal.[84] Millar, who made it to the final ten, wore her one-piece on national television. As noted, she was thankful for the opportunity to set an example for young girls.[85] She interpreted her actions, as did her religious community, as a way to witness to her convictions.

Some contestants communicated via their dress choices that they belonged to a certain religious community and that even in the pageant they must uphold its standards. Millar; Kylie Kofoed, Miss Idaho 2010; and Anna Nelson, Miss Wyoming 2009, were just three Latter-day Saint (LDS) pageant contestants to garner praise for their modest swimsuit choices.[86] LDS news outlets, and even some evangelical ones, poured accolades on church members who refused to back down.[87] Their choice allowed them to stand out in the crowd. Pageantry became a means for conveying their uniqueness and their ability to succeed in spite of (or because) of it. The LDS church and others applauded their daughters for standing up for church teachings, holding them up as examples for integrating faith into one's everyday life.

Perhaps not coincidentally, the only two Mormon Miss Americas won before two-piece swimsuits reconfigured the swimsuit competition.[88] Colleen Hutchins, Miss America 1952, and Sharlene Wells, Miss America 1985, did not face the same dilemma about attire that their Mormon sisters after them did. As two-pieces grew in popularity on the pageant stage, even Mormon participants found it hard to model modesty. By 2012, a move among contestants at the Utah state pageant to consider the swimsuit a "costume" enabled many to justify less modest attire than they would wear to the pool.[89] They wanted to win Miss America, and they realized that the one-piece was a liability. Participants wished to honor their church and their convictions, but also respect their equally strong ambitions for themselves and their church mission.[90] This tension they faced was not a simple choice between belief and fame, but a choice between different kinds of belief and ambition.

The talent competition provided another opportunity for contestants to testify to their religious beliefs. Some, like Miss America 2007, Lauren Nelson, spoke generally about using their God-given gifts to honor God. Nelson, a United Methodist, asserted that her church in Oklahoma nurtured her love of singing.[91] Others, however, saw an opportunity to evangelize for God through their song choice. The *Alabama Baptist* praised Alison McCreary's decision to sing a Christian song, noting, "One of the most obvious testimonies of her faith came in the talent competition of the Miss America pageant when she sang, 'How Great Thou Art.'"[92] Miss America 1995, Heather Whitestone, and Miss America 2009, Katie Stam, chose Sandi Patti's rendition of *Via Dolorosa* as their talent song. Whitestone performed a ballet en pointe depicting the words of the song, and Stam sang the piece. Both spoke of God's hand in their talent performance in particular and in their pageant participation more generally.[93] They joined the ranks of other competitors on every level who decided to make a faith statement with their performance choice. Of course, their selection also signaled their determination to mark their personal identity as a believer.

If the talent competition gave Christians a stage for evangelism, the platform component offered them the world. Beginning in 1989, each contestant at every level of competition chose an issue as "her" cause.[94] This community service requirement seemed tailor-made for Christians. Young women advocated for character education, abstinence, and literacy—to name a few. Beginning in 2007, the new Miss America also served as the goodwill ambassador for the Children's Miracle Network. For Christians, the introduction of the platform and the work with the Children's Miracle Network further legitimized the program, distinguishing the Miss America competition from other beauty events. In fact, the pageant hosted a second competition based solely on a contestant's community service. Finalists for the Quality of Life Award were announced each year during contest week, with the top three receiving scholarship dollars.[95]

Christians used their platforms to live out their faith on the national stage, and their faith communities held them up as examples. For example, the Woman's Missionary Union (WMU) of the Southern Baptist Convention (SBC) celebrated Deidre Downs, Miss America 2005, in a feature article.[96] Downs, a Baptist from Alabama, spent uncounted hours advocating for her platform, "Curing Childhood Cancer." The story recounted her work with cancer patients at Camp Smile-A-Mile as well as the success of Alabama's Curing Childhood Cancer license plate, which Downs designed. Downs and others obtained the one thousand people needed for the state to produce the tags. When the article was published in 2007, more than $250,000 had been raised for cancer research. The piece did more than list her accomplishments, however. It probed deeper to explore Downs' motivation for helping others, highlighting her childhood conversion and her desire to serve the "least of these" described in Matthew 25:40.[97] Cindy Townsend, the author of the piece, held up Downs as an example to be emulated by the Christian readers of *Missions Mosaic*. She hoped Downs' story inspired others "to find their mission in life, to discover their God-given purpose and wake up every day desiring to fulfill that purpose."[98] Townsend implied that being Miss America was God's mission for Downs.

Other religious groups also held up Miss America as an example. Mormons reacted similarly to the crowning of Sharlene Wells. Wells, Miss America 1985, was the daughter of Elder Robert E. Wells of the First Quorum of the Seventy.[99] The LDS magazine, *Ensign*, lauded her public witness, both spoken and lived.[100] Wells spoke boldly to the press about abstaining from drugs, alcohol, and premarital sex. She said she wanted to be a role model. Her church applauded her decision to speak about her LDS affiliation and to stand by her religious convictions in the national spotlight. In fact, her father likened her year of service as Miss America to a year on mission, saying, "Personally, I look on it as any parent sending a missionary into the mission field."[101] The LDS community celebrated Wells for maintaining her religious standards throughout her reign, seeing it as an opportunity for the world to learn more about the church.

The Christian example of some Miss Americas provoked critique. For example, Erika Harold faced opposition, including conflict with the Miss America Organization, when she promoted chastity before marriage as part of her platform.[102] Harold, Miss America 2003, garnered much praise from Christians for refusing to back down.[103] A member of Urbana Assembly of God, Harold enjoyed the support of her parents and her minister. All claimed to see God's hand at work in her life. Her pastor, Gary W. Grogan, noted, "As a church, we see the sovereignty of God in her selection as Miss America. We believe that, as with Esther, Erika has been called to the kingdom for such a time as this."[104] Harold, and her religious community, understood her pageant journey and her faith journey as part of the same story.

When Harold failed to win Miss Illinois during the first two years she competed, she believed she was being punished for standing up for her faith.[105] Her Pentecostal tradition had a long history of both rejecting and embracing culture, and she reflected that paradoxical history.[106] Harold took a break from pageantry the next year before returning to, and ultimately winning, the competition. Faced with opposition to her participating in pageants as a Christian, she stated, "I am under no illusion that I won because of beauty or talent. God has creative ways of using people to make a difference. We should never limit Him to traditional ways we conceive of ministry."[107] Her faith community, including her pastor, agreed. As Grogan said, "The Lord rewards those who stand for Him . . . It's one thing to be bold in church; it's another thing in the public arena. She's reaching more lost people in a year than the average preacher will in a lifetime."[108] Like so many other religious Miss Americas, Harold and her religious community believed her role as Miss America to be divinely appointed.

In addition to print media, Christian radio and television programs interviewed Miss Americas past and present, praising them for making a difference through their examples and community service. Rather than disgracing a young woman, the Miss America title elevated her to a position of leadership. In many ways, it uniquely qualified her since she was used to being in the spotlight and leading by example. For instance, Miss America 1973, Terry Meeuwsen, became the cohost of the Christian Broadcasting Network's program *The 700 Club*, showing the heights to which a community would lift a pageant winner. In addition to her regular duties, Meeuwsen hosted Miss America winners on her show regularly, asking them about their Christian witness. She commiserated with them about the grueling duties of a Miss America. Once, she gathered with three other "formers" to wish Miss America a happy ninetieth birthday and to explore "why the pageant is far more than just a beauty contest."[109] With local churches, pastors, and denominational publications, Meeuwsen validated participation.

The presentation of the Miss America Organization as a venue for evangelism provided the perfect justification for churches and church-related publications to promote contestants. Some religious communities seized the opportunity to invite participants to speak and perform. Terry Meeuwsen, Miss America 1973, estimated that she spoke in churches about twice a month during her reign. Beyond the local church, some Miss Americas had the opportunity to speak, sing, or testify at larger gatherings of Christians such as denominational meetings and interdenominational revivals or conferences. For example, Miss America 1971, Phyllis George, spoke at a Billy Graham evangelistic crusade's Youth Night Service in Baton Rouge, Louisiana during her reign. The number of microphones on the podium signals the size of the arena, and, by extension, the audience being addressed. Some contestants noted that hearing a Miss America (or Miss [State] Pageant) speak about her faith or reading a Miss America's story encouraged her to compete. To name just two examples, Tara Holland, Miss America 1997, credited her participation to reading the autobiography of Cheryl Prewitt, Miss America 1980, and Rebecca Eileen Trueblood, Miss Idaho 1989, recalled the example of Kellye Cash, Miss America 1987, speaking at a youth festival.[110] The support of churches, Christian organizations, and Christian media provided a steady stream of contestants for pageants, all intent on making a difference.

Figure 4.4. Christian Miss Americas were often invited to speak at churches, Youth for Christ events, and other religious gatherings. Pictured here is Phyllis George, Miss America 1971, speaking at a Billy Graham crusade.

At times, the praise of pageant contestants and of their high morals spread outside the Christian community. Rabbi Yonason Goldson used his blog to commend Heather Whitestone and Erika Harold for their beliefs on abstinence. In a post titled "The Private Life of Miss America," he called their "nonconformity" "inspirational."[111] The *Chicago Tribune* ran a story about Erika Harold's abstinence message, noting the positive response she had received from America's youth at some of the schools that had invited her.[112] *Jet* magazine featured Debbye Turner on the front, arm stretched toward heaven, with the cover story "New Miss America Says, 'Beauty is Content of Character.'"[113] Still, the Christian community accounted for a lot of the publicity.[114] Christian Americans commended young women for their witness despite the seeming conflicts of interest.

Thus some Christian pastors, organizations, and denominations eventually joined forces with pageants. Pageants emerged as benign events that in their judgment could be used for good. At least three things are in play. First, denominations and universities claimed their winners publicly because of the "proud parent syndrome." Religious groups, no less than parents, wanted to publicize their daughters' success. For example, when Samford University alumna Deidre Downs took the Miss America 2005 title, Samford published a piece in the campus newspaper, the *Belltower*. In addition, the Baptist school hosted a luncheon to honor Downs.[115] In essence, the Christian community celebrated pageant wins as they would academic, athletic, or altruistic accolades. They capitalized on the young woman's fame, featuring "their beauty" in church publications, denominational literature, and campus newsletters. Smart, attractive, successful women were commodities even in the religious world.[116] Their presence provided churches credibility in the religious marketplace as they competed for members and students. Even churches and universities who refused to openly advocate pageants claimed their winners and sought to benefit from them.

Second, at least since the postwar years, some Christians encouraged young women to participate because they saw pageantry as an avenue for evangelism. The pageant became yet another competition for claims on national identity and civic presence.[117] Committed young women jumped at the chance to showcase their faith on stage. Even when pastors, churches, and religious mentors did not explicitly encourage young women to enter beauty competitions, most sanctioned the contests. With beauty an established commodity for evangelism, partnering with pageants seemed not only logical, but also desirable.[118]

Third, post-1965 churches appeared to join forces with pageants to pre-serve traditional forms of femininity from the perceived threat of feminism. This was not an official alliance, of course, but evidence suggests that Christians united with pageants more in the wake of feminism than they had previously. In other words, churches saw pageants as purveyors of tradition. And in many ways they were right. The Miss America contest adapted slowly to changes in the culture, maintaining its role of promoting the girl-next-door. In tumultuous times, pageants offered a taste of the familiar. Its ceremony harkened back to a simpler time that may have proved comforting to many conservative (mostly white) Christians in America.[119]

Thus Christians invited young pageant participants to speak and perform in their churches, promoting them as role models. Though this happened prior to 1965, the shift in pageant culture that allowed women to speak more openly about their religious views made the arrangement more natural. Perhaps this new focus prompted some Christians, whether consciously or not, to see the Miss Americas as the type of American woman they wanted their daughters to be. Certainly Vonda Kay Van Dyke and Terry Meeuwsen were less threatening (and represented them better) than Betty Friedan and Gloria Steinem.[120] The Miss America ideal represented a kind of sanctified feminism.

These three reasons, and perhaps many others, go hand in hand. Christians in America rallied around their contestants, encouraging them to embrace the pageant and all of its benefits. Win or lose, all Christian pageant representatives seemed loved.

Making Meaning: Religion in the Public Sphere Post-1965

The religious landscape of America in 1921 differed greatly from that of 2018. Slaughter's careful crafting of the pageant into something respectable did not by itself lead to the moment when Vonda Kay Van Dyke spoke openly about her faith. Many factors prepared her (and others) to speak in new ways. At least three trajectories in American religious history paralleled some of the changes in the pageant and helped make them more palatable to Christian Americans.

First, beginning with the Cold War, religion gained an ever increasing role in American public discourse. It became accepted that public figures would speak about their relationship with God, at least in general terms as a means of combating "godless communism."[121] For example, "In 1949 . . . President Harry Truman told Americans that 'the basic source of our strength as a nation is spiritual. . . . Religious faith and religious work must be our reliance as we strive to fulfill our destiny in the world.'"[122] Then, at his inauguration in 1953, President Dwight D. Eisenhower offered a prayer. Evangelist Billy Graham helped rally the nation into churches, encouraging cooperation among American Christians to be united in their opposition to communism. Church attendance rose from 49 percent in 1940 to 65 percent in 1970.[123] These forces contributed to an increase in religious discourse, especially Protestant, Catholic, and Jew, in American life.[124] The Miss America contest, experiencing its golden years in the 1950s and 1960s, offered another venue for Americans to show off the success and character of their young women. When Van Dyke spoke about her Christianity in 1965, the country was prepared not only to accept her, but to praise her.

Second, the rise of the feminist movement in the 1960s affected the pageant and Christians' response to it. On the one hand, the women's movement authorized and accelerated the impulse for women to hold public roles. On the other hand, it induced fear that women would forget their place as the moral guardians of society.[125] The Miss America competition offered an in-between space that allowed women greater public freedom even as it offered a buffer against an overly aggressive Gloria Steinem–type of public presentation. Pageants provided a compromise. In a period when many women in society questioned traditional gender roles and demanded more access to education, jobs, and power, Van Dyke's espousal of conservative Christian values seemed an untapped resource. She modeled a "new woman" that Christian parents could commend to their daughters.[126] In other words, pageants provided women opportunities for advancement, but not in a way that threatened Christian patriarchy.[127] America was not as united as they attempted to show in the 1950s and 1960s. The Civil Rights Movement and the rise of feminism prompted fear in many Americans. Controversy surrounding equal rights displayed America's disunity, and some would suggest hypocrisy, to the world.[128] Christians found space in beauty pageants that allowed them to feel safe and secure in these turbulent times.

Finally, the prevalence of evangelicals in popular culture in the late twentieth and early twenty-first centuries prompted them to talk about God and God's role in everyday activities in a way formerly untenable. While many forces made this alliance possible, the mainstreaming of evangelicalism allowed this once estranged religious group cultural power and influence. As such, these (largely conservative) Christians sought to enforce their worldview onto America at large, using all of the tools at their disposal to reach the world for Christ.[129] These contestants and their communities embraced the idea of pageant participation with the larger purpose of evangelism in mind.

Christian Miss Americas routinely paraded their faith down the runway and into the world beyond.

Of course, this newfound freedom had its limits. So, what about pageants made them acceptable in the eyes of many contenders and supporters? Pageants offered enough respectable aspects (talent, community service, scholarship) to outweigh its questionable ones (commodification of female bodies, self-promotion). As evangelicals flooded the political arena in the form of Jimmy Carter's presidency and the rise of the Religious Right, previously unthinkable alliances emerged as evangelistic opportunities. Evangelicals Christianized rock music, romance novels, and movies—so why not pageants? These Christian additions to popular culture provided vehicles for evangelism just like the Miss America contest. For conservative Christians in general and evangelicals in particular, popular culture was neither good nor bad.[130] Within American popular culture were neutral events, objects, and spaces that could be used for Christ when Christians were intentional about their goals and took action to achieve them.

Multiple Voices: A Test Case

Not all Christians supported pageants, and pageants did not always welcome Christians. Multiple voices contributed to the conversation about this unlikely match. One example from the 2009 Miss USA pageant highlighted the complexities well. Though different in some respects from the Miss America Organization, the Miss USA pageant was similar enough to justify comparisons regarding Christian–pageant interaction. The underlying issue of women's beauty display and the marketing of their bodies existed in both and provides the basis for some comparisons to be made. To be sure, the difference between the Miss USA and Miss America competitions matters greatly to those who participate in them. Most notably, Miss America contestants performed a talent, advocated a community service platform, and underwent a more substantial interview than Miss USA contestants. Most pageant viewers, however, conflated the two pageants in their minds. The distinctions so important to Miss America contestants sometimes went unnoticed by their supporters. Carrie Prejean's story received much publicity, and the response to it highlighted the diversity of opinions among Christians.

Carrie Prejean, Miss California USA 2009 and first runner-up to Miss USA 2009, sparked commentary throughout the blogosphere for her answer to an onstage question about same-sex marriage. Celebrity blogger Perez Hilton asked Prejean, "Vermont recently became the fourth state to legalize same-sex marriage. Do you think every state should follow suit? Why or why not?"[131] She answered:

> Well, I think it's great that Americans are able to choose one or the other. We live in a land that you can choose same-sex marriage or opposite marriage. And you know what, in my country, in my family, I think that I believe that marriage should be between a man and a woman, no offense to anybody out there. But that's how I was raised, and that's how I believe that it should be—between a man and a woman.[132]

Hilton later confirmed that Prejean's answer cost her the crown.[133] Reactions to the chain of events that eventually cost Prejean the Miss California USA crown as well were as diverse as judge and contestant.

On one side of the aisle stood Prejean's supporters. She became a hero in the evangelical community seemingly overnight. *Focus on the Family*'s James Dobson praised her for preaching a sermon with her life, her pastor Miles McPherson compared her to Esther, and the National Organization for Marriage hired her to appear in an ad called "No Offense."[134] On the other side, Prejean experienced attacks because of her stance on marriage, dodged insults regarding her breast enhancement surgery, and endured a firestorm over some photos of her in which she was scantily clad. Rumors (later confirmed) of a sex tape added fuel to the fire.[135]

Christians and non-Christians weighed in on both sides of the debate. Since the support of Christians in pageants has already been established, it remains only to parse some of the opposition. Some Christian bloggers posed questions about whether Prejean should have been competing in the pageant at all, criticizing beauty pageants in general. For example, in a blog post titled, "The Other Miss California Controversy," Katelyn Beaty pinpointed the crux of the issue:

> What has surprised me about the Christian media's response is a seemingly inconsistent sexual ethic at play: Celebrating Prejean as the lone voice for biblical convictions in a public square where it's now bigoted to oppose same-sex marriage, while never questioning if a Christian woman like Prejean should be participating in the Miss USA pageant in the first place.[136]

Others shared Beaty's concerns. Warren Throckmorton queried, "Is anyone else puzzled by the response to our new family values spokeswoman?" Though mild in his criticisms, he concluded: "But unless religious conservatives have some kind of answer to our girls about how they can lionize a Miss USA contestant and stress modesty at the same time, I do not see the virtue in giving her the platform."[137] Their voices joined others asking for a closer inspection of Christian pageant culture.[138]

Of course, the Miss America contest also received criticism from evangelical Christians. For example, in a brief essay by Marc Gibson, he condemned Christian participation in beauty pageants. "Over the years, Christians have been teaching their children how to live holy lives in an unholy world. Our young folks learn that there are many activities in this world that are not fit for Christians to participate in," he argued. "One of those things is the ever-popular beauty pageant."[139] The problem with such competitions, he continued, was that "the physical form and beauty of a female girl or woman's body is put on display as an object to be judged. Clothing, or lack thereof, is worn to immodestly highlight the attractive features of the female body for all to observe."[140] "Faithful Christians," he intoned, eschewed associating with such "worldly" pursuits. Gibson felt compelled to write because Jennifer Berry, a member of a Church of Christ, had recently been crowned Miss America 2006. When Berry was Miss Oklahoma, one of her traveling companions was a deacon's wife. Both had received positive press from the *Christian Chronicle*, another Churches of Christ publication. Gibson lamented this encouragement, claiming, "In the past, brethren would have been ashamed to report such a thing."[141] He cited Scripture as he asked, "Has a love for this present world turned our ears deaf to the divine standards of morality and godliness?"[142] Promises of evangelistic opportunities or free publicity for the Churches of Christ failed to lure Gibson from his quest for holiness. He urged others to beware the traps of immodesty and worldliness.

Others offered a more nuanced critique. For example, after Vanessa Williams lost her crown, Tom Minnery of *Focus on the Family* defended the pageant against accusations that "*Penthouse* poses differ[ed] only in degree from the sexual titillation of the swimsuit competition."[143] While he praised the pageant "for standing fast and acting decisively," he also urged contest officials to consider the relationship of enterprises like the Miss America Organization to publications like *Penthouse*.

> While we do not necessarily endorse swimsuit competitions, the efforts to compare them with clinically explicit lesbian sex pictures are feeble and ridiculous. There is cause for the pageant executives to consider how much they, like Guccione, use sex to sell their product, but the pornographic *Penthouse* is worlds away from the beauty and talent pageant in Atlantic City.[144]

In the end, he blamed Williams, not the pageant, for the missteps that occurred. Comparing her to Eve, he noted, "There is always a price to pay for perverting God's purposes and the beauty of his created order. Miss Williams learned the price quickly."[145]

One of the longest, most pointed, and theologically rich Christian critiques of beauty pageants does not address a specific winner at all. In Harvey
Cox's 1961 article, "Miss America and the Cult of the Girl," he argued, "The
Girl is an idol" that "*functions* in many ways as a goddess."[146] "The truth
is that The Girl can*not* bestow the identity she promises," Cox wrote. "She
forces her initiates to torture themselves with starvation diets and beauty par-
lor ordeals, but still cannot deliver the satisfactions she holds out."[147] The Girl,
as any idol, distracts the believer from God who "is the center and source of
value . . . The identity he confers frees men from all pseudo-identities to be
themselves, to fulfill their human destinies regardless of whether their faces
or figures match some predetermined abstract 'ideal.'"[148] Thus Cox noted
the formational power of pageants, both for participants, and worshipers,
and calls for a reordering of one's devotion and re-centering of one's identity.
These examples demonstrated the cacophony of voices surrounding Christian pageant participation.[149]

For Such a Time as This: The Esther Narrative

Christian pageant contestants were sometimes compared to Queen Esther
in the Bible. This seemed particularly true of contestants who faced controversy, whether it was with the pageant or secular culture. Assertions that
God placed them in their positions "for such a time as this" gave credibility
and solidarity to their struggles.[150] Both Erika Harold, Miss America 2003,
and Carrie Prejean, Miss USA 2009, were compared to this biblical queen.
At times, Christians used the rhetoric to justify beauty pageants, claiming
that the book of Esther narrates the first beauty pageant ever held. The language of election was also applied to evangelical women outside of pageants.
Notably, evangelical Christians used the Queen Esther story to validate their
support of Sarah Palin for vice president in the 2008 election.[151] Though not
usually in favor of women holding such a high public office, the nation, some
Christians asserted, needed Palin's gifts and God had set her apart to serve.
If such verbal gymnastics sounded like special pleading, looking at the *actual*
story of Esther in Scripture confirmed it. Indeed, the biblical account highlighted different, often overlooked, similarities between modern-day beauty
competitions and King Ahasuerus' pageant.

At least three thorny issues for Christians appeared in Esther. These
ideas make comparing positions like Miss America to that of Queen Esther
undesirable. In addition, recounting some of the darker themes of the story
might prompt some consideration of the dangerous parallels between the
two. First, the story in Esther was one of male control of women's bodies

under the auspices of national security. Queen Vashti lost her position as queen because she refused to dance naked before the king and his drunken guests at a banquet. Second, women did not choose to participate in the king's beauty pageant. "Beautiful young virgins" were brought to the king from throughout the kingdom, and he chose his queen from among them. Again, this was not an innocent parade of beauty. Each virgin slept with the king, and he selected the one that "pleased" him to be queen.[152] The rest remained in his harem. Finally, in this biblical narrative, the power derived from pleasing men with one's body proved limited. The women in the story, both Vashti and Esther, were at the mercy of King Ahasuerus. Any control they possessed came through him and thus could be taken away at any time. Again, the dangers of Christians using this scriptural text as a template for women to follow were numerous.

The comparison of this text to the modern-day pageants by conservative Christians was a good one, but not for the reasons they supposed. Esther was chosen "for such a time as this," but she did not choose her exploitation. One could argue that women involved in beauty pageants actively participated in their objectification. Women involved in beauty pageants also found national ideals mapped onto their bodies. They became commodities with men as the consumers. One final similarity should be noted. In beauty pageants, the power granted to women was limited. It was not necessarily limited by men, but certainly women found their pageant credentials did not unlock every gate, as occasionally asserted.

Conclusion

After a rocky start, the relationship between Christians and pageants enjoyed praise in denominational publications from the *Alabama Baptist* to *Today's Pentecostal Evangel*. In many cases, the religious media ignored or justified the apparent contradictions between their conservative theology and pageant participation. Most notably was a failure to comment on conservative Christian notions of modesty with regard to the body and the seeming incompatibility of participating in an event in which women were judged on their bodies. Christian leaders and other religious pageant supporters behaved as if the religious opportunities and rewards of pageantry outweighed any costs. Almost all of them that noted drawbacks focused on issues of display and exhibition with few questioning the commodification or commercialism also inherent in the contest. One issue dominated their vision and drove their conversations, making it easier to justify any surface contradictions between church teaching and pageant preaching.

However, not all Christians agreed. Some called Christian pageant participants out on what they determined to be hypocrisy. Others merely raised questions about the benefits of pageantry. A media explosion surrounding the ethics of pageantry led to articles on the blogs of *Baptist News Global*, *Her.meneutics*, and *GetReligion.org*, among others. The fact that these Christian media outlets felt compelled to weigh in on this issue testified to the public appeal of pageants among Christians. Their voices indicated that the story of Christians and the Miss America Pageant was not a monolithic one. It also showed that pageants were important enough to warrant their hostile attention.

Not deniable, however, was the fact that Christians who once opposed the Miss America competition came to sing its praises. The organization once targeted as a source of corruption for America's young women became seen as a celebration of Christian ideals such as hard work, helping others, and honoring God-given gifts. Christian communities increasingly saw the Miss America competition as a source of empowerment and religious opportunity for their daughters. The benefits were so great that it seemed a natural fit for many Christian young women even as some struggled to make sense of the seeming contradiction between the teachings of their church and the expectations of the pageant. The approval of Christian communities not only celebrated current pageant contestants but encouraged other young women to seek accolades through pageantry as well. In other words, Christian churches ensured a steady stream of Christian competitors who sought to fulfill their God-given purpose through pageantry. And, on the face of it, it appeared that many Miss Americas post-1965 saw pageantry as a religious opportunity, providing them a platform from which to preach the goodness of God's love and faithfulness through even the most trying of circumstances.

Thus the faith *of* the pageant enabled faith *and* the pageant, which encouraged faith *in* the pageant. The faith of individual contestants served as a lens through which they experienced and understood their pageant participation. Their pageant "testimonies" reinforced both the faith *of* and faith *and* the pageant.

5

Faith in the Pageant

"It's more than just a job to me. To me, the Miss America experience is the opportunity to be a part of a ministry."

—Caressa Cameron, Miss America 2010[1]

During her reign as Miss Alabama and subsequently as Miss America 1995, Heather Whitestone, a Baptist, traveled the nation promoting her platform of youth motivation titled "Anything is Possible." The first Miss America with a disability, Whitestone encouraged youth to focus on their abilities rather than their disabilities, claiming that her religious faith was a powerful motivator for helping her achieve success.[2] Pageant winners like Whitestone became local celebrities, often finding their way into schools, churches, Kiwanis meetings, and other community events. She used her national status as Miss America as a platform to promote her religious convictions.

Whitestone was neither the first nor the last Miss America to mix faith and celebrity.[3] Miss America 1980, Cheryl Prewitt (Pentecostal); Miss America 1996, Shawntel Smith (Pentecostal); and Miss America 2007, Lauren Nelson (Methodist) were just three of the many local and national winners who construed pageantry as part of their religious journeys. In the latter half of the twentieth century and into the twenty-first, Christian women took to the stage with a mission in surprising numbers. To be sure, not all Christians approved of pageants. Equally important, not all women who participated in beauty contests claimed to be Christian. Still, more than half of the winners post-1965 professed Christianity.[4] And all of them donned a swimsuit and bared their bodies as part of the credentialing process.

The crowning of Miss America 2002 took place on September 22, 2001, less than two weeks after the September 11 terrorist attacks on the United States. After the competition, the contestants compiled a book of "fifty-one stories documenting the quest of the Class of 2001 to impart hope and healing during a year of service like no other."[5] The book revealed that thirty-five of the fifty-one contestants (68.6 percent) alluded to their faith in their three- to four-page "testimony."[6] Participants wrote of praying together, "God [creating] us all for *such a time as this*," and God choosing "the perfect woman to be Miss America."[7] Chapter titles included "Renewed Faith" and "Blessings in Disguise."[8] Such a cursory look at each individual's reflection does not offer conclusive evidence that she was a Christian, but it does at least intimate that contestants perceived faith to be an advantage.

At first, Miss America's faith earned nationwide attention by accident. Miss America 1965, Vonda Van Dyke (Methodist, Miss Arizona), was the first winner to speak about her faith commitments publicly. At that time, Miss America contestants signed a contract agreeing not to talk about religion or politics, but when emcee Bert Parks asked Van Dyke whether her Bible served as her good-luck charm, she seized the opportunity. She answered, "I do not consider my Bible a good-luck charm. It is the most important book I own."[9] After seeing the positive responses from the American public to Van Dyke, pageant officials decided to change the rules.[10] Van Dyke paved the way for many Christians who took the stage after her, including Whitestone. Those Christian winners received overwhelming support and encouragement from their religious traditions, and some even cited their pageant careers as preparation for Christian ministry.

While much changed in the pageant during its history, one thing stayed the same: the consistency with which pageant winners discussed their purpose in seeking the title. Their stories describing their pageant participation dripped with religious language. Women have long been seen as the moral guardians of society.[11] They were expected to teach and embody religious values to the next generation by setting a good example for others to follow.[12] Christian pageant contestants highlighted their piety and emphasized how pageants allowed them to fulfill this role of moral exemplar. Likewise, the talents chosen, answers given in interviews, and responses to onstage questions suggested an affiliation with Christianity and a desire to impart one's faith through performance. Christian Miss Americas, just like born-again Christians, had a story, or perhaps two stories, to tell.

As part of their narratives, these pageant participants provided explanations of the merits of beauty competitions. The contests offered more than shiny headgear. Pageants, contestants claimed, gave them a venue to develop confidence, practice community service, and celebrate women's scholarship. The contests also provided an outlet for living out their faith and, at times, a springboard into various types of full-time Christian ministry.[13] Further, given the time in which young women were involved, pageant participation provided a foundation in their religious identity formation.[14] It told them who they were even as it shaped who they were becoming.

Contestant stories followed a predictable outline, one in which they overcame some kind of trial to receive glory as Miss America and then used their newfound fame to give the glory back to God. This configuration echoed common tales of conversion experiences, following the classic model in which testimonies were delivered in churches, moving from crisis to faith to reward.[15] Participants' prayers reveal the depth to which faith informed their practice. Participants often saw pageantry as an opportunity that could be a test of faith, a platform for personal growth, or an opportunity for evangelism. God directed, God led, or God commanded, it was always God-ordained.

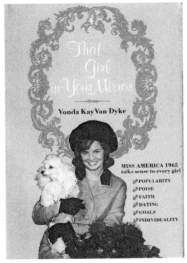

Figure 5.1. Cheryl Prewitt, Miss America 1980, and Vonda Kay Van Dyke, Miss America 1965, were just two Miss Americas who chose to record their pageant testimonies in print.

All conversion stories were inherently normative, pageant testimonies included.[16] They acted "as both a narration of events and a confession of belief."[17] In telling their stories, contestants wished "to know the self better in order to know God better" and "to help others follow a similar path of liberation and salvation."[18] Participants narrated two conversions. They testified to the power of both God and of the pageant in their lives. Lines blurred when trying to separate the two confessions. The Miss America competition and God's purpose intertwined.

To be sure, not every Christian contestant articulated a "call" to pageants or interpreted their experience in Christian terms. Some saw a disconnect between their participation and their faith. Others did not think much about it. Some used religion "strategically." In addition, some Christian women dropped out of pageantry all together. Contestants often interpreted their forays in retrospect. Consequently, they may have superimposed religious language to validate their participation or denied incentives in light of rewards (or the lack thereof). Paying attention to the complexity and multiplicity of motives and testimony timelines of Christian Miss Americas adds further dimension.

Likewise, not all Christians approved of pageants, at times speaking out against them. The story of faith and the pageant is not a monolithic one, but it is one that moves generally from protest to support.[19] And this, in part, is due to the deep value that Christian women placed on their pageant participation. Dissecting the predictable and repeated pattern used by Miss Americas in pageant "testimonies" reveals characteristics of Christianity that made this unlikely relationship of Christians in the pageant possible.

Christianity and "Our" Miss Americas

Perhaps no one was more convinced that God was directing her pageant heels than Miss America 1980, Cheryl Prewitt.[20] A Pentecostal from Mississippi, Prewitt claimed that the healing of God allowed her to participate and eventually win. Not only that, she believed that her healing happened in order that she might testify on the national stage to God's goodness and power. She remained so confident that she would win that reflecting upon her crowning moment, she declared, "I wasn't shocked. I didn't cry. But oh, I was happy. Happier than I'd ever been in all my life."[21] Prewitt used her story as evidence of God's power.

After an automobile accident at age eleven, physicians told her that she might never walk again. While further medical intervention enabled her to walk, Prewitt possessed a decided limp because her crippled leg healed two inches shorter than the other. She later learned that her injuries meant she might not be able to have children. Soon after, she attended a Kenneth Hagin healing meeting in Jackson, Mississippi. There, according to her, she experienced the miracle for which she had been praying and believing. As she described it:

> Soothing warmth, as though I'd been immersed in a hot tub, enveloped me. For a moment I seemed to lose track of time. I was aware in my mind that Mr. Hagin was still by my side, but somehow I no longer heard a word he was saying. It was as though I had slipped away to some faraway bright-shining place—a private place inhabited only by myself and Jesus. I felt overwhelmed, filled to overflowing, with His Presence—with His power, compassion, and love. More than anything else, His love.[22]

After falling to the floor "as though in a deep sleep," Prewitt sat up to find that her left leg now extended as far as her right. She believed that God healed her for a "bigger reason" than just her desire for healing. As she wrote, "The ultimate reason for answered prayers of any kind (especially miracles) is to serve as a sign to others (especially nonbelievers) of God's existence and love."[23] Her healing, as she understood it, proved crucial to her testimony and, later, to her mission to become Miss America.

Prewitt recounted a similar revelatory encounter about her pageant participation. She believed that God called her to compete for a higher purpose than the mere hope of a crown or the benefit of scholarship money (one of her initial reasons for entering). Shortly after praying that God would show her what he wanted her to do with her life, she was "struck with the realization that my involvement in pageants could, in fact, be a means to an end—that is, if my ultimate goal was to win the title of Miss America!"[24] She questioned, "Could trying for the title of Miss America be what God wanted me to do with my life; that is, if my purpose was to use the position as a means of witnessing for Him on a world-wide scale? The more I thought and prayed about it, the more certain I became that it was."[25]

Prewitt submitted herself to the process, enduring a rigid training plan. She dedicated herself to getting rid of "two small paunches of ugly fat" on her thighs. She read newspapers and magazines to prepare for the interview. The Mississippi pageant board held mock interviews with Prewitt, videotaping her "performance" so that she could study and perfect every word, sentence, and gesture. They even helped her tame and groom her accent.[26] She felt God wanted her to compete and thus left nothing up to chance. She worked as if her life depended on it, taking on the time commitments and lifestyle changes required of student athletes.

In the midst of all of the focused hard work, Prewitt turned to God for guidance. She developed a pageant prayer during her second year vying for the title of Miss Mississippi. As she sought to live into God's purpose for her, she found herself praying, "Lord, this is Your pageant. If I can do more good for You—reach more people—as Miss Starkville than as plain old me, then let me win. Otherwise, don't."[27] She repeated that prayer at the Miss Mississippi Pageant, changing only the titles. While preparing for Miss America, Prewitt did more than pray and prep. She drew on Scripture to confess. Referring to her confessions as "positive talking," she pointed to Mark 11:23 as her evidence that "not only do you have to believe, you've got to *say* what you believe. Confess it to others."[28] She continued, "The way I figure it, confessing with your mouth helps your mind to become convinced. It also serves to surround you with continual positive vibrations—like a protective screen—that prevent Satan from sabotaging your mind with negativity."[29] Another Scripture passage that took on new meaning was Hebrews 11:1. In seeking to receive comfort from this text, she accepted that she would win Miss America and presented that notion as fact to more and more people. Her "positive talking" led to "positive knowing." As she wrote later, "It was almost as though I had already won the title—it just hadn't happened yet in time and space."[30] Prewitt drew on everything she knew about God, faith, hard work, and pageants to ready herself for competition.[31]

She recited her prayer at Miss America too. Shortly after praying, "Lord, this is Your pageant. If I can do more good for You—reach more people—as Miss America than as Miss Mississippi, then let me win. Otherwise, don't," Prewitt received the crown and entry onto an even broader stage.[32] She believed God meant for her to win Miss America, but she did more than just believe it in the abstract. In her mind, belief fostered action. She knew that she must offer the best testimony of God's grace, love, and healing possible and worked hard to represent herself, and her God, well. As she noted when faced with a difficult diet and exercise plan, "If the press picks up on the story of my healing, I've got to have the best looking legs in town!"[33] Conservative Christians like Prewitt felt extra pressure to do well because they represented not only themselves but also their church, and ultimately, God.[34] Prewitt was willing to do whatever it took to testify to God's goodness in her life. She saw God's hand every step of the way, drawing comfort from her expectation of God's presence and perfect divine will. Pageants offered her the platform.

Even if some of Prewitt's religious claims were "extreme," she was not alone in her religious defenses of beauty competitions.[35] Prewitt asserted that becoming Miss America was part of God's perfect plan for her. In her mind, she confessed her belief and worked hard to make it a reality. Once crowned Miss America, she used the opportunity (and all doors it opened) to testify to God's healing power. She, like many pageant contestants both before and after, embraced the crown as her anointing, an ordination to a ministry. Numerous Miss Americas spoke or wrote about God's directing their pageant steps too. And the validation of pageantry became almost second nature within and among religious communities across the nation after Vonda Kay Van Dyke's onstage answer in 1965. Examining participants' words alongside those of their religious communities proves crucial for understanding contestants' motivations, how they represented their faith traditions, and how they interacted with the goals of the pageant.

Pageant stories resembled call and conversion narratives. One Miss America wrote about her "baptism into the Miss America routine."[36] At the same time, their testimonies went beyond a simple conversion into the Miss America program. Contestants also spoke of being called in a religious sense. Teresa Scanlan, Miss America 2011, declared that her win was "to fulfill His [God's] plan," and Tara Holland, Miss America 1997, believed "I was one of those that was called to do pageants."[37] Many claimed that the experience gave their life new meaning, delivered them from undesirable circumstances, or provided opportunities for spiritual growth. Conservative Christian women across the nation embraced the organization wholeheartedly, seeing the competition as a way to communicate their faith. Pageants offered a tool just like radio, television, or rock music—all productive public venues for twentieth-century Christians—for communicating the gospel.[38] Christians maintained a strong presence in this purportedly secular enterprise. Among the winners (and even some of the losers), religious language of divine direction and purpose enveloped the arena.

Cheryl Prewitt moved from a physical disability to restored health. Her strengthened faith in God led her to see pageants as a venue for evangelism. Despite skepticism encountered along the way, she stayed true to her convictions, crediting God with her healing and her ministry as Miss America and beyond. Prewitt's story of triumph over adversity reveals a testimony pattern. Participants encountered a crisis, expressed a resurgence of faith (often in the form of a "call" to pageantry), and experienced an outpouring of rewards. They then testified to God's goodness even as they endured tests of faith. Finally, they received affirmation that their witness made a difference. God's will was done. Many Christian winners' narratives took similar form in their biographies and autobiographies. Their testimonies and prayers relayed much about their theology. This paradigm offers a clearer picture of how Christian women talked about God's work in the world they inhabited. The particularities of their faith tradition were evident even as commonalities became evident across traditions. Likewise, their stories illustrated how religion functioned in the everyday life of Christian pageant contestants and how they interpreted their pageant participation. Testimony marked them as part of a unique community even as participants strived to broaden their experience with others.[39]

Crisis and Call

Like Christians, especially evangelical Christians, describing how they found Jesus, Christian Miss America contestants spoke of "converting" to pageantry in almost salvific terms. While the extent of their crises pre-pageantry differed, many described their life pre-Miss America as lacking in purpose and direction. Competition gave them a reason to push past their obstacles—physical and otherwise. The pageant thus offered the formation and affirmation one would expect from a religious community. The call to pageants became a turning point or touchstone that Christian Miss Americas felt the need to describe in detail. Perhaps because some of the mores associated with the contests seemed to contradict those of conservative Christianity, many participants sought to justify their participation. Though often articulated in retrospect, the event gave them a renewed vision and, for some, became a part of their conversion story as well. For others, the experience represented the overcoming of an impediment or provided an escape from a directionless life. While contestants were clear that Miss America was not what "saved" them, many recognized it as a crucial component of their faith journey and a ministry.

This pattern held true for Terry Meeuwsen, Miss America 1973. Before competing, Meeuwsen traveled as a folk singer with The New Christy Minstrels, believing her life "glamorous and exciting."[40] And yet her existence felt empty. Despite achieving her dream of singing professionally, she was headed down a path of destruction. Her life was in shambles as she struggled with days on the road, a time full of drugs, sex, and alcohol. Thanks to some new friends, however, Meeuwsen's life gained a new direction and took on a whole new meaning:

> My life was a little like a mountain stream. It was moving along swiftly and steadily, but the hills were so steep and the trees so thick that I couldn't see where I was going. I couldn't see where I would come out. And then suddenly, the trees were fewer, the sun began peeking through, and there in the distance, in the bright sunlight, I saw the end: my reason for being. It was Jesus Christ and I found Him in Plainview, Texas, which was our next stop.[41]

With a little help from some "Jesus Freaks," Meeuwsen experienced a conversion that led her away from time on the road and, eventually, back to the way of beauty contests that she thought she had left behind.[42] In pageants, she found her ticket to a different life. "The Miss America pageant," she later reflected, "is one of the few platforms available for young Christian women to win significant educational scholarships while gaining incredible exposure to realize their dreams without compromising their beliefs."[43] Her story bore a striking resemblance to those told by many of her colleagues. The organization, they believed, offered them a mission in the midst of their uncertain futures.

Another young woman who seized the opportunity to change her fortune was Heather Whitestone. She was first runner-up to Miss Alabama twice before finally clinching the title. Her persistence paid off when she was crowned Miss America 1995. Her failed attempts made an interesting side story, but the crux of her pageant testimony was the bigger obstacle she overcame: deafness. A childhood illness left Whitestone unable to hear at the age of eighteen months. She worked to be part of the hearing world, relearning how to speak and discerning how to read lips. Whitestone found an outlet in ballet and began dancing at the age of five. While at one time she dreamed of being a professional ballerina, she eventually found a new dream in pageants and imagined the thrill of dancing on national television before millions. Beauty contests offered her proof that she could belong.[44] The Miss America crown also gave her "a bigger voice to encourage people to follow the dreams God had given them."[45] However, even in this arena of performance Whitestone remained acutely aware of her deafness. Trying to hide her deafness, she struggled with the interview portion of the competition most. Even though Whitestone was an excellent lip-reader, sometimes judges spoke too quickly or their lips were hidden, making it difficult to answer their questions. Not until she confronted the judges about her inability to hear did Whitestone find success. Like other Christian Miss Americas who overcame struggles, she understood her win as proof that with God one could overcome even the toughest of circumstances. Whitestone claimed her hard work and determination resulted in her becoming the first Miss America with a disability.

Other Miss Americas had less serious crises that prompted their pageant performances. Still, there remained a need to explain one's pageant participation. For Vonda Kay Van Dyke, Miss America 1965, the obstacle was her attitude. After a couple of losses, Van Dyke believed her pageant days were over. As she recounted in *That Girl in Your Mirror*, "I was through with pageants or any other kind of competition. I didn't have enough talent, or enough poise, or whatever else I needed. I didn't have anything! How foolish I must have looked!"[46] Eventually, she surmised that she had lost because she "hadn't done her best" and because she "was aiming for the wrong goal and for the wrong reasons."[47] As Van Dyke recounted, "The prize was the only thing I could see. I didn't really appreciate the competition or the opportunity it offered me. I had to have it and I wanted it all for myself. I had never even asked myself whether I was doing the right thing—and I had never asked God how He felt about it."[48] Van Dyke discerned that God wanted her to compete again. "'All right,' I said, when I felt that my prayers were answered, 'I lost when I did things my way. Now we'll try Your way—but I don't see what difference that's going to make. If I'm not good enough, I'm not good enough.'"[49] Van Dyke rededicated herself to pageant preparation with the fervor of a backslider returned to the straight and narrow. She worked especially diligently on her talent, practicing and perfecting her ventriloquist act with a job at Legend City Music Hall. With a newfound focus on doing her best, Van Dyke determined that "I was going to try to please God by making the most of a good opportunity to share my talents."[50] Like so many others, she realized that a crown was not the only reward that pageantry had to offer.

Participants claimed the competitions afforded them a multitude of opportunities for growth and advancement. Some contestants, like Meeuwsen, saw pageantry as a way out of their previous disillusionment, a new endeavor to match their new Christian lifestyle, a new chance at success. Others, like Prewitt, understood pageants as a mandatory response to God's goodness in their life. For Prewitt and Meeuwsen, the crisis was a spiritual one tied in part to an experience that deepened their faith. Others, like Whitestone, faced physical crises that their faith helped them overcome. For these contestants, their physical restrictions made winning Miss America an impossible dream. Nevertheless they felt compelled to overcome the obstacles and compete for themselves and others. Still more, like Van Dyke, saw an opportunity to trust God's guidance and hone God-given talents. They believed that God's hand extended into every aspect of their lives, pageantry included.

Self-understanding presented only one way to interpret contestants' experiences. Many times, young women were already involved in pageants, or had been at one time, prior to their "call." Though they articulated an encounter with God that gave them a renewed vision for competing, it did not spark their initial entry onto the stage. Rather, it provided them an explanation—whether before, during, or after their crowning moment was up for interpretation—that helped explain their continued attempts at the crown. What some might call obsession, these Miss Americas labeled as religious commission.

Faith: Answering the Call, Committed to the Process

According to Christian contestants, they launched or continued their competitive careers with renewed fervor after experiencing their "call." Like a new Christian "on fire for Jesus" lived for worship and Bible study, these contenders ate, slept, and breathed pageants and contest preparations. Some were true pageant converts, novices who had to learn the ropes. Others had grown up on the pageant circuit and now saw the competitions with fresh eyes. They worked hard to accomplish their goals, believing God would bless their efforts. In other words, contestants testified to working with God to achieve God's purpose.[51] Of course, since people interpret their lives retrospectively, it was probable that many of their interpretations drew in factors— like faith—not in play originally. In their testimonies, however, they claimed their call gave their pageant careers a greater sense of purpose.

These Christian young women approached the events with a belief that their participation was for the greater good. Some competed one year and won Miss America. Others persisted for seven without ever winning. As they sought the crown (or crowns) it took to work their way to the top, they used religious language to describe their experience. They acknowledged that God used even their defeats to teach them life lessons and further sharpen their faith (and their skills). For some young women, pageants provided a unique test of faith and perseverance in the face of obstacles, as they trusted God's perfect plan. Evangelical contestants in particular felt compelled to testify about their participation. Even though their individual testimonies reflected the particularities of various faith traditions, the consistency with which the narratives appeared confirmed a common tendency to ascribe religious meaning to this secular event.[52]

Debbye Turner, Miss America 1990, received many lessons in patience during her years of participation. "It all happened in God's timing," she said. "I wouldn't have been ready if I had won sooner."[53] Though she began competing in pageants to finance her education, she later confessed, "I do a lot of motivational speaking now, and I tell people I didn't win Miss America because I was the prettiest or most talented girl there. I believe it was God's design for my life. So He gave me the favor and the grace that I needed. That's why I won."[54] She worked for seven years, competing in two different states before winning a title. After three failed attempts to secure the Miss

Arkansas crown, Turner entered the pageant circuit in Missouri where she was attending veterinary school. She won Miss Columbia, the state crown, and, eventually, the Miss America title. Like any Christian waiting on God to answer one's prayers, Turner hoped she would get her heart's desire. And, like many pageant contestants, her reasons for participating were complex and varied. Turner offered some insight into the many layers of her pageant journey during the national competition:

> Well, you know I've tried to win a state title for seven years now. I guess I just don't give up easily! I also wanted to do it for the scholarships. Veterinary school is very expensive. But most of all I wanted to be Miss America because I want to show that a girl who had nothing can become something. I want to use it as a chance to share my faith in God.[55]

Scholarships, a desire for upward mobility, and an opportunity for religious testimony: all of these reasons enticed Turner to compete and each of them played a role in her success. That she admitted her desire to win money should not negate her commitment to share her faith. Turner's record of talking about God and performing Christian rap (even, on occasion, in public schools) bore testimony to her sincerity.[56] Other contestants invoked similar reasons for competing and equal dedication to accomplishing the task.

Figure 5.2. Debbye Turner, Miss America 1990, competed for seven years before she clinched the title. A born-again Christian, Turner threw up her hands to praise God upon hearing she had won.

Heather Whitestone approached the competition with extreme focus and determination, but after placing first runner-up twice at Miss Alabama, she almost stopped competing.[57] The disappointment of defeat made her many sacrifices, especially the large amount of time she invested, seem pointless. Her support system, however, refused to believe that her pageant career was over. One family gave her an airplane ticket to Atlantic City in hope that she would leave inspired to try again. Whitestone confessed that God spoke to her in Atlantic City and through hundreds of others who believed in her mission when she had given up hope.[58] Later, she recounted some of these events, highlighting one transformational moment.

Whitestone found herself in the convention hall shortly after the conclusion of the Miss America 1994 Pageant. She asked one of the workers who was cleaning up if she could walk on the stage. She climbed on the runway with her mother "and suddenly felt confident and relaxed."[59] In this moment, Whitestone recommitted herself to the pageant with renewed fervor.

> In an instant, all my old insecurities vanished. I felt the presence of God right there beside me, and he spoke to my heart: *Go back and continue with your hard work, this is the time for you, this year.* I didn't know then if I would be Miss America, I just knew I was supposed to work toward Miss Alabama with renewed energy. I thought God wanted me to witness for Jesus on whatever stage I found myself. In his wisdom, I don't think God wanted me to know I would be Miss America. If I'd known, maybe I wouldn't have worked so hard, or maybe I'd have become snobby. God wanted me to depend upon him completely, to have complete trust in his plan.[60]

Whitestone returned to Alabama confident that God wanted her to compete. She thrust herself into pageant preparations. In the midst of exhausting mock interviews, community appearances, and talent rehearsals, she maintained her focus "to witness for Jesus on whatever stage" she found herself. For Whitestone, part of answering the call meant enduring the threat of possible defeat, trusting that God would use her, win or lose. Like a Christian returning to church, she recommitted her life to pageants. As she saw it, she took solace in the knowledge that God's plan would prevail, convinced that she would understand the purpose later.

Vonda Kay Van Dyke, Miss America 1965, was also unsure what the outcome would be, but she later claimed that after she adjusted her attitude, she approached the pageant with new eyes. She embraced this newfound view, seeing it as an avenue to share her faith, grow as a person, and entertain others. In other words, she lived for the process, not just the outcome. As Van Dyke recalled, "Maybe I would find the opportunity that meant more to me than any of the others—it could happen during a beauty pageant as well as anywhere else on this earth. I just might be given a chance to share the most important gift of my life—my faith in God."[61] She did not give up the hope of winning, but she valued the adventure, looking for ways to minister along the way. Like Christian in John Bunyan's *Pilgrim's Progress*, completing the journey well was as important as the destination.

By focusing on what God wanted and how she could impact others, Van Dyke testified that she received more blessings and affirmation than when she was only in it to win.[62] Like so many others, she later claimed that prayer offered her comfort and direction. She wanted an onstage question about her faith so she prayed before walking out for her interview questions. She prayed, "Father, give me confidence and help me to perform to the very best of my ability, and if there be any way that I can witness, give me the words to say. Amen."[63] Her chance came in the form of her second question. Bert Parks said, "I understand that you always carry a Bible with you as a good-luck charm. Tell us about your religion."[64] Van Dyke believed God provided both the question and the answer when the words came so easily.

> I do not consider my Bible a good-luck charm. It is the most important book I own. I would not describe my companionship with God as a religion, but as a faith. I believe in Him, trust in Him, and pray that even tonight His will may be done.[65]

Van Dyke had the chance she wanted. Her bold statement of faith changed the face of the pageant.

Young women like Van Dyke sought to live an exemplary pageant life. They had faith in the pageant or, more specifically, faith that God could work through it. Just as conversion narratives were offered retrospectively, contestants usually recounted their pageant testimonies when their stage days were over. They narrated their pageant career as one describes a faith journey, acknowledging that it was important to allow themselves to grow and not expect to achieve "perfection" all at once. For some, like Prewitt, their Miss America story was inextricable from their faith story. For others, the pageant enhanced their faith. Still more found the competition provided an outlet for them to put their faith in action. They described pageantry as a rewarding experience that deepened their faith and expanded their influence.

Rewards: Of Crowns, Causes, and Spiritual Capital

A religious testimony always ended with evidence that one reaped benefits from her conversion. Pageant narratives proved no different. Converts extolled the benefits of the competition both tangible and intangible. Winners and losers alike spoke fondly of their time on the circuit, using their narratives to invite and spur on new initiates. They encouraged other young women to join them on the runway, heralding the scholarships and professional opportunities participation afforded. These rewards coupled with a penchant for performance and a desire to make the world a better place appealed to many. While disappointment often followed a failure to earn the crown, competitors still noted the value of friendships begun, doors opened, and differences made.

Pageantry offered young women an opportunity to earn heavenly rewards in addition to earthly distinction.[66] Of course, accepting that pageantry was God's will for them was easier when one won a contest and received the accompanying accolades. Winners pointed out that they gained more than a title; the Miss America crown opened doors and provided opportunities not available to the vast majority of seventeen- to twenty-five-year-olds. The Miss America crown served as an ordination of sorts, offering young women credentials and influence that rivaled seminary degrees in many church cultures. After a woman received the Miss America crown, she represented all of the competitors just as a minister represented a congregation. Christian winners felt a responsibility to use the crown they had been given to glorify God. Just as in traditional conversion narratives, the testimonies were intended to point beyond themselves. They served as inspiration to others to "go and do likewise."[67]

Other than scholarships, the crown represented the most obvious reward. More than the physical crown, contestants competed for what the crown represented: access to a grander stage. For Nicole Johnson, Miss America 1999, and many others, the crown provided a way to advocate for a cause. Johnson adopted diabetes education as her platform and rejoiced that she had the chance to spread awareness of this disease during her reign. Reflecting on her work at an American Diabetes Association event, she noted, "For the first time as Miss America I was doing the work that I believe God had been preparing me for all along. One of the most difficult things, I think, is trying to figure out God's plan or purpose for your life. Many people search their whole lives for it. Well, with God's grace, I had found my purpose—or at least an important part of it."[68] Johnson, who suffered from Type I diabetes, enjoyed sharing about how God had given her the grace to continue living her life. She educated others of the warning signs of diabetes, raised money for diabetes research, and promoted early detection and prevention of this vicious disease. The crown gave her entry to work with many organizations already tackling these issues and gave them a spokeswoman with name and brand recognition. Johnson's claim that she sought the crown to advocate a cause was not unique. Since the competition began requiring contestants to choose a platform in 1989, many aspiring philanthropists made their way to the runway. Miss Americas Debbye Turner, Tara Dawn Holland, Erika Harold, and Teresa Scanlan were just some of the many looking for a louder microphone.[69] As Holland remarked, "No other program gives such a voice to a woman . . . I realized that this was my opportunity to make a difference for everything from literacy to abstinence. There is something about the crown that makes people listen to what you have to say."[70]

In addition to their platforms, many Miss America hopefuls claimed another cause: evangelization.[71] In a blog posted the day before she left for the Miss America competition, Teresa Scanlan wrote, "Why am I competing in the Miss America competition over the next ten days? Because God has placed me in this position to show His love."[72] She knew that God wanted to use her, praying, "I am clay in your hands, your humble servant, willing to do whatever you wish for me in your perfect plan."[73] She understood that God worked in mysterious ways, including through pageants. Scanlan went on to claim the ninetieth-anniversary Miss America crown and with it a national stage to be a witness. She was not the only one to laud pageants as an opportunity to evangelize. Even those who failed to receive the top prize expressed delight. For example, Miss Oklahoma 1998 rejoiced that she was able to share her faith with other contestants.[74]

This call to testify often mingled with a contestant's official platform. Christian contestants chose issues ranging from abstinence to character education to autism awareness. Like their foremothers in nineteenth-century reform movements, Christian contenders sought to make the world a better place because of their commitment to Christ.[75] They found this work a privilege, a reward that allowed them to be useful.[76] Prior to the advent of official platforms, Van Dyke, Meeuwsen, Prewitt, and others spoke of their desire both to witness for Christ and to make a difference in the world. Their testimonies made clear that the advent of pageant as mission field preceded the Miss America Organization's focus on volunteerism. Participants found their reward in the form of opportunities to stand for Christ and also at the same time realize their personal identity.[77]

For others, the rewards of pageantry proved more personal and even intangible. Some fell into their roles, seeing God's design in retrospect. Jane Jayroe, Miss America 1967, noted the amount of personal growth she experienced during the pageant, claiming that it prepared her for a life of ministry. Her story of God's involvement differed a bit from many of her Miss America

peers, but she considered her win no less ordained. From agreeing to participate in the Miss Oklahoma City contest to her eventual arrival in Atlantic
City, Jayroe never believed that she could capture the crown on the first try.
Indeed, when she won Miss Oklahoma City she claimed she was "the most
surprised girl in the audience."[78] Jayroe went on to become Miss Oklahoma
1966, all the while protesting, "I knew I would not win."[79] For her, this was
further evidence of God's masterful plan.

Later, Jayroe expressed many of the same feelings as she faced in the
Miss America competition, stating, "I was prepared to lose. Winning was out
of the realm of my thinking. Winning the Miss America crown happened
to perfect people and even in my most confident moments I was not even
close to perfect."[80] She considered her shy disposition an impediment. Yet
she noted, "I was determined to do my best and that was always my prayer. I
never prayed to win."[81] Ultimately her best proved good enough as she found
herself the talent winner, a top ten finalist, a top five finalist, and finally Miss
America.[82] Her doubt that she could win followed her even into the final
moments of competition. Jayroe recalled, "When the judging got down to
just Miss California and me, I was still okay with the fact that I now had won
the coveted first runner up spot."[83] As she walked down the Atlantic City
runway with the crown on her head, she claimed, "I was so stunned I could
hardly breathe. I was not supposed to win."[84] Jayroe began her yearlong reign
in a state of disbelief, sobbing in the hotel room the night of her coronation
as she considered what she had gotten herself into.[85]

Jayroe soon accepted her responsibility as Miss America as God-ordained.
After the luncheon the next day, she received a phone call from her childhood pastor, the Reverend Leonard Gillingham. As she recounted:

> To this day, I do not remember any part of the actual conversation with
> Leonard, but what I experienced was grace . . . I knew that when my parents
> left me in a few hours to return home, I would not be alone in New Jersey,
> New York, or any other place on earth . . . I had the ultimate friend, God.
> I did not have to be everything to everybody . . . It was enough for the
> moment just to belong to God and experience His power and grace. Even
> though I was not prepared on the external for this big role, God had been
> preparing me internally for years . . .[86]

Like so many Miss Americas before and after her, Jayroe found solace in
God's perfect plan. During her year of service, she did not overcome her
shyness, but she knew that God used her in spite of it. She hoped her foray
in the pageant world had benefited others, but *she* knew she had benefited
tremendously.

Pageants provided ample room and opportunity for growth. Many relished the journey, talking of friendships made, charities started, and personal goals achieved. However, Christian pageant winners described their rewards as not only earthly but heavenly. While crowns, scholarships, and camaraderie offered abundant reasons to enter pageants, they were not the only motives contestants cited for their participation. Many commented that the crown provided the key to a bigger stage, one on which they could make a difference beyond the walls of the convention center and thus one which allowed them to grow spiritually. Spiritual capital in the form of church invitations and other opportunities to minister also contributed to the incentives. Sometimes their spiritual capital helped them earn more spiritual capital.[87] It might have even helped some secure their crown and access to a wider stage. Contestants may have recognized the opportunity for Christian service in the midst of their experience or in retrospect.[88] Common experience suggests that their motives were mixed, like all human action, but in their minds evangelism was a very compelling motive.[89] They claimed that the chance to evangelize launched them to careers of service after Miss America and their faith helped them cope with tests and trials.

Tests and Trials: God's Faithfulness in the Midst of Struggles

No testimony would be complete without confirming God's faithfulness through the trials and temptations along the way. Most conversion narratives, or faith journeys, including biblical ones, involved a trial: the whale swallowed a disobedient Jonah, Paul was shipwrecked and imprisoned, and Ruth lost her family and homeland. Contestants interpreted their life experiences in light of this pattern, modeling the customary narrative with which they were intimately familiar. Pageant winners felt overwhelmed with their responsibilities and often found their faith tested as much or more during their year of service as they did en route to the crown. Almost without exception, Miss America winners described some kind of conflict or disappointment with the Miss America Organization, the American public, or their overcrowded schedule. Some relished the opportunity to stand strong in their beliefs against cultural (or pageant) expectations. Others struggled to maintain their faith in the face of loneliness, reporters, and the public spotlight. Still more faced disillusionment about their effectiveness.[90] Most, it seemed, tried to balance a belief that the opportunity came from God with the frustration of their new job. Put differently, Christian Miss Americas tried not to express regret at being Miss America because doing so could be interpreted as questioning God's sovereignty. Yet all realized, at some point, that being American royalty was not all roses and parades.

For Erika Harold, Miss America 2003, this realization came early in her reign. Harold, whose official platform was preventing youth violence, endured a conflict with pageant officials when she decided to advocate sexual abstinence as well. Less than a month into her year of service, they instructed her to stick to the teen violence platform only. Harold refused to back down, telling the *Washington Times*, "I will not be bullied."[91] While the two parties resolved the conflict quickly, the scuffle appeared in the media for months. Christian publications praised Harold's bravery. Mainstream media offered varying accounts. Some defended Harold's right to free speech while others accused her of having a secret agenda since she did not compete with an abstinence platform.[92] Harold spoke boldly about her decision to stand for sexual purity but tried to keep her message positive rather than denigrating those who disagreed with her. After crowning her successor, Harold spoke about her decision not to speak harshly of those who told her to keep her views about sex to herself.

> Well, I knew that God wanted me to stand firm in what I believe in, but I also knew that He wanted me to carry myself in a gracious and dignified way. It would have undermined my testimony if, while I was saying, "I'm going to stand up for what I believe in," I was behaving at the same time in a manner that appeared un-Christian to the people in the Miss America organization. God puts us in places to be able to witness to people who may oppose us. During the course of the year they had opportunities to see me present the abstinence message and to see that it's something that's received well by young people. It gives them hope. And I think that may have changed the way the Miss America organization views the abstinence issue.[93]

Harold took pride in her ability to stand firm. She told *Pentecostal Evangel*, "If you're a Christian it needs to be manifest in every aspect of your life. If you encounter any adversity in life, God can use it."[94] Harold presented her pageant career as proof, believing that God had worked through her to reach countless youth with her message, "Protect Yourself, Respect Yourself." The concept of premarital virginity, however irregularly practiced, represented a deep-seated ideal in conservative Christian culture.[95] Miss Americas like Harold who advocated abstinence were embracing and replicating part of their culture, which strengthened their position as icons and role models.

The knowledge that someone was always watching alongside the fear (and reality) of criticism haunted other Miss Americas. Heather Whitestone, Miss America 1995, faced disapproval from some in the deaf community because of her commitment to speak instead of using sign language. She felt her platform message was overshadowed by this controversy and considered resigning her title. Instead she turned to God. "I poured out my heart to him and gave him the responsibility of my new job . . . his dream for me."[96] Whitestone believed God answered her prayer. "He reminded me that he allowed trials in my life for his reasons, and he wanted me to learn to depend upon him completely." As a result, she continued her mission as Miss America, noting that doing so "enabled me to handle difficult situations gracefully instead of with anger and bitterness. I heard the criticism, but I continued to offer a positive message . . ."[97] She ended her speeches by addressing some of the controversy head-on and tried to focus on the positive responses she received. The crown provided opportunities that were simultaneously burdens and blessings.

Many found their year as Miss America to be quite isolating as they realized they had few people in whom they could confide about their frustrations. At times, they even lamented their new role in the spotlight. Miss Americas often found themselves lonely, but they were rarely alone. One particularly humorous example makes the point. Whitestone found the pressure to always be "on" and never make a mistake difficult, recalling one occasion when she lost her temper. At the governor's inauguration in Alabama, a group of women swarmed her asking for autographs. When she slipped away to the bathroom, one pushed a piece of paper under the stall! As she walked to the sink to wash her hands, women continued mobbing her. She turned and yelled, "Stop it!"[98] Guilt and sadness at one's failure to be gracious and fulfill unrealistic expectations accompanied many Miss Americas.[99] For Christian Miss Americas like Whitestone, the stakes seemed even higher.

Their schedules sometimes had them making multiple appearances a day and boarding multiple planes a week. Even winners who had close friends and family found little time or energy to keep them informed. As Jane Jayroe, Miss America 1967, related, "Being Miss America was a lonely existence. Even when I experienced a thrilling occasion there was no one to share it with personally or even by phone. Oklahoma was in a different time zone and my family and friends were already in bed by the time I arrived at my hotel."[100] Caressa Cameron agreed. Like many of her sisters, she turned to God for companionship. In an interview with Terry Meeuwsen, she confessed, "There's just sometimes that you're just by yourself and to know that God is there and to be able to pray and to have these conversations with him—it's less lonely."[101] Angela Perez Baraquio, Miss America 2001, decided to rely on God from the start. She remembered seeking comfort throughout the competition, praying, "Come, Holy Spirit, fill the hearts of your faithful." After winning, she insisted upon attending Mass the next day before flying to New York for her appearances. She wanted to "keep her connection with God in the forefront of her year as Miss America."[102]

This connection to God served as a source of grounding not only in the midst of criticism and loneliness, but also in busyness and exhaustion. Terry Meeuwsen, Miss America 1973, described one event where she "almost collapsed" because she was "emotionally drained." Both she and Nicole Johnson, Miss America 1999, spent some of their reign in the hospital.[103] Even though most Miss Americas avoided the hospital (as patients), many battled other minor illnesses and learned to live on little sleep. Sharlene Wells, Miss America 1985, testified that being Miss America was akin to "spending a year at boot camp," adding, "Physically, the pace is a killer. Mentally, it's an obstacle course."[104] Heather Whitestone recalled: "Like a car gasping on gasoline fumes, I was running on empty . . . I wanted to rest."[105] Contestants expressed a deep-felt need to push to make a difference for God in spite of their tired, fragile bodies. Even the stamina of youth had its limits.

Winners clung to any and all evidence that their sacrifices were worth it. When Jayroe lamented the constant smiling required of her and longed to do something more important, a letter put her seemingly trivial job in perspective. A Navy officer reminded her that even a smile could be a big thing: "I have seen and spoken to you at least five times since you came aboard the ship and each time you spoke and smiled back. You seem to be just as happy to be here as the crew—there seems to be a smile upon each and every face since you arrived."[106] Though a small action, this assurance that her work mattered helped Jayroe and other Miss Americas continue their work as goodwill ambassadors. Jayroe, Whitestone, Meeuwsen, and Wells were some of the many Miss Americas who gained strength and encouragement from letters that praised their morals, their platform, or their message. Raising awareness and monetary contributions also contributed to their feelings of success. Nicole Johnson remarked: "One of my primary goals as Miss America was to campaign for greater investment in diabetes research and prevention. While money is certainly not the only measure of success, I think it says a lot that during the time I held the title, more money was raised for diabetes research than had—or has—been raised for the cause of any other Miss America."[107] Miss Americas craved the reassurance that their hard work was not as pointless as it sometimes felt. Like votes for a politician or laughter for a comedian, pageant contestants sought palpable evidence of their success.

Perhaps most affirming for the winners was when they received confirmation that others saw Christ in them. Cheryl Prewitt, Miss America 1980, shared the story of William Stephens, an admissions counselor at Mississippi State University who helped her prepare for the Miss Mississippi pageant. During a church appearance where Stephens served as Prewitt's accompanist, he joined the church. Prewitt rejoiced with him.[108] Prewitt also recounted the response of one journalist who heard her testimony about God's healing in her life. Just as she wondered whether "any of them had felt just a touch of truth" and if "God had somehow been glorified," she heard one reporter comment, "You know, it's the darndest thing. To hear her speak, she could almost make a believer out of me!"[109] For tired Miss Americas, moments like these made up for the many hours of long rehearsals and countless appearances. Sacrifices and trials paled in comparison.

In addition to sharing their faith with others, participants argued that their faith grew in the process. Like many Miss Americas, Katie Stam, Miss America 2009, traveled 20,000 miles a month and thus could not always attend church. Most likely, her travels meant that she rarely attended. She claimed that her "personal time with God," including phone devotionals and prayers with her boyfriend, allowed her relationship with God to grow.[110] Others asserted that they gained strength from appearances in churches and other religious groups where they felt freer to share. Christian Miss Americas also cited the positive examples of other Christians, Miss Americas and otherwise, who found themselves in the public eye as inspirational. Many felt compelled to describe how they managed their personal piety in the land of rigorous schedules, pageant officials, the media, and personal doubts. Being "on" seemingly round the clock presented a special trial for these women thrust into the public eye.[111]

A year of service required much energy, commitment, endurance, and, Christian Miss Americas argued, faith. It was not unusual for Miss Americas to long for and even celebrate the end of their reign even as they acknowledged that it had forever changed them.

> Halfway through the year, I found myself feeling anxious for the year to end so I could slip back into the woodwork. After a little soul-searching, I realized that this was totally unrealistic and would be very ungrateful of me. The Lord has given me much more than I deserve . . . For those of us who have the truth to guide us, who understand what life is about . . . it is inexcusable for us to sit back and let others carry the load. I believe we must all be willing and prepared to share our beliefs with others.[112]

Winners felt their crown came with enormous responsibility. They recounted not only their increased faith in God, but faith and assurance that some good was being accomplished through their efforts regardless of how frazzled they felt or how much controversy they faced. Confronted with the pressure to perform their expected roles on cue, winners sought solace and direction in times of distress. In fact, this insistence that God worked through all circumstances extended even to pageant participants who did not walk away with the Miss America crown.

Losing Faith

> I listened and believed. From my very first memories, I'd been told that if two or three people pray together, God will answer their prayers. I knew people all over the world prayed for me, and I believed God would respond to those prayers. I also prayed that if I didn't make Miss America, God would help me handle it. But I felt that with all the people I had praying for me, together with my own hard work and the signs that had led me into the pageant world, I was destined for the Miss America crown.[113]

Many times those who felt "destined" for the Miss America crown walked away without it. Rebecca Trueblood, Miss Idaho 1989, was one such competitor. Pageant losers, however, also experienced a keen sense of God's sovereignty. They spoke of praying for God's will, and many who struggled to accept their loss still acknowledged that God was working through the winner. Some clung to their pageant prayers and pageant testimonies, noting that they too had been called to compete for a higher purpose, reinterpreting their calls in light of their new circumstances. Others named what God accomplished through their pageant participation. Indeed, statements made by Miss America contestants who failed to win the national crown emphasized God's hand in the pageant and in their lives through the process of competing. For example, Julie Payne, Miss Oklahoma 1998, joined hands with Miss Maryland to pray for the new Miss America just moments after the announcement. She had prayed that "God would use her to glorify him" and felt her prayer was answered. "I had opportunity to share with some girls who aren't Christians. I hope there were some seeds planted there," Payne noted.[114] Payne was not the only individual who felt fulfilled despite losing the title. Katie Millar, Miss Utah 2006, relished her opportunity to take a stand for modesty on the Miss America stage. When chastised by a man for blowing Utah's shot at a Miss America, she responded, "I'm sorry, sir, I can't change who I am. I guess no crown is worth it."[115] Millar believed God had used her and felt no shame that the crown did not follow.

One of the most intriguing of these testimonies is that of Miss Idaho 1989, Rebecca Eileen Trueblood. As many individuals competing for the crown, Trueblood believed that God wanted her to be Miss America. Indeed, she had a conversion experience that highlighted God's involvement in her decision to participate. Trueblood outlined in some detail her call to pageants, even going as far as to name the first chapter of her book "The Calling." After hearing Kellye Cash, Miss America 1987, speak of God using her during her reign, Trueblood wondered if God had been preparing her for the contest. The feeling that she was meant to try for the title kept coming back to her so she prayed, "Lord, if You want me to run for this thing, please give me a sign. A *big* one! I don't want any questions in my mind."[116] A few months later a woman approached Trueblood while she was getting a haircut and said, "I'm with the Miss California Pageant board, and I've been watching you today. I really feel you should enter a pageant. I'll give you any amount of help I can. I don't know what it is, but I just really felt I needed to tell you that."[117] Trueblood acknowledged this as a sign but soon realized that most of the preliminaries had already taken place. She put thoughts of competing aside until a newspaper article noted that her hometown pageant, Miss Treasure Valley, was the very last preliminary of the year in Idaho. She decided to enter, praying as she filled out her application, "Lord, help me not to offend anyone with this. Help this to be the right thing to do. I don't want people to think I'm doing this for my glory. Help them to see You through me."[118] Trueblood narrated her pageant journey as one with a mission.

That mission resulted in her winning the Miss Treasure Valley crown and, eventually, the crown of Miss Idaho 1989. Reflecting on her win at the state pageant, Trueblood noted, "I felt that all of my life had been a preparation for this. All the experiences I'd had growing up, all the rough times in my life, everything led up to this moment. And I wondered, as I looked forward to the challenge of Atlantic City, could God want me to be the next Miss America?"[119] She accepted that God's hand directed her pageant participation, believing that God wanted to use her to make a difference in people's lives as Miss America. Whenever she got discouraged by all of the hard work and tight schedules, she remembered all of the people praying for her and cheering for her success.[120] She logged numerous runs, appearances, and practice interviews just like her fellow contestants from other states. She considered her call from God to be unique, however, until confronted by the accounts of other Christian contestants.[121]

Trueblood discovered that many of the other Miss America contestants were Christians who "had felt called to enter the pageant. Many of them had people praying for them. Any one of these Christian girls would use the office of Miss America to witness for God."[122] As the practices drew to a close and the competition began, Trueblood prayed that she would remain focused on God, reflecting on how "strange to know that the other Christian girls in the pageant were probably praying the same prayer."[123] She wondered whether she would win, praying to at least make top ten so that she could sing "God Bless America" on television, but when the names of the finalists were called, Rebecca Eileen Trueblood's was not among them.

When Trueblood lost, she grieved. She received the award for the best interview, but that did little to soothe her pain. At first she continued to pray, but her prayers had changed. She questioned God, "How could You let this happen? How could You have brought me so far and now nothing?" Trueblood felt that she had not only let herself down, but that she had disappointed her family, friends, and her entire state as well. She wondered how she had misinterpreted God's will for her and felt deserted by God, believing that her prayers reached no higher than the ceiling.[124] With time, the pain faded and Trueblood accepted that God's will had been accomplished even though it had not been what she wanted.[125]

Trueblood reinterpreted her loss as an important life lesson. She recounted her dream of singing professionally and her fear that she would have nothing to say during a concert because her life had been so good. Before losing the pageant, Trueblood questioned how she could relate to someone with hurt in their lives.

> But now, after losing the pageant, I felt I could instantly relate to people who had worked with all of themselves for something and lost. Maybe everyone hadn't experienced Miss America, but many, *many* people had experienced the loss I felt. I knew I could take in their feelings and experiences, and people would have a connection with me. For the first time since the Miss America Pageant, I felt at peace. The hurt remained, but I knew I'd be able to keep it in a tiny corner of myself. I had a reason. I could heal. "Thank You, Lord," I whispered. "Thank You."[126]

For Trueblood, this life-altering experience caused pain and disappointment, but she considered herself no less called than Debbye Turner, the Christian who won Miss America the year Trueblood competed. She claimed that God used the experiences of competing for the Miss America crown to prepare her for future ministries.

Trueblood was not alone in seeing God's hand at work even when it resulted in a pageant loss. Marti Sue Phillips, Miss Florida 1979, had a similar experience. When she placed fourth runner-up to Cheryl Prewitt, her disappointment faded quickly. After hearing Prewitt share part of her testimony with the media, Phillips approached Prewitt in tears, saying:

> "Oh, Cheryl," she cried, throwing her arms around me, "I prayed tonight to God that I'd win—but that if He could be better glorified by someone else that she would win. It was such a noble prayer," she laughed, "and to tell the truth, when I didn't win, I wasn't much comforted by it. But now, after seeing the way you handled that press conference, after hearing your testimony—now I know why you're the one who won! Oh Cheryl, I'm so happy for you—and for all the good that's going to come from your reign as Miss America!"[127]

Responses like this propagated the belief that everything in the world happened because it was God's will. This belief in the sovereignty of God was popular among conservative Christians and informed the worldview of many young pageant contestants. Many who admitted confusion about why they were called to pageantry only to lose found or invented explanations for how God used their participation. They confessed other values that they gained from pageants. They noted that competition made them better people by helping them grow in their faith and in other areas. Indeed, pageants were often credited with things usually attributed to God—changing their lives and giving them newfound purpose. For God to call multiple people to compete, there had to be more to it than the crown.

A Place to Belong: One among Many

Many women remained dedicated to the Miss America Organization even after they "aged out." They sponsored and organized pageants, recruited contestants, hosted fundraisers, and trained a new generation of contestants. The stage, like a baptistry, initiated them into their new life. They belonged. They were "pageant girls." Their stories testified. Even losers recognized the importance of the competition in their formation. Former contestants joined around the positive features of pageantry, regaling others with examples of its formational role in their lives. The pageant saved them. The pageant provided for them. The pageant encouraged them. Of course, most acknowledged that it was God working through the pageant, but this did nothing to diminish their devotion to the Miss America program. Women, young and old, had faith in the pageant process and faith that God's will was being done in it. In short, the pageant provided them a community. It gave them a place to belong, and they wanted to share that comfort, security, and acceptance with others.

However, their testimonies and pageant prayers did more than connect contestants to the pageant community. They served a dual purpose. Testimonies not only tied contestants to the pageant community but also united them to the Christian one. Their testimonies linked them to a long history of individuals who recounted their religious experiences in scripted ways.[128] Testimony was intricately related to identity. For example, in Pentecostalism, testimonies "strengthened personal identity by narrating God's wondrous handiwork in individual lives," "strengthened collective identity by sealing the link between the individual and the group," and "clothed individual lives with timeless significance."[129] Pageant testimonies did all of these things on multiple levels, giving participants assurance that they belonged and that their lives mattered.[130] The written accounts served as a part of their testimony, further solidifying the narratives' importance.

The stories were important for the communal and individual identities that they affirmed for young women, but also for their ability to recruit others to the organization. Several Miss Americas recalled hearing a former winner speak (or reading her autobiography) before they had even considered pageantry. Indeed, some credited that moment as instrumental in their own decision to pursue the crown.[131] Just as details of religious conversions often sparked additional ones, hearing the testimonies of those who allowed God to use their pageant experience encouraged other Christians to participate. This form of evangelism was fundamental to conservative Christian culture.

In addition to these traditional functions of testimonies, pageant testimonies fulfilled (at least) one other role. They offered a religious justification for participation in the Miss America contest. On the one hand, this is not surprising since evangelical Christians in particular saw God in all aspects of their life and expected God to use their gifts and talents to serve. On the other hand, pageant participants engaged in behavior and activities not usually sanctioned by the evangelical community. The testimony provided evidence of God's favor in an attempt to reconcile the seeming disconnect between evangelical teachings and pageant participation. The story of one's call to compete demonstrated that God continued to work in unexpected ways and through unexpected avenues. Still, the unusual circumstances demanded an explanation much like those given by the extraordinary women called to preach in the nineteenth century.[132] In both circumstances, a gifted individual was called to use those gifts in service to the kingdom despite contradicting either religious or cultural mores. The use of the testimony by pageant contestants sealed its destiny as a pageant formula. The competitions were commemorated by many evangelicals as events in need of evangelists.[133] To those who participated it served as both a reassurance of their devotion and as inspiration to those looking for a similar experience.

Pageant testimonies, like traditional conversion stories, offered feelings of belonging and evidence of God's favor and intervention. Christian contenders infused their narratives with spiritual significance, conflating religious testimony with a secular enterprise. Their words both set them apart and joined them together as they proclaimed the good news that you can achieve anything God has for you. Pageants might not be your mission field, they implied, but God has a mission field for you. Contenders saw their experience as unique even as they demonstrated that it could be mapped onto others. Even more important and more simply, these testimonies confirmed that pageants constituted an acceptable mission field.

Other Voices

To be sure, not all Miss Americas presented themselves as straight-laced "goody-goodys." For example, Miss America 1976, Tawny Godin, shocked pageant followers when she admitted to smoking marijuana and confessed socially progressive views such as having "nothing against homosexuals."[134] Miss America 1982, Elizabeth Ward, purportedly slept with Bill Clinton and later posed for *Playboy* (though both happened after she handed over her crown).[135] And, most famously, Miss America 1984, Vanessa Williams, gave up her crown owing to nude pictures later published in *Penthouse*.[136] Then there is at least one "goody-goody" who did not want to be Miss America. Bette Cooper, Miss America 1937, decided to deny her win ever happened. She was crowned Miss America, but failed to show up to her first official appearance the next morning. Rumors abounded as to why, but Cooper claimed, "It was all my father's decision. He thought I should go back to school."[137] Only seventeen years old when she won, Cooper escaped back home to live her quiet life free from the demands of Miss America duties. When *People* magazine contacted her for a 2000 story, she replied, "There is no Miss America here."[138] These stories highlight some of the diversity among the winners.

Equally important, not all Christians interpreted their Miss America experience in the same way. As shown, some contestants claimed a call to pageantry. They maintained that competing strengthened their faith and allowed them to minister. Others believed that Christianity and beauty contests were compatible, but noted more mundane reasons like scholarship funds for competing. They embraced the opportunities for ministry along the way, but viewed them as an added benefit. Still more acknowledged their Christianity but did not discuss their year as Miss America in religious terms. Some quit competing, disillusioned or disheartened by the messages received from participating.[139] Finally, some Christian contestants were eventually disquieted about their participation and sought to understand their motivations and explain their uneasiness. One example makes this point.

Shelli Yoder, Miss Indiana 1992 and second runner-up to Miss America 1993, described the complexity of her pageant memories: "Talking openly about the good, the bad, and the in-between is like reuniting with an old friend. My pageant past is multilayered and peculiar—complete with big hair and oddly enough, a significant amount of gratitude."[140] Yoder experienced tremendous support from her small town of Shipshewana, Indiana. She described how its "500 citizens, predominately Amish and Mennonite," celebrated her win with "welcome home parades . . . exquisitely handcrafted gifts, horse and buggy rides . . . and homemade Amish peanut butter."[141] At that point in her life she found her Mennonite tradition and her pageant participation surprisingly compatible. "There was no gray ambiguity . . . Legalism stood firm. Religion and Miss America seemed to embody the pursuit of perfection. To become Miss America was to become America's ideal, God's ideal, or so I thought."[142] With the distance of time, however, Yoder expressed concern about what the pageant taught her.

"But what cannot be ignored or denied," she wrote, "is the objectification imbedded in the phenomenon of Miss America, a reflection of the broader culture."[143] In reading her reflection, it became clear that analyzing her experience ten years later was painful. Yoder internalized the mixed messages sent by pageants and expressed guilt at the role she played in perpetuating them. She summarized the tension well:

> The inherent danger in this violation is that it is couched in terms of women's liberation . . . Miss America is now marketed as the world's leading provider of scholarships for women, but Miss America's relationship with education creates mixed messages of women's liberation and sexual objectification. As long as women are able to name and claim the conditions, the misogyny is no longer labeled as objectification but earns the dangerous label of women's liberation via empowerment.[144]

Yoder's pageant "testimony" stands in stark contrast to many of the others, but she too experienced a conversion at the hand of the pageant. The pageant changed her, and in many ways, her faith. And what is religious autobiography if not a mixture of success and failure, unbridled praise and suspended disbelief? Interspersed with Yoder's frustrations with the pageant was a layer of thankfulness for the experience and what it taught her. The pageant was formational. She simply questioned the extent to which that formation was good.

Perhaps Yoder's account would be different had she won the coveted crown of perfection or had she never received theological education. Perhaps Van Dyke's would be different if she had not taken top prize. Perhaps the "truth" however elusive lies somewhere in the middle. Or, more simply, maybe one's religious tradition set the parameters within which she experienced and recounted her participation. Evangelicals like Van Dyke might have felt compelled to justify or narrate every experience in terms of their Christianity. Mainline Christians like Yoder (who was preparing for ministry in the United Church of Christ when she wrote her piece) may have been influenced by new knowledge (for Yoder, feminism) rationally and critically to explain their experience. Regardless, the spiritual journey of Christian beauty queens existed in tension just as stories of religious conversion, attempted conversion, and de-conversion did. There was no one way to narrate experience.

Conclusion

Christians found a welcome home in pageants, employing the language of their religious traditions to describe the competition's impact on their lives. Their testimonies followed a predictable pattern that moved from crisis to faith to reward, echoing the conversion accounts so popular among evangelical Christians. These narratives allowed room for the particularities of one's tradition to be incorporated, but the basic pattern of God redeeming seemingly unredeemable circumstances always emerged. According to the contestants, God called individuals to the pageant and then worked through them to accomplish much good. In the process, contestants gained many rewards, both spiritual and physical. In short, Miss America contestants saw pageantry as a religious opportunity that was at times a test of faith, a platform for personal growth and identity formation, or an opportunity for evangelism.

Likewise, these pageant narratives served a purpose similar to their religious counterparts. They marked the individuals testifying as set apart and gave the young women a sense that they belonged to a unique community. Talk of rewards and newfound direction also offered incentives for others to join. Miss America competitors longed to bring new members into the fold even as they reached beyond their target audience of potential converts to make the world better for everyone. Contestants needed the pageant. It was part of God's plan and therefore inescapable. These accounts and the actions they represented linked competitors to a long line of evangelicals who used the tools at their disposal to reach others with the gospel.

Christian contestants used pageant testimonies, including their pageant prayers, to explain and validate their participation. In telling their stories, Christian Miss Americas narrated their pageant involvement and their year of service as a story laden with God's direction. Even in the midst of confusion, conflict, loneliness, and exhaustion they articulated God's hand at work, noting small and large ways they made a difference in the lives of others. For Christian competitors, the process provided and indeed was a religious opportunity. For many, their time as Miss Americas served as the beginning of their ministry. The pageant runway launched former competitors on career in fields as diverse as politics, medicine, and full-time Christian ministry. Even those outside traditional fields of "missions," however, often described themselves as ministers or representatives of the gospel, crediting not only God but also pageants with preparing them for their vocations. Their prayers, it seemed, had been answered through faith *in* the pageant.

Conclusion

Born Again: Miss America 2.0

M iss America is many things and runs the risk of being everything—and thus nothing. In fact, many people consider Miss America as trivial, inconsequential, and, now, an outdated affront.[1] But Miss America, like America itself, has been reinventing itself, and in doing so has become a trope, a deep and complicated trope, for what America is and hopes to be.[2] In 2018, Miss America tried to recreate herself yet again, billing the new and improved contest as Miss America 2.0. This rebirth occurred after the ousting of Sam Haskell from his position as Miss America's CEO. Leaked emails revealed that Haskell and others had engaged in derogatory talk about current and former Miss Americas. Gretchen Carlson grabbed the reins and, along with some of her Miss America sisters, sought to redeem the Miss America Pageant by giving it what they deemed a much-needed makeover.[3]

Most notably, Carlson announced in June 2018 that Miss America would no longer have a swimsuit competition.[4] In addition, it would henceforth be referred to as the Miss America Competition rather than the Miss America Pageant. Candidates, not contestants, would interview for the job of Miss America. Other changes followed: candidate sashes contained the name of the state they were representing rather than "Miss [State]," the evening wear competition was transformed into a red carpet walk in which candidates spoke about their platforms, and the talent portion of Miss America went from 35 percent of a candidate's overall score to 50 percent. This was, of course, merely the latest in a series of attempts to update Miss

America as America's "ideal." And, like previous changes implemented in the pageant, it was met with mixed reviews.

People representing an assortment of opinions about Miss America 2.0 descended on Atlantic City for pageant week in September 2018. The reigning Miss America, Cara Mund, had spoken out against Carlson's leadership. Some newly appointed board members had resigned. Some state pageants were pressing for more information, and talk of secret meetings was communicated in slightly hushed tones. Signs with Gretchen Carlson's face on them and the caption "So Fake" appeared around town as if on cue, and the Miss America statue at Kennedy plaza was awarded a blue sash that read "Gretchen Sucks."[5] Both acts communicated the disdain with which some fans viewed Carlson. In their minds, she had single-handedly ruined the pageant.

An air of uncertainty clouded the week. Some fans wondered if the pageant would survive without the one thing that had been there since the beginning while others were sure that it would not. There was concern about the "girls" who had trained for one kind of contest and would be competing in another. That it was not fair to change the rules midstream was a common refrain. Increased empowerment rhetoric saturated the week from introductions to the printed program to onstage presentations to the merchandise to the television broadcast. Miss America 2.0 was sleek and modern. She was agent, not object. But grumbling—and a lawsuit—continued even after pageant week. The controversy over the "soul" of the pageant paraded on, each side convinced that they knew who Miss America should be. Such mixed reviews harken back to the earliest days of the pageant. Dropping the swimsuit competition appeared to be just the latest in a long history of gimmicks to make the pageant relevant, relatable, and respectable. It was yet another attempt to keep the pageant alive.

In the early twentieth century, burlesque faced a similar dilemma. It existed in a saturated market where everything it offered could be found elsewhere. But instead of vying for respectability, burlesque went for spectacle. "The true strip was burlesque's last-ditch and ultimately unsuccessful strategy to stay alive. It represents not the symbol of burlesque's golden age—although it is remembered as such—but rather its ultimate failure to sustain a performance medium sufficiently distinct in its appeals from other forms to draw an audience."[6] The tactic did not work, and, today, burlesque is remembered for what it was at the end and not what it was in its heyday. One wonders if a similar thing will happen to Miss America.[7]

Miss America was birthed during this time period. The pageant found a way to thrive despite not offering the same level of "tease" available elsewhere.

However, it eventually faced the same dilemma to remain relevant in a world where all that it offered was available somewhere else. The glitz. The glamour. The sex. The service. The entertainment. The competition. The beauty. And, these things were bigger, better, brighter, and bolder in other spheres. And yet Miss America survived. The Miss America Pageant wove these threads together in a unique way, offering competitors the chance to be crowned Miss All-Around. The woman chosen excelled at everything American culture valued, not just one component. She had it all. That is why Miss America worked. And it is why Miss America endured. Miss America pointed beyond herself to a nation ever conflicted about who it was and how to hold the things it valued in tension. If one person could embody and enact these contradictions, surely the nation could as well. The trick was to find something that could bind them together.

Miss America is sex, yes. Plain and simple. But so is everything else. Sports is sex. Beer is sex. Music and movies and television and politics is sex. Sex pervades schools, churches, and little girls' dance classes. America, if it is obsessed with anything, is obsessed with sex. Sex lurks behind every corner, enticing and encouraging Americans to believe in its power to solve all things. Health in America is not about health; it is about looking good so that sex abounds. At their core, Americans want to be desired and desirable. Indeed, it is hard to find anything in American culture that is not about sex or using sex. And yet the lie of sex is that it is never enough. It is empty and shallow and meaningless when it is merely paraded about for consumption in the public sphere. Sex becomes a commodity rather than a covenant, something to be bought and sold rather than something to be shared. Miss America was no different. Behind all the talk of virtue and civics was sex. These were woman to be ogled. Period.

But America's Puritan dance with sex meant that Miss America could never be just a pole dance in primetime. Miss America needed to appear chaste and virginal, even if it was all a ruse. Miss America was Sunday school, not Saturday night. She was a carefully constructed celebration of beauty to be admired, not a cheap thrill to be used. She spoke of everything but sex even as she embodied the very essence of sex. The lines were blurry, intentionally so, as Miss America was asked to walk a tightrope between acceptable and unacceptable forms of display for "respectable" women. Miss America could never be naked, but she had to be beautiful. She also had to be sexy, even if the sexy was all hemmed in.

In the end, if Miss America was only about sex, then Miss America would have become a peep-show queen or simply a historical artifact like burlesque. But Miss America lived on, and Miss America's longevity raises the questions why. Leonard Horn, onetime CEO of Miss America, mused, "As far as the Miss America Pageant is concerned, indifference is our worst enemy—and people are *not* indifferent to the program."[8] If Miss America was sex and only sex, it would have passed away with age, as do all beauties. But Miss America was persistent; she refused to die. She has grown old and aged well because she relied on more than beauty, knowing that sex alone was not enough to save her. Miss America is far, far more than just sex. It is sex, yes. But it is not sex in the abstract; it is sex in relationship. It is sex rooted in something deeper.

Sex lives on the same street as entertainment. Indeed, they have become close neighbors. What is true for American culture is especially true for Miss America. Sex drove entertainment. Miss America used sex to entertain. They were intertwined in an almost seamless way. Sure, contestants sang. Sure, they played the piano. Sure, they twirled batons. There was suspense when the contestants had to answer on-the-spot questions and dread when the question was particularly dicey. The audience, both live and television, waited with bated breath at the announcements of the finalists, and then, two hours later, the winners. But this high holy moment of entertainment was clothed in formfitting gowns and swimsuits, both topped off with perfectly made-up faces, flirtatious glances, and a pair of heels for good measure. Drama was all visual. Drama had big blue eyes and blonde hair. Drama came in pretty packaging.

But it was entertainment and not just sex. Entertainment was an industry, and Miss America became a part of the American landscape of entertainment. She was accepted and expected. Miss America was not relegated to a dark alley; she existed on a stage framed by a spotlight. She was meant to be seen, not hidden, relishing her fate as entertainer. In some ways, Miss America operated like a serial television show with Americans tuning in year by year. It was a condensed version of *Survivor* with contestants voted off the island of competition in rapid succession until only one was left standing. Or *The Bachelor* where fans became overly invested in who proceeded to the next round, shedding tears when their favorite was eliminated. It was *Gilmore Girls* providing a picture of community both ridiculed and craved by Americans. Or *Jeopardy* with its head-to-head competition. It was *America's Next Top Model*, *America's Got Talent*, and *Good Morning America* wrapped up in one. Miss America played every key on the keyboard of entertainment, combining elements of live theater, game shows, reality television, drama, and even a little comedy to create an entertainment genre all its own. Miss America defied categorization. It was, put simply, Miss America. And it was entertainment at its finest.

But as powerful as sex and entertainment are—and, no doubt, they are a formidable pair—the holy trinity for American fixation demanded one more member: competition. Once Miss America figured out how to leverage America's addiction to competition, it was able to mix a cocktail that simply could not be resisted. Indeed, it was guzzled by America, even those who found the combination off-putting and hard to swallow. Competition added a layer of meaning to the pageant. Miss America was not the fleeting, empty lust of sex. It was not the mindless escape of consuming entertainment. It was a contest, based on skill and "pluck," to determine who was the best. And Americans loved awarding hard work and grit with a little hardware, be it a Super Bowl ring or a Miss America crown. America loved events that ended with a clear winner.

Miss America was competition. Indeed, pageants were fiercely competitive enterprises that demanded skills, training, and strategy. Looking good was not enough. One must prove herself near perfection in all phases of the contest. Women competed in talent, evening wear, and interview. They competed to develop the best platform and provide the most community service. They used competitive tactics such as self-promotion, competitor manipulation, and competitor derogation (and, more rarely, outright aggression) to get themselves ahead.[9] Competitors drafted coaches, amassed fans, and endured stringent training. Behavior and proper "form" was learned and perfected as women quite literally performed the roles expected of them. And, like their counterparts in sports and politics, Miss America hopefuls were in it to win it.

Sex, entertainment, competition. What could be more powerful? Well, only one thing. There's only one card that could trump this trinity, one single phenomenon for Americans more central than their dance with sex, their addiction to entertainment, and their love of competing. Religion. Religion is what is at the core of who America is, and always has been. Since the first Pilgrim climbed aboard a rickety boat bound for the New World, America has been defined by religion.[10] What that has meant has shifted, as has the religious makeup of America, but that Americans care about religion, and have held on to it more deeply than their European counterparts, has not.[11] Faith and identity go hand in hand for Americans even if that faith is not a traditional faith but a civil religion of sorts. And yet Christianity still looms large on the American religious landscape.[12] Even those who do not claim or practice Christianity feel its influence as sacred and secular meet in the marketplace.

American Christianity holds within it the other attractions of the pageant—sex, entertainment, and competition. It has used sex and is sexualized with women in its most conservative spaces fulfilling gendered roles with similar restrictions and expectations to those in the pageant. American Christianity is also entertainment. From Aimee Semple McPherson riding a motorcycle into the pulpit to fog machines that rival rock concerts, American Christians package the gospel message to be consumed. And Americans wanted their particular gospel to be consumed, not someone else's. From the frontier to the present, Methodists, Baptists, Catholics, Pentecostals, and a host of other churches vied for adherents. Religious competition is fierce in the flooded market, so representation in the public sphere, be it politics, entertainment, or, yes, even Miss America, felt all the more critical.

So, it is no surprise that religion stands at the core of Miss America. Religion capitalizes on all that is American in Miss America. It sanctifies the sex, ritualizes the entertainment, and justifies the competition. Religion makes Miss America.

In Miss America, the faith(s) of America in all their complexities get played out on the stage under the spotlight. Miss America carried with it a sense of reverence and sacredness. In many ways, it functioned as a civic ritual, with God and country fused in nearly seamless ways at times with pageant leaders casually referencing Scripture at the national pageant and ministers serving as judges. Equally important, contestants often narrated their pageant participation as a religious opportunity, a chance to gain access to a bigger stage to serve, mentor, or evangelize. Pageantry was a vehicle to deepen, embody, and share their faith. Thus pageant contenders claimed that Miss America served as a site of individual moral formation. At the root of contestants' reasons to compete was their desire to remake themselves. Along the way, many found God as well, claiming their faith gave them a larger purpose for participation. The pageant gave them a platform for ministry and their faith claims gave them justification to grace the stage.

But religion is but a proxy. Religion is not what is at the mysterious center of Miss America. Miss America captivates because of the way religion enables self-discovery and the making of identity. Nothing is more American than becoming a self. Thus for two hours, once a year, America tunes in to see someone become a self. Religion enables that woman to be both smart and beautiful, to hold together all that is mapped upon her in that moment, to be America *and* to be a woman, *and* to be a self. Religion is the proxy, the conceptual space, that enables a woman to stand for America, in a skimpy swimsuit, and to do so without being just an object. Of course, the reality is that there are competing selves, each wanting to be declared the ideal. And, in the individual quests for self in the pageant, the temptation exists to forego self-discovery and become the expected self. When one achieves success, such a sacrifice is more easily accepted and readily embraced. When the pursuit to be crowned perfection falls short, contestants often note a feeling of deep loss and lack of self.

In the end, Miss America is a commentary on the quest of America for transcendence. Miss America's God is one that encourages a nation to sacrifice one of its own to stand in that gap, embodying all of the contradictory pieces, feeling the weight of responsibility, and adapting to fit the changing needs of a shifting nation.[13] And it prompts its young women to accept the challenge, all while smiling and being thankful for the privilege. We may not have Manifest Destiny, but we do have Miss America.

Appendix

Miss Alabama Contestant Survey[1]

Please circle or check the response that best describes your situation. For open-ended questions, use the space provided or the back of the survey. If you use the back of the survey, please identify clearly the question to which you are responding. The survey should take approximately 15 minutes.

1. How many times have you participated in the MAP?

This was my first time	2	3	4	5 or more

2. What, if any, is your religious affiliation? Please specify the particular denomination, religious body, or group to which you belong (e.g., Christian—Baptist, Jewish—Reformed, etc.).

3. If you are a member of a religious tradition, does your church or religious group support your participation in the MAP? Are they . . . ?

Very unsupportive	Moderately unsupportive	Neutral	Moderately supportive	Very supportive

4. If your religious tradition supported your preparation for and participation in the MAP, how did they show their support? Please check all that apply.

Sponsored a prayer service for you
Placed you on the prayer list
Had a send-off party for you
Sponsored a page in the MAP program book
Supported the MAP golf tournament
Printed congratulations in the bulletin or newsletter
Other (please indicate how)

5. How many times per week do you attend worship services or other religious functions?

None	2	3	4

6. How would you describe yourself?

Not Religious	Some-what Religious	Religious	Very Religious

7. Are you currently, or have you ever been, involved in religious organizations at your school?

Currently involved	Used to be involved, but not now	Never involved

8. If you are involved in a religious organization on your school campus, how many times a week do you participate in religious functions with these groups?

1–2	3–4	5–6	7–8	8 or more

9. If you are a member of a religious organization at your school, does that organization support your participation in the MAP? Are they . . . ?

Very unsupportive	Moderately unsupportive	Neutral	Moderately supportive	Very supportive

10. If your school religious organization supported your preparation for and participation in the MAP, how did they show their support? Please check all that apply.

Sponsored a prayer service for you
Placed you on the prayer list
Had a send-off party for you
Sponsored a page in the MAP program book
Supported the MAP golf tournament
Printed congratulations in the bulletin or newsletter
Other (please indicate how)

11. How many preliminaries did you compete in this year?

1–3	4–6	7–9	10–12	12 or more

12. What did you hope to accomplish through your participation in the MAP? Circle or check all that apply. Feel free to explain any of your answers.

Gain scholarship money
Promote my platform
Have fun
Meet new people
Make a difference
Be a witness to my faith
Gain interview skills
Improve my talent
Other (please specify)

13. Approximately how much scholarship money have you won since becoming involved in the MAP system?

Less than 1,000	1–5,000	5–10,000	10–15,000	More than 15,000

14. If you do not win the MAP this year, do you intend to participate again next year?

Yes	No	Maybe

15. How many public appearances have you made since winning your title?

None	1–5	5–10	11–15	15 or more

16. What percentage of your public appearances were in churches or for religious organizations?

None	25%	50%	75%	100%

17. What do you most like about the MAP pageant or about being a MAP contestant?

18. What do you like least about the MAP pageant or about being a MAP contestant?

19. What, if any, religious opportunities have you gained from being in the MAP?

20. Do you feel or sense tensions between your religious tradition and the MAP? If so, what are some of them?

21. How would you describe the relationship between religion and the MAP?

22. Would you be willing to talk further with me about your participation in the MAP?

Yes	No	Maybe

If so, please list your contact information below, indicating the method by which you prefer to be contacted.

Name
E-mail
Phone

Thank you for your time and help. Please return completed surveys and signed consent forms in the enclosed envelope. My contact information is below should you need to contact me.

Mandy McMichael
[address]
[phone number]
[e-mail]

Notes

Introduction

1 Here I am referring to beauty pageants, competitions designed to determine the most attractive participant, but it is important to note that prior to the prominence of beauty pageants in American culture the word "pageant" had a very different connotation. "Since the early nineteenth century, pageants have held a special place in the development of 'female rites.' First used by women reformers, church groups and by schoolteachers to present dramatically social ideals and female solidarity, the female rites of pageantry as an organizational style unique to women's groups and clubs developed naturally into a part of the organized women's movement." Cynthia Patterson and Bari J. Watkins, "Rites and Rights," in *Women in American Theatre*, ed. Helen Krich Chinoy and Linda Walsh Jenkins (New York: Theatre Communications Groups, 1981), 29. See also David Glassberg, *American Historical Pageantry: The Uses of Tradition in the Early Twentieth Century* (Chapel Hill: University of North Carolina Press, 1990); and Linda J. Lumsden, *Rampant Women: Suffragists and the Right of Assembly* (Knoxville: University of Tennessee Press, 1997). For a fascinating argument about how a tool for inspiring cooperation between women gets co-opted into one of competition, see Jennifer Jones, "The Beauty Queen as Deified Sacrificial Victim," *Theatre History Studies* 18 (June 1998): 99–106. Kimberly A. Hamlin draws on Jones' argument and extends it in her essay "Bathing Suits and Backlash," in *The Politics of Sex, Beauty, and Race in America's Most Famous Pageant*, ed. Elwood Watson and Darcy Martin (New York: Palgrave Macmillan, 2004).

2 Jones in "Beauty Queen" notes, "No longer an isolated event that happens once a year and involves only fifty women, today, a hundred thousand women compete in Miss

America feeder pageants each year, not to mention Miss USA, Miss Teen America, Miss Black America, Mrs. America, Miss Hemisphere and Miss Universe. Beyond the national pageants, nearly every American woman attended, or attends, or will attend a school in which a prom queen or a homecoming queen is chosen" (99).

For the sake of ease and consistency, I refer to contestants by their competition names. Though many Miss Americas used their maiden name professionally after they married, not all of them did. In addition, the marriages of pageant winners, like those of other women, sometimes ended in divorce. Winners could change their names multiple times in the course of their careers. Referring to women by their "pageant name" streamlines the narrative. There are two exceptions to this formula. First, when a Miss America wrote a book under her married name, I reference the book using that name in the endnotes and bibliography. Second, if someone else referred to a Miss America winner or contestant by her married name and I quote that person directly, I do not change the name.

3   The history of the pageant is treated in a number of works including Sarah Banet-Weiser, *The Most Beautiful Girl in the World: Beauty Pageants and National Identity* (Los Angeles: University of California Press, 1999); Lois W. Banner, *American Beauty* (Chicago: University of Chicago Press, 1983); Ann-Marie Bivans, *Miss America: In Pursuit of the Crown* (New York: MasterMedia Limited, 1991); Frank Deford, *There She Is: The Life and Times of Miss America* (New York: Viking Press, 1971); Angela Saulino Osborne, *Miss America: The Dream Lives On: A 75 Year Celebration* (Dallas: Taylor, 1995); and A. R. Riverol, *Live from Atlantic City: A History of the Miss America Pageant before, after and in spite of Television* (Bowling Green, Ohio: Bowling Green State University Popular Press, 1992). The controversy surrounding the temporary closing of the pageant is addressed more fully in chs. 1 and 4 of this volume.

4   Deford, *There She Is*, 3.

5   No less than Bert Parks, longtime emcee of the pageant, referred to the pageant as a "nonevent, a beautiful piece of fluff, two hours of no message, two hours of good news—because there's no news in it—two hours of going back in time to perhaps a time that never was, and that we always dreamed would be, a time for pure, unadulterated girl-watching, and appreciating, and for all of the values that connect with that marvelous pastime." Bert Parks, "And Now, a Few Words from the Emcee . . . ," *New York Times*, September 10, 1977, 21.

6   My book joins a growing body of scholarship on beauty pageants in general, and the Miss America Pageant in particular. Books include Banet-Weiser, *Most Beautiful Girl*; Rebecca Chiyoko King-O'Riain, *Pure Beauty: Judging Race in Japanese American Beauty Pageants* (Minneapolis: University of Minnesota Press, 2006); Maxine Leeds Craig, *Ain't I a Beauty Queen?: Black Women, Beauty, and the Politics of Race* (New York: Oxford University Press, 2002); M. Cynthia Oliver, *Queen of the Virgins: Pageantry and Black Womanhood in the Caribbean* (Jackson: University of Mississippi Press, 2009); Riverol, *Live from Atlantic City*; Blain Roberts, *Pageants, Parlors, and Pretty Women: Race and Beauty in the Twentieth-Century South* (Chapel Hill: University of North Carolina Press, 2014); Rochelle Rowe, *Imagining Caribbean*

Womanhood: Race, Nation, and Beauty Contests, 1929–1970 (Manchester: Manchester University Press, 2013); Karen W. Tice, *Queens of Academe: Beauty Pageantry, Student Bodies, and College Life* (New York: Oxford University Press, 2012); and Christine R. Yano, *Crowning the Nice Girl: Gender, Ethnicity, and Culture in Hawai'i's Cherry Blossom Festival* (Honolulu: University of Hawai'i' Press, 2006). Two edited volumes that contribute to the conversation are Colleen Ballerino Cohen, Richard Wilk, and Beverly Stoeltje, eds., *Beauty Queens on the Global Stage: Gender, Contests, and Power* (New York: Routledge, 1996); and Elwood Watson and Darcy Martin, eds., *The Politics of Sex, Beauty, and Race in America's Most Famous Pageant* (New York: Palgrave Macmillan, 2004).

7 My use of the generic moniker "Christian" will be addressed more fully in chs. 4 and 5. Here it suffices to note that the diversity of Christian denominations represented in the pageant demanded a broad umbrella term.

8 That American culture is beauty obsessed has been well documented. See, for example, Rita Freedman, *Beauty Bound* (Lexington, Mass.: Lexington Books, 1986); Kathy Peiss, *Hope in a Jar: The Making of America's Beauty Culture* (New York: Metropolitan Books, 1998); and Deborah L. Rhode, *The Beauty Bias: The Injustice of Appearance in Life and Law* (New York: Oxford University Press, 2010)—to name just three I engage in this volume. The privileging of beauty in the pageant is discussed in ch. 1.

9 Melinda Beck et al., "A Controversial 'Spectator Sport,'" *Newsweek*, September 17, 1984, 56.

10 For a helpful overview, see the section "Feminist Debates over Beauty and Representation," in Banet-Weiser, *Most Beautiful Girl*, 10–13. With Banet-Weiser, I believe it important to "find a way to critique cultural discourses and practices that objectify, alienate, or otherwise fragment the female body without treating the contestants themselves as somnolent victims of false consciousness" (14). And yet, with Bonnie J. Dow, I see the potential limits of such a framework when pushed. See Bonnie J. Dow, "Feminism, Miss America, and Media Mythology," *Rhetoric and Public Affairs* 6, no. 1 (2003): 127–49. I engage these differences of opinion in my discussion of sex in the pageant in ch. 1.

11 Many women in the stories depicted here indicated that the advantages of pageant participation outweighed the disadvantages. Perhaps this simple acknowledgment provides a model for understanding how women work within structures seen by outsiders as oppressive, religious or otherwise. Rather than discounting or ridiculing expressions because they conflicted with stated beliefs (or societal expectations), I strive to understand why women felt compelled to remain in seemingly restrictive positions—be it a particular religious community, a beauty pageant, or both at once.

    In other words, I worked to listen to the women's voices, exploring the incongruities between belief and practice for these (mostly) conservative Christians. As Laurie Maffly-Kipp pointed out in the introduction to *Practicing Protestants*, "practices both mediate religious culture (thereby regulating behavior) and express creativity, improvisation, and resistance." That is, people's practices do not always match their beliefs.

In fact, they say one thing and do another all the time. I discovered that Christianity as practiced by beauty pageant contenders and their supporters expressed much "creativity, improvisation, and resistance." Laurie F. Maffly-Kipp, "Introduction," in *Practicing Protestants: Histories of Christian Life in America: 1630–1965*, ed. Laurie F. Maffly-Kipp, Leigh Eric Schmidt, and Mark R. Valeri (Baltimore: Johns Hopkins University Press, 2006), 7. See also Mark Chaves, "Rain Dances in the Dry Season: Overcoming the Religious Congruence Fallacy," *Journal for the Scientific Study of Religion* 49, no. 1 (2010): 1–14. This article helped me articulate the incongruence between belief and practice. Chaves' assertion that "religious incongruence is not the same thing as religious insincerity or hypocrisy" rang true. In fact, he notes, religious beliefs and practice rarely correspond; religious incongruence is the norm.

Many works in religious studies take seriously the diversity of women's voices and experience. Two in particular were instrumental in shaping my own study of women from predominantly conservative Christian traditions: R. Marie Griffith, *God's Daughters: Evangelical Women and the Power of Submission* (Los Angeles: University of California Press, 2000); and Elizabeth H. Flowers, *Into the Pulpit: Southern Baptist Women and Power since World War II* (Chapel Hill: University of North Carolina Press, 2012).

12   Most obviously, the official Miss America website, missamerica.org, promotes this vision of the pageant. For an overview of how the media has contributed to this understanding of Miss America as an opportunity for female empowerment despite feminist critiques to the contrary, see Dow, "Feminism, Miss America."

13   Shirley Monty, *Terry* (Waco, Tex.: Word Books, 1982), 33.

14   Cheryl Prewitt with Kathryn Slattery, *A Bright-Shining Place: The Story of a Miracle* (Garden City, N.Y.: Doubleday, 1981), 236–38.

15   Miss Alabama survey responses. As part of my research, I surveyed the Miss Alabama Pageant contestants for four years (2006–2009, see appendix). While I did not consider the response rate high enough to use the aggregate data as evidence to make sweeping arguments, I do incorporate individual responses into this account as evidence for my arguments when relevant. The answers encountered there also prompted more questions and suggested new avenues for research. Per the consent forms signed, no names will be used without permission. Julie Byrne's book *O God of Players: The Story of the Immaculata Mighty Macs* (New York: Columbia University Press, 2003) provided a helpful example for writing and conducting a survey. See also ch. 1, n. 9 in this volume.

16   Julie Hoffman, "Charles' criticism of Miss America Organization misguided, harmful says Julie Hoffman," *Press of Atlantic City*, January 27, 2019. In each new iteration of the pageant, the rhetoric of female empowerment grew. "The Miss America Organization will continue to welcome those who want to make Miss America more inclusive, diverse and relevant to a new generation of young women and create a path for more doctors, lawyers, educators, scientists, ministers and moms to make a difference in their community."

17 A number of Miss Americas have written books in which they recounted their experiences, both good and bad, of their time as Miss America. Many, as will be explored later, discussed the impact of their Christian faith on their participation. See, for example, Phyllis George, *Never Say Never: Ten Lessons to Turn You Can't into Yes I Can* (New York: McGraw-Hill, 2003); Sharlene Wells Hawkes, *Living in but Not of the World* (Salt Lake City: Deseret Book Company, 1997); Jane Jayroe with Bob Burke, *More Grace than Glamour: My Life as Miss America and Beyond* (Oklahoma City: Oklahoma Heritage Association, 2006); Nicole Johnson, *Living with Diabetes: Nicole Johnson, Miss America 1999* (Washington, D.C.: Lifeline Press, 2001); Prewitt, *Bright-Shining Place*; Kate Shindle, *Being Miss America: Behind the Rhinestone Curtain* (Austin: University of Texas Press, 2014); Marilyn Van Derbur, *Miss America by Day: Lessons Learned from Ultimate Betrayals and Unconditional Love* (Denver: Oak Hill Ridge Press, 2012); Vonda Kay Van Dyke, *That Girl in Your Mirror* (Westwood, N.J.: Fleming H. Revell Company, 1966); and Heather Whitestone with Angela Elwell Hunt, *Listening with My Heart* (New York: Doubleday, 1997).

18 "Focus on the Family transcript," Tara Dawn (Holland) Christensen website, http://taradawnchristensen.com/Focus_on_the_Family_Transcript.htm.

19 See the Miss America website, missamerica.org.

20 Bernie Wayne, "Miss America," quoted in Bivans, *In Pursuit of the Crown*, 3. In thinking about the construction of womanhood and the models of femininity rewarded in pageants, I relied on Joan W. Scott's understanding of gender as "a constitutive element of social relationships based on perceived differences between the sexes" and "a primary way of signifying relationships of power." "Gender, then, provides a way to decode meaning and to understand the complex connections among various forms of human interaction." Thus my attempts to grasp the complexities at work in the production of and promotion of womanhood through the pageant was aided by gender as a "category of historical analysis," which highlighted "the reciprocal nature of gender and society." The Miss America Pageant constructs gender and gender constructs the Miss America Pageant. Joan W. Scott, "Gender: A Useful Category of Historical Analysis," *The American Historical Review* 91, no. 5 (1986): 1053–75, here 1067 and 1070.

21 In June 2018, Gretchen Carlson, the new CEO of the pageant, announced the elimination of the lifestyle and fitness in swimsuit competition. Though participants continued to compete in swimsuit at their state preliminary pageants, it was not part of the Miss America 2019 pageant held in September 2018. See ch. 1 as well as the conclusion for a more thorough engagement of this change in the competition. For one of the many articles that addressed this shift, see Jessica Bennett, "Goodbye, Swimsuit Competition. Hello, 'Miss America 2.0,'" *New York Times*, June 5, 2018.

22 Johnson, *Living with Diabetes*.

23 Mia Watkins, "Miss Alabama 2014 Caitlin Brunell Wins Quality of Life Award at Miss America Competition," al.com, September 10, 2014.

24 When the Miss America Pageant mandated that contestants adopt a platform for their year of service (1989), the link between church and pageant grew even stronger

25   Beck et al., in "Controversial 'Spectator Sport,'" noted, "Pageantry magazine esti-
      mates that between county fairs, high-school homecomings and endless rounds of
      preliminaries and feeder pageants, an estimated 750,000 contests are held across the
      country each year. The competitions span every conceivable religious, ethnic and
      physical group and, it seems, every taste . . . Across the country, contestants number
      into the millions every year, some barely out of diapers" (56). The staying power of
      pageants is evidenced by the continuing establishment of new pageants, with Miss
      America launching Miss America's Outstanding Teen in 2005 and Pure International
      Pageants—whose tagline is "It's not just a crown. It's a calling!"—joining the stage in
      2011. See maoteen.org and pureinternationalpageants.com.

as contestants used the opportunity to live out their faith on the national stage. This
community service requirement seemed tailor-made for Christians and will be discussed more fully in ch. 4.

26   As Rita Freedman noted in her work *Beauty Bound*, "There has been a phenomenal
      growth in children's beauty contests since those protestors picketed the Miss America
      Pageant in 1968. Paradoxically, during the very years when the women's movement
      became a pervasive social force, beauty pageants for children, shown in the illus-
      tration, also gained in popularity. The Miss Hemisphere Pageant, with numerous
      divisions for girls ages three to twenty-seven, has mushroomed in size from a few
      hundred contestants in 1963 to hundreds of thousands of participants today. It is
      billed as the largest single beauty pageant in the world. Toddlers barely out of diapers
      (sometimes wearing false eyelashes and tasseled bikinis) are paraded before judges
      who scrutinize their 'beauty, charm, poise and personality.' The separate 'masters'
      division for boys up to age nine attracts far fewer contestants" (123). The TLC series,
      Toddlers and Tiaras, which ran from 2009 to 2016, highlighted this trend of child
      beauty pageants in American pageantry.

27   A plethora of books, blogs, and websites offer advice on how to achieve a pageant-
      perfect look. Two venues dedicated to all things pageants are pageantrymagazine
      .com and pageantplanet.com. See also Peggy Orenstein, *Cinderella Ate My Daughter:
      Dispatches from the Front Lines of the New Girlie-Girl Culture* (New York: HarperCol-
      lins, 2011), 73–76.

28   Banet-Weiser, *Most Beautiful Girl*, 50; Deford, *There She Is*, 154–55; and Jill Nei-
      mark, "Why We Need Miss America," *Psychology Today* 31, no. 5 (1998): 72. "As
      of 1994, only the Louisiana Pageant was still under the auspices of the Jaycees."
      Osborne, *Dream Lives On*, 145. Incidentally, Louisiana is one of only four southern
      states to never win the national pageant.

29   Beck et al., "Controversial 'Spectator Sport,'" 56.

30   As will be addressed later, the South and Midwest regions of the United States pro-
      duced more Miss America winners than the other regions. Still, pageants are largely
      considered a *southern* phenomenon. Most notably, this southern flavor of pageants is
      addressed by Charles Reagan Wilson. See "Beauty, Cult of," in *The New Encyclopedia
      of Southern Culture*, Volume 13: *Gender*, ed. Nancy Bercaw and Ted Ownby (Chapel
      Hill: University of North Carolina Press, 2009), 30–40; and "The Cult of Beauty," in

Charles Reagan Wilson, *Judgment and Grace in Dixie: Southern Faiths from Faulkner to Elvis* (Athens: University of Georgia Press, 1995), 144–58. Wilson writes, "With the Americanization of the South—and the southernization of the United States—in recent decades, southerners have become identified with love of beauty pageants . . . Beauty pageants in the South are part of a regional cult of beauty," "Beauty, Cult of," 34–35. Wilson is not the only one to notice the South's penchant for pageant success and excess, however. See, for example, Beck et al., "Controversial 'Spectator Sport'"; Deford, *There She Is*, 82; and Neimark, "Why We Need," 43.

31 Roberts, *Pageants, Parlors*, esp. ch. 3, "Homegrown Royalty: White Beauty Contests in the Rural South," 105–48.

32 Deford, *There She Is*, 82.

33 For one account of why parents might enroll their daughters in "high-pressure, appearance-driven 'glitz' beauty pageants," see Martina M. Cartwright, "Princess by Proxy: What Child Beauty Pageants Teach Girls about Self-Worth and What We Can Do about It," *Journal of the American Academy of Child and Adolescent Psychiatry* 51, no. 11 (2012): 1105–7. Cartwright argues that "some pageant parents exhibit a unique form of ABPD (achievement by proxy distortion) [she calls] 'princess by proxy.'"

34 The pursuit of outward beauty over inner character has proven more important in the twentieth and twenty-first centuries than in centuries before. As Joan Jacobs Brumberg noted in her work, *The Body Project: An Intimate History of American Girls* (New York: Vintage Books, 1997), "The traditional emphasis on 'good works' as opposed to 'good looks' meant that the lives of young women in the nineteenth century had a very different orientation from those of girls today" (xx–xxi). See also Patrice A. Oppliger, *Girls Gone Skank: The Sexualization of Girls in American Culture* (Jefferson, N.C.: McFarland & Company, 2008); and Orenstein, *Cinderella Ate My Daughter*.

35 Orenstein, *Cinderella Ate My Daughter*, 40. In other words, female characters needed to be relatively attractive for the viewers to like them. *Sesame Street* creators researched every aspect of their newest female addition from the size of her nose to the length of her lashes. Abby, a "pretty" pink "fairy in training," proved to be all the designers hoped and more (39–41).

36 Orenstein, *Cinderella Ate My Daughter*, 39–43.

37 Rhode, *Beauty Bias*, 26.

38 Neimark, "Why We Need," 42. "The fact is, Miss America informs us about our culture's ideals and conflicts . . . The Miss America contest has always knit together in its middle-class queen the deep schisms in American society. Whether her contestants flaunt pierced belly buttons or Ph.D.s in veterinary medicine, wear pants or ballgowns, Miss America is a mirror of America, even now."

39 With Scott, I understand "experience is at once always already an interpretation *and* is in need of interpretation. What counts as experience is neither self-evident nor straightforward; it is always contested, always therefore political. The study of experience, therefore, must call into question its originary status in historical explanation.

This will happen when historians take as their project *not* the reproduction and transmission of knowledge said to be arrived at through experience, but the analysis of the production of that knowledge itself . . . Experience is, in this approach, not the origin of our explanation, but that which we want to explain. This kind of approach does not undercut politics by denying the existence of subjects, it instead interrogates the processes of their creation, and, in so doing, refigures history and the role of the historian, and opens new ways for thinking about change." Joan W. Scott, "Experience," in *Feminists Theorize the Political*, ed. Judith Butler and Joan W. Scott (New York: Routledge, 1992), 22–40, here 37–38. In other words, women's experiences in beauty pageants demand explanation and analysis. Why do they experience it as they do and how does it contribute to the meaning-making in their lives? What led to their desire for these experiences? How do their other identity markers (geographical, racial, religious, etc.) interact with and influence their identity as a pageant contender? And what do their experiences have to teach us about what it means to be a woman in America and the impact of pageantry on Americans, male and female? See also Banet-Weiser's discussion of "Methodological Dilemmas, or What to Do with Women's Experience," in *Most Beautiful Girl*, 13–18. As she notes, "The pageant contestants embrace and resist different identities, identities that are constituted through the structuring of the pageant itself. And, through the words of the pageant contestants and accounts that rehearse why these women are participating in the pageants, we can understand the discursive processes that are both visible and invisible, and reactionary and potentially liberatory—processes that are part of the construction of the beauty pageant and, in the larger culture, of the beauty system itself" (18).

40 See, for example, Harry Stout, *The Divine Dramatist: George Whitefield and the Rise of Modern Evangelicalism* (Grand Rapids: Eerdmans, 1991).

41 Within the field of American religious history, my work, like much of the scholarship that privileges women's religious experience, was inspired in part by Ann Braude's now-famous piece, "Women's History *Is* American Religious History." Braude urged scholars to view women's experience as normative and to consider how their stories challenged, redefined, or solidified the dominant narrative(s) of American religious history. Her approach coupled with a penchant for exploring "lived religion" changed how many scholars approached women's religious history. Ann Braude, "Women's History *Is* American Religious History," in *Retelling U.S. Religious History*, ed. Thomas A. Tweed (Los Angeles: University of California Press, 1997), 87–107. See, for example, the essays in Catherine A. Brekus, ed., *The Religious History of American Women: Reimagining the Past* (Chapel Hill: University of North Carolina Press, 2007); and Michael S. Hamilton, "Women, Public Ministry, and American Fundamentalism, 1920–1950," *Religion and American Culture: A Journal of Interpretation* 3, no. 2 (1993): 171–96. Hamilton encouraged historians to look at women's stories, arguing that "scholars have elbowed women to the margins of the histories of Fundamentalism far more thoroughly than men ever pushed women to the margins of the movement itself." For one of the many works that influenced my understanding of lived religion, see David D. Hall, ed., *Lived Religion in America:*

Toward a History of Practice (Princeton, N.J.: Princeton University Press, 1997). My work exists within this now-established field of study.

Chapter 1: Miss America as Sex

1   Deborah L. Rhode, *The Beauty Bias: The Injustice of Appearance in Life and Law* (New York: Oxford University Press, 2010), 23.

2   Miss America Pageant, Planet Hollywood Resort & Casino, Las Vegas, January 15, 2011, on-site visit.

3   The Black-Eyed Peas, "The Time (Dirty Bit)," on *The Beginning*, released November 5, 2010.

4   To be sure and as will be discussed, at various times the Miss America Pageant sought to downplay or deny the role of sex in the pageant. As will be demonstrated, however, sex appeal has always contributed to the pageant's ongoing attraction. As Banet-Weiser argued, "Sex is forcibly called up through the swimsuit competition, not only because of the sexualized body that is evaluated, but also because of the silence of the contestants. Voices may be heard during each individual parade in front of the judges (and the voice may even be the recorded voice of the contestants), but the contestant herself does not speak during this particular competition . . . This fragmentation works in conjunction with the voicelessness of each contestant, where denying the contestants their voice contains the female body by reducing it to an isolated sexuality, one with no voice and no chance to talk back. It is, in other words, a body spoken for or on behalf of." Sarah Banet-Weiser, *The Most Beautiful Girl in the World: Beauty Pageants and National Identity* (Los Angeles: University of California Press, 1999), 75–76. Banet-Weiser's astute book, esp. ch. 2, "Anatomy of a Beauty Pageant," proved a crucial conversation partner for my analysis of Miss America as sex. At times, my work corroborates hers, at points it extends it, and, more rarely, it refutes it. Such contradictions arise because of shifts in the pageant in the twenty years since the publication of Banet-Weiser's groundbreaking work. For example, my description of the swimsuit walk at the 2011 pageant contradicts her argument that "the swimsuit competition is not about the sensual movement of the body: breasts are not supposed to jiggle, butts and thighs are to remain firm. Firm, rigid flesh represents and reflects the intense discipline of each contestant—and, importantly, firm flesh does not merely reflect the physical discipline it takes to create such a body. Rather, tight and contained flesh represent a tight and contained moral subjectivity" (68). And while true that jiggling breasts, butts, and thighs are still frowned upon, the movement of the hips, the seductive tuck of the leg, and the skimming of the hip and waist with one's arm and hand all while sexually explicit music played in the background suggests movement in the pageant's stance on sex, or, at the least, an openness to the contestants' bodies being consumed by the public in whatever way pleased them. Thus, the pageant seemed to move away from its dedication "to the repression of sexual excitement—of both the contestants and the (male) audience members" (71). I do not mean to suggest that the pageant was the equivalent of a striptease or that its only concern was sex. Rather, pageant officials saw in sex, both

the careful packaging and display of it, and the purposeful containment of it, a strategy for success that they used to their advantage. And as American culture became more comfortable with the display of women's bodies, and sex in the public square, so did the pageant.

5 Miss America Pageant, Planet Hollywood Resort & Casino, Las Vegas, January 11–15, 2011, on-site visit. By the Miss America 2018 Pageant, none of the national contestants chose to compete in a one-piece swimsuit. Miss America Pageant, Boardwalk Hall, Atlantic City, September 6–10, 2017, on-site visit. A quick Google search for tips on how to win a beauty pageant yields plentiful results in the form of blog posts, podcasts, and pageant coach websites. Such pageant "tricks" are also discussed in some pageant books. See, for example, "That Miss America Look," in Nancie S. Martin, *Miss America through the Looking Glass: The Story behind the Scenes* (New York: Little Simon, 1985), 114–16; Ginie Polo Sayles, *How to Win Pageants* (Plano, Tex.: Wordware Publishing, 1989); and Ann-Marie Bivans, *101 Secrets to Winning Beauty Pageants* (Secaucus, N.J.: Carol Publishing Group, 1995).

6 Miss America Pageant, Planet Hollywood Resort & Casino, Las Vegas, January 15, 2011, on-site visit.

7 Official photographs are available for purchase on the Miss America website. And, despite eliminating the swimsuit portion of the competition in 2018 and launching Miss America 2.0, fans can still (as of January 28, 2019) buy swimsuit photos of contestants who competed in previous years.

8 Judith Butler, *Gender Trouble: Feminism and the Subversion of Identity* (New York: Routledge, 1999), preface and part 3. Butler's theory of gender as performed and performative proves useful in considering how gender is both enacted and reinscribed through cultural rituals like beauty pageants. That is, pageants simultaneously re-created and reinforced gendered identities. For further discussion of how Butler's theory intersects with beauty pageants, see Banet-Weiser, *Most Beautiful Girl*, 11–12. To read more about the performance of a particular version of femininity in the pageants, see Sarah Banet-Weiser and Laura Portwood-Stacer, "'I just want to be me again!' Beauty Pageants, Reality Television and Post-feminism," *Feminist Theory* 7, no. 2 (2006): 255–72; and Bonnie J. Dow, "Feminism, Miss America, and Media Mythology," *Rhetoric and Public Affairs* 6, no. 1 (2003): 127–49.

9 This pursuit of the perfect body by pageant contestants reflected broader cultural trends that placed a premium on beauty. In fact, this trend toward garnering praise for one's beauty began early for women. For how and why women in the twentieth century sought to discipline their bodies to fit an ideal, see Joan Jacobs Brumberg, *The Body Project: An Intimate History of American Girls* (New York: Vintage Books, 1997), esp. ch. 4, "Body Projects." For a fascinating account of modern women's relationship to their bodies, see Susan Bordo, *Unbearable Weight: Feminism, Western Culture, and the Body* (Los Angeles: University of California Press, 1993), esp. part 2, "The Slender Body and Other Cultural Forms." For an investigation of "body work" as a negotiation of "gendered identity," see Debra L. Gimlin, *Body Work: Beauty and Self-Image in American Culture* (Los Angeles: University of California Press, 2002),

esp. the introduction. Gimlin discovered that some women found this "work" to be a source of empowerment in the face of difficult-to-achieve beauty ideals. For an opposing view that suggests "that beauty practices are not about women's individual choice or a 'discursive space' for women's creative expression, but . . . a most important aspect of women's oppression," see Sheila Jeffreys, *Beauty and Misogyny: Harmful Cultural Practices in the West* (New York: Routledge, 2005), 2. Chapter 1 of Jeffreys' work, "The 'Grip of Culture on the Body': Beauty Practices as Women's Agency or Women's Subordination," "examine(s) the ideas of the radical feminist critique of beauty and show(s) how these came to be challenged both by the new liberal feminism and by its counterpart in the academy, a variety of postmodern feminism that emphasizes choice and agency in a similar way" (6). For a fascinating study on "sexualized girlhood" and how the media bombards young girls with messages that their looks are of primary importance, see Peggy Orenstein, *Cinderella Ate My Daughter: Dispatches from the Front Lines of the New Girlie-Girl Culture* (New York: HarperCollins, 2011).

10   Katelyn Beaty, "Miss America and the Bikini Question," *Christianity Today*, January 20, 2011.

11   The pervasiveness of beauty culture in America has been well documented. For insight into America's beauty culture, see Kathy Peiss, *Hope in a Jar: The Making of America's Beauty Culture* (New York: Metropolitan Books, 1998). For the most comprehensive social history of beauty in America, see Lois W. Banner, *American Beauty* (Chicago: University of Chicago Press, 1983). Banner argues that "the identification of women with beauty has a lengthy tradition in Western culture" (10) and demonstrates that "the pursuit of personal beauty has always been a central concern of American women" (1). In other words, attractiveness denoted a feminine quality that women pursued and men admired. Banner's groundbreaking work was republished in 1984 and 2006 and continues to be cited in works on beauty, including those listed here. For a discussion of black beauty culture in America, its emergence, and its ideals, see Maxine Leeds Craig, *Ain't I a Beauty Queen: Black Women, Beauty, and the Politics of Race* (New York: Oxford University Press, 2002). For a more general examination of "beauty as a central dimension of femininity," see Rita Freedman, *Beauty Bound* (Lexington, Mass.: Lexington Books, 1986), x. For a comprehensive look at appearance-related bias, see Deborah L. Rhode, *The Beauty Bias: The Injustice of Appearance in Life and Law* (New York: Oxford University Press, 2010), esp. ch. 1, "Introduction"; and ch. 2, "The Importance of Appearance and the Costs of Conformity."

12   As A. R. Riverol wrote, women "were emancipated from the status of domestic work horse and rabbit only to attain that of financial commodity . . . Yet the exploitation of young American females had to be done in keeping with the virtues of Victorian maidenhood. America's best representative product had to be labeled 'Maid in U.S.A.' The answer was the beauty contest . . . For the amusement of an audience, babies, cattle, pies, and women were judged as the best in their respective fields. The human auction blocks had been closed, yet the beauty contest had replaced

them by transforming women from the prize to the priced." A. R. Riverol, "Myth America and Other Misses: A Second Look at the American Beauty Contests," *ETC: A Review of General Semantics* 40, no. 2 (1983): 207–17, here 209. However, official Miss America publications, including their website, employed a rhetoric of female empowerment to attract competitors, volunteers, and donors. Bonnie J. Dow explored some of this rhetoric and how Miss America has been presented by the media in her article "Feminism, Miss America, and Media Mythology."

13 A. R. Riverol, *Live from Atlantic City: A History of the Miss America Pageant before, after and in spite of Television* (Bowling Green, Ohio: Bowling Green State University Popular Press, 1992), 12–25, here 21.

14 "Bather Goes to Jail; Keeps Her Knees Bare," *New York Times*, September 5, 1921, 4. In "Bathing Suits and Backlash," in *The Politics of Sex, Beauty, and Race in America's Most Famous Pageant*, ed. Elwood Watson and Darcy Martin (New York: Palgrave Macmillan, 2004), Kimberly Hamlin comments, "Apparently, it was more acceptable to Atlantic City officials for women to parade in front of judges and spectators in their bathing suits than to swim in the ocean in them" (37). See also Angela J. Latham, "Packaging Woman: The Concurrent Rise of Beauty Pageants, Public Bathing, and Other Performances of Female 'Nudity,'" *Journal of Popular Culture* 29, no. 3 (1995): 149–67, here 165.

15 Riverol, *Live from Atlantic City*, 22–23.

16 In "Bathing Suits and Backlash," Kimberly Hamlin demonstrates this point well: "In the 1920s, just as women achieved unprecedented personal, professional, and political power, the Hotelman's Association of Atlantic City stumbled on something that Hazel MacKaye and the suffragists already knew: namely, that pageants are a highly effective form of propaganda. Instead of welcoming women into politics and the professions, the Miss America Pageant encouraged women to compete against each other for a crown and then return home to live quietly ever after. The first Miss America Pageants praised and represented only those young women who looked nothing like flappers or suffragists and who posed little or no threat of emerging in the public sphere. That such an image of womanhood was, by all accounts, unanimously agreed on by promoters, fans, and judges and celebrated across America testifies to its broad-based appeal. In the 1920s, crowning a passive, traditional, 'unpainted' and 'unbobbed' girl soothed a nation struggling to accept the changing gender roles brought by suffrage, world war, and the flapper and provided a cookie-cutter version of America's ideal woman" (45–46).

17 Hamlin, "Bathing Suits and Backlash," 45. "From descriptions of Gorman's appearance and stature, it is apparent that the judges were not interested in celebrating the new, emancipated women of the 1920s but in promoting images of the girls of yesterday: small, childlike, subservient, and malleable" (35).

18 Frank Deford, *There She Is: The Life and Times of Miss America* (New York: Viking Press, 1971), 117; Banner, *American Beauty*, 268–69; Hamlin, "Bathing Suits and Backlash," 35–36: "Mary Pickford became famous playing wide-eyed innocent adolescents . . . Beyond legitimizing the pageant and allaying middle-class reservations

about it, Gorman's selection and her similarities with Pickford testify to the pageant's conservative and reactive nature." See also Gaylan Studlar, "Oh, 'Doll Divine': Mary Pickford, Masquerade, and the Pedophilic Gaze," in *A Feminist Reader in Early Cinema*, ed. Jennifer M. Bean and Diane Negra (Durham, N.C.: Duke University Press, 2002), 360–61: "Pickford appealed to and through a kind of cultural pedophilia that looked to the innocent child-woman to personify nostalgic ideals of femininity . . . the articulation of Pickford as an antimodernist, Victorian indebted model of femininity served as one antidote to a perceived crisis in feminine sexual behavior. It is well documented that in the 1910s and 1920s, the flapper and the new woman symbolized American women's perceived transgression of the traditional feminine sexual norms of passivity and restraint."

19 "'Miss Indianapolis' Is Prettiest Girl: Thelma Blossoms Wins First Two Events in Atlantic City Beauty Show," *New York Times*, September 8, 1922, 13. "I have traveled afar, but this is the greatest treat I was ever afforded. It will be almost a super-human task to choose the prettiest, and I am glad I have not the responsibility of judging officially. To me, however, Miss Washington most greatly appeals. She represents the type of womanhood America needs, strong, red-blooded, able to shoulder the responsibilities of homemaking and motherhood. It is in her type that the hope of the country rests." Banner and Hamlin mistakenly cite the September 8, 1921 *New York Times* rather than the 1922 article cited here. As such, Banner, Hamlin, and PBS's American Experience ("People and Events: The First Miss America Beauty Pageant, 1921") have attributed Gompers' reference to Miss Washington as a reference to Margaret Gorman as I have above. However, Gorman competed as Miss Washington at the 1921 pageant. In 1922 she competed as Miss America and placed first runner-up. There was another contestant, Evelyn C. Lewis, representing Washington, D.C. in 1922. Consequently, Gompers could have been referring to Evelyn Lewis rather than Margaret Gorman. Whether discussing Lewis or Gompers, the point that onlookers and judges valued traditional versions of femininity remains. Banner, *American Beauty*, 341, n. 44; and Hamlin, "Bathing Suits and Backlash," 49, n. 38.

20 "In the absence of any direct signals of ovulation or fertility, the man is forced to use indirect cues such as physical attractiveness to assess the reproductive value of the woman. It is the fundamental assumption of all evolution-based theories of human mate selection that physical attractiveness is largely a reflection of reliable cues to a woman's reproductive success." Devendra Singh, "Adaptive Significance of Female Physical Attractiveness: Role of Waist-to-Hip Ratio," *Journal of Personality and Social Psychology* 65, no. 2 (1993): 293–307, here 293. Singh uses measurements of Miss America winners and *Playboy* centerfolds as one study in a three-part study to show "that men judge women with low WHR as attractive" (293). He notes that "in Western societies, a narrow waist set against full hips has been a consistent feature for female attractiveness" (296) and "the fact that WHR conveys such significant information about the mate value of a woman suggests that men in all societies should favor women with a lower WHR over women with a higher WHR for mate selection or at least find such women sexually attractive" (305). See also Devendra Singh

and Patrick K. Randall, "Beauty Is in the Eye of the Plastic Surgeon: Waist-Hip Ratio (WHR) and Women's Attractiveness," *Personality and Individual Differences* 42 (2007): 329–40; and Steven M. Platek and Devendra Singh, "Optimal Waist-to-Hip Rations in Women Activate Neural Reward Centers in Men," *PLoS ONE* 5, no. 2 (2010): pe9042. At least one study has questioned "that there is something special—evolutionarily hard-wired or otherwise—about a specific female waist-to-hip ratio of 0.70 as a preference of American heterosexual males." See Jeremy Freese and Sheri Meland, "Seven Tenths Incorrect: Heterogeneity and Change in the Waist-to-Hip Ratios of Playboy Centerfold Models and Miss America Pageant Winners," *Journal of Sex Research* 39, no. 2 (2002): 133–38, here 133. Despite Freese and Meland's argument that there is a wider range of WHR among Miss America and *Playboy* centerfold models than noted by Singh, I was convinced by the other evidence presented by Singh and his fellow researchers that men consistently demonstrate a preference for women with a 0.7 WHR over those with 0.8 or higher WHR and that a lower WHR among women correlates to being perceived more attractive and of greater "reproductive value" by men. I would be interested for other scholars to repeat some of Singh's experiments with women who have a WHR of less than 0.7 to see if 0.7 is still the preferred WHR. Still, the point that winners of the Miss America Pageant had low WHR holds true using either set of numbers. And, in the early years, the celebration of winners as homemakers and mothers was merely coded language for women men found attractive and desirable.

21 "Advertisers could hardly fail to realize the success of cigarette advertising using cards with photos of buxom women on them. Early in the century perfume cards usually featured cherubic children; by the 1880s fashionable women had replaced them as subjects." Banner, *American Beauty*, 261–64, here 262.

22 "Florenz Ziegfield made the chorus girl 'respectable' in the 1910s by divesting her image and figure of working-class culture . . . Hers was the sage, non-threatening sexuality of the middle-class girl next door, not the predatory sexuality of the burlesque poster." Robert Clyde Allen, *Horrible Prettiness: Burlesque and American Culture* (Chapel Hill: University of North Carolina Press, 1991), 272; Banner, *American Beauty*, 263.

23 "Ironically, a period that began with cosmetics signaling women's freedom and individuality ended in binding feminine identity to manufactured beauty, self-portrayal to acts of consumption." Peiss, *Hope in a Jar*, 135. "In the 1920s and 1930s, cosmetic producers, advertisers, and beauty experts shifted the burden of female identity from an interior self to a personality made manifest by marking and coloring the face: Makeup was a true expression of feminine identity, not its false mask, and the makeover was a means of individual self-development." Peiss, *Hope in a Jar*, 166.

24 Banner, *American Beauty*, 207–8. "Feminism had succeeded in the early twentieth century because it had galvanized the universal American belief in women's moral superiority to bring women out of the home and into reform work. A corollary of that success was the identification of beauty with the natural woman as well as the notion that every woman could be beautiful. With the demise of the moral

superiority argument in the 1920s, such identification was seriously undermined. But the possibility that every woman might be beautiful, once raised, did not disappear. With its powders and lotions, its cosmetics and hair dyes, the commercial culture of beauty then became the major claimant to the means of beauty for all woman. When in the 1920s women no longer were seen as possessing a superior spirituality, their outward appearance could be viewed as more important than their inner character, and external means could become central to improving their looks."

25 Arguably, no amount of "agency" felt or expressed by the contestants completely eliminated the fact that their bodies were marketed and objectified in the pageant. As Dow notes, "Indeed, the role of agency within feminist theory is complicated. On the one hand, if patriarchy were as powerful as is sometimes implied, women's agency (and, by extension, feminism) could not exist. On the other hand, if women's agency were as powerful as is sometimes implied, there would be no need for feminism. The truth lies somewhere between the two: patriarchy is powerful, but not so much so that resistance is impossible, and women do exercise agency, but often within a limited field (limited not just by patriarchy, but by race, class, and sexuality as well)." Dow, "Feminism, Miss America," 147. Hamlin employs Bourdieu to argue that "it only has to be pointed out that this use of the body remains very obviously subordinated to the male point of view." "Bathing Suits and Backlash," 46. Banet-Weiser's work includes "the contestants' experience as evidence for the cultural practices that both sustain and construct beauty pageants," but even she admits it is a dilemma. "I must find a way to critique cultural discourses and practices that objectify, alienate, or otherwise fragment the female body without treating the contestants themselves as somnolent victims of false consciousness." *Most Beautiful Girl*, 14. This tension is one that persists in the pageant, and, in many respects, has gotten stronger over time as contestants became more vocal about their participation as a source of empowerment, not oppression.

26 Deford, *There She Is*, 124–25.

27 Deford, *There She Is*, 125–26.

28 Hamlin, "Bathing Suits and Backlash," 44. "The main difference between the pageants of the early 1920s and those of the latter half of the decade was not so much an increase in commercialism but the fact that contestants started to profit from the title and seek public acclaim for themselves."

29 "Attacks Bathing Review: Preacher Says Atlantic City Event Endangers Youthful Morals," *New York Times*, September 11, 1923, 15; "Criticism Well Deserved," *New York Times*, April 21, 1924, 16; "Attack Beauty Pageant: Philadelphia Women Sign Protest to Atlantic City Authorities," *New York Times*, March 1, 1927, 3; "Women Open Fight on Beauty Pageant: Tell Atlantic City Officials That Contests Harm Entrants and Commercialize Shore," *New York Times*, November 18, 1927, 12; "Bishop Condemns Beauty Pageant," *New York Times*, November 20, 1927, 10.

30 "Attacks Bathing Review."

31 "Women Open Fight."

32 "Women Open Fight"; Southern Baptist Convention, "Resolution passed at the Southern Baptist Convention, 1926," *SBC Resolutions*, May 1926.

33 "Attack Beauty Pageant." "Proclaiming the demoralizing effect of the annual pageant to be an established fact, the meeting 'considered it unworthy of a great resort like Atlantic City to adopt a method of advertising which involved the exploitation of young women.'" The paper reported that the women in attendance at the meeting were "leaders in educational, civic, religious and social organizations." "Ignores Pageant Protests: Atlantic City Chamber Minimizes Criticism of Beauty Contest," *New York Times*, March 2, 1927, 26. This article notes that the protest of the Philadelphia women was not the first such criticism of the pageant. Angela J. Latham discusses Mae West's unpublished play that criticized pageants in her work, *Posing a Threat: Flappers, Chorus Girls, and Other Brazen Performers of the American 1920s* (Hanover, N.H.: Wesleyan University Press, 2000), 91–93.

34 The issue of the pageant's disappearance from 1928 to 1932 and 1934 is a complex one. The Miss America website notes that "unfortunate happenings with the press and ever increasing pressure from women's groups and church officials make pageant organizers fearful that the pageant was beginning to give the city a bad name. Despite a $7,000 profit on the 1927 event alone, they voted 27–3 to discontinue the famed Atlantic City Pageant." Further, the website dubbed the 1933 return of the pageant a "financial disaster," in part due to "lack of adequate publicity." This relaunching, of course, took place in the midst of the Great Depression. Deford claims, "It was abandoned because the key persons in the resort, the hotel operators, who had once championed it, soured on it." For more see Deford, *There She Is*, 129–30. Riverol concludes, "Whether the pageant sponsors buckled to this outside pressure and bad press, or whether, indeed, it was because of financial considerations is inconsequential." Riverol, *Live from Atlantic City*, 23–24. Hamlin argues that it was the increasing boldness of the winners that led to the pageant's demise (see n. 28 in this chapter). As Hamlin goes on to argue, "Thus, the pageant ended up encouraging what it had attempted to throttle—the rise of independent, ambitious women in the public sphere." She concludes, "As contestants began to capitalize on the profit and fame the title 'Miss America' could bring them, Atlantic City leaders suspended the pageant indefinitely." "Bathing Suits and Backlash," 44–45. Most likely it was a combination of factors that led to the pageant's demise. It is undeniable that the pageant faced criticism, but that criticism did not appear out of nowhere in 1927. Likewise, pageant supporters routinely dismissed that criticism as invalid and unimportant. See, for example, remarks by Frederick Hickman, president of the Atlantic City Chamber of Commerce, in March 1927. "I am satisfied that this action was initiated by some one who has never seen the pageant and was not familiar with the conditions under which the beauties compete and are entertained. Instead of having a demoralizing effect, the opposite is true, because it has been demonstrated to the young women of the country that the popular girl is the one who represents the highest ideals." "Ignores Pageant Protests." It is also the case

that the pageant faced its fair share of "scandal" in the early years. See, for example, Deford, *There She Is*, 130–33.

35 See n. 21 in this chapter. The continued use of attractive female images to market goods is well established. The use of beautiful women in advertising also serves to market particular versions of femininity. Over time, these images have become more sexually explicit. The narrow versions of womanhood portrayed in the media has had negative effects on women's self-image. See, for example, Cecelia Baldwin, *How the Media Shape Young Women's Perceptions of Self-Efficacy, Social Power and Class: Marketing Sexuality* (Lewiston, N.Y.: Edwin Mellen Press, 2006); John Alan Cohan, "Towards a New Paradigm in the Ethics of Women's Advertising," *Journal of Business Ethics* 33, no. 4 (2001): 323–37; Terry D. Conley and Laura R. Ramsey, "Killing Us Softly? Investigating Portrayals of Women and Men in Contemporary Magazine Advertisements," *Psychology of Women Quarterly* 35, no. 3 (2011): 469–78; Indhu Rajagopal and Jennifer Gales, "It's the Image That Is Imperfect: Advertising and Its Impact on Women," *Economic and Political Weekly* 37, no. 32 (2002): 3333–37; and Lorna Stevens and Jacob Ostberg, "Gendered Bodies: Representations of Femininity and Masculinity in Advertising Practices," in *Marketing Management: A Cultural Perspective*, ed. Lisa Penaloza, Nil Toulose, and Luca Massimiliano Visconti (New York: Routledge, 2012), 392–407.

36 Of the pageant's revival, Deford wrote, "*Miss America* had a large debt outstanding left over from the 1920s, and while many of the town's most solid citizens had their names on the note, the banks were not disposed to put pressure on them. Under the circumstances, it seemed more agreeable to see if the Pageant could not be re-established and work itself out of the hole. The scheme became more attractive because Corcoran, a popular local figure, was out of work. One man who was privy to all these proceedings even says, 'Don't believe anything else. The only reason the Pageant was started up again—the one reason we have a *Miss America* here today—is because a bunch of his friends were trying to help Eddie Corcoran get a job.'" Deford, *There She Is*, 151.

37 Ann-Marie Bivans, *Miss America: In Pursuit of the Crown* (New York: MasterMedia Limited, 1991), 12–13.

38 Bivans, *In Pursuit of the Crown*, 13–14. See also Sarah Banet-Weiser, "A Certain Class of Girl: Respectability and the Structure of the Miss America Pageant," in *The Most Beautiful Girl in the World: Beauty Pageants and National Identity* (Los Angeles: University of California Press, 1999), 31–57. For Lenora Slaughter's role in this quest for a certain "class of girl," see 37–42. For more on Slaughter's reforms in the pageant, see Angela Saulino Osborne, *Miss America: The Dream Lives On: A 75 Year Celebration* (Dallas: Taylor, 1995), 86–90; and Deford, *There She Is*, 149–60. The pageant already had a rule that Miss America contestants could not be married. It was not until 1951 that they instituted a rule that winners could not get married during their year as Miss America. Riverol, *Live from Atlantic City*, 42.

39 Bivans, *In Pursuit of the Crown*, 14.

40 Bivans, *In Pursuit of the Crown*, 16.

41 Deford, *There She Is*, 157. Osborne, *Dream Lives On*, 128–30 and 186–92. See also Harvey Cox, "Miss America and the Cult of The Girl," *Christianity and Crisis* 7 (August 1961): 143–46.

42 Deford, *There She Is*, 158–59; and Susan Dworkin, *Miss America, 1945: Bess Myerson and the Year that Changed Our Lives* (New York: Newmarket Press, 1999), 98–102.

43 See Banet-Weiser, *Most Beautiful Girl*, 81–86 and 146–50; and Latham, "Packaging Woman." Latham argues, "The status of women as emblematically portrayed by both the celebrated bathing beauty and the pitiable chorus girl poignantly bespeaks the complexities of an era in which woman's sacrifices may truly have outweighed her gains . . . Unfortunately, the entertainment industry, while offering employment, notoriety, even 'royalty' status to women, further enslaved them. These means of woman's enslavement were more insidious than conditions of unemployment and obscurity. In effect, her body came up for public auction" (165–66). Rita Freedman also offers a helpful discussion of the careful distinctions made between pornography and pageantry. "Those who seek admiration as a beauty object but fear exploitation as a sex object must be careful not to cross the line. The demands of beauty and the taboos of pornography require a balancing act that often throws women off balance . . . The fake wholesomeness of beauty pageants has been called the flip side of pornography. Like a pair of contradictory myths, each side of the image depends on the other. Both distort the female body, making it harder for women to sustain a positive view of themselves." Freedman, *Beauty Bound*, 42.

44 See missamericafoundation.org. *Last Week Tonight* host John Oliver investigated Miss America's claim to be the largest provider of scholarships to women in the world. He satirizes, "Currently the biggest scholarship program exclusively for women in America requires you to be unmarried, with a mint condition uterus, and also rewards working knowledge of buttock adhesive technology." John Oliver, "Miss America Pageant: Last Week Tonight with John Oliver," *Last Week Tonight*, hbo.com/last-week-tonight-with-john-oliver. While there are still questions about how Miss America counts the scholarship amount awarded, it does appear to remain the largest provider of scholarships to women in the United States. See Ed Mazza, "John Oliver Explains Everything That's Wrong With The Miss America Pageant," *Huffington Post*, September 22, 2014; Amy Kuperinsky, "Miss America Organization Responds to John Oliver's Segment on Pageant," September 24, 2014, nj.com; and John V. Santore, "Miss America Unclear on Amount Awarded in Scholarships," *Press of Atlantic City*, January 5, 2015. This claim by the pageant to be "the largest scholarship foundation in the world for young women" goes back to at least 1971 and my guess is it dates back even further. Grace Lichtenstein, "Miss New York: On the Road to Success or Exploitation?" *New York Times*, September 7, 1971.

45 Deford, *There She Is*, 64. "Nineteen forty-six was also the year when Lenora heard E. B. Steward, the president of Catalina, the bathing suit firm that was one of *Miss America*'s sponsors, roar on one occasion, 'It's not a bathing suit, dammit. You bathe in a tub. You swim in a swimsuit.' Lenora liked this definition and promptly decreed that thereafter there would be no such thing as bathing suits at *Miss America*."

46 Deford, *There She Is*, 180; and Sam Roberts, "Yolande Betbeze Fox, Miss America
Who Defied Convention, Dies at 87," *New York Times*, February 25, 2016.

47 Banet-Weiser, *Most Beautiful Girl*, 44. After Betbeze refused to pose in a swimsuit,
Catalina Swimsuits pulled their sponsorship of the pageant and launched its own
pageant. Originally known as Miss United Nations, the pageant eventually became
the Miss Universe Organization, which was owned by Donald Trump from 1996
to 2015. The title that corresponds to Miss America is Miss USA, a precursor to
Miss Universe.

48 The protest songs written for the 1968 protest of the Miss America Pageant capture
this sentiment brilliantly. The opening lines to one song, sung to the tune of "A
Pretty Girl Is Like a Melody," were "A pretty girl is a commodity with stock to buy
and sell . . ." Another song included the lines, "We're gonna tell all the ad men here
they've used us long enough . . . Now you can't use us any more . . ." Robin Morgan, "Protest Songs for the Miss America Protest," n.d., box S17, "Demonstrations:
Miss America 1968" folder, in Robin Morgan Papers, David M. Rubenstein Rare
Book and Manuscript Library, Duke University, Durham, North Carolina. This box
has fifty-eight documents related to the protest and the pageant. As Rita Freedman
notes in *Beauty Bound*, "When beauty is assigned to the feminine role it becomes
a primary asset, a basic commodity of gender exchange, and a key to economic
survival" (116). Banet-Weiser, *Most Beautiful Girl*, 59 and 63; Rebecca Chiyoko
King-O'Riain, "Making the Perfect Queen: The Cultural Production of Identities
in Beauty Pageants," *Sociology Compass* 21 no. 1 (2008): 74–83; Hamlin, "Bathing
Suits and Backlash," 45; and Mary Louise Roberts, "Gender, Consumption, and
Commodity Culture," *American Historical Review* 103, no. 3 (1998): 817–44. For a
fascinating discussion of commodifying "women's bodies in the service of commodity crop farming," see Blain Roberts, *Pageants, Parlors, and Pretty Women: Race and
Beauty in the Twentieth-Century South* (Chapel Hill: University of North Carolina
Press, 2014), 128–32. "Beauty contest sponsors offered women's bodies as commodity crops, which tempered the troubling implications of the bathing beauty ritual"
(107).

49 Kelsey Wright, "Sexual Objectification of Female Bodies in Beauty Pageants, Pornography, and Media," *Dissenting Voices* 6, no. 1 (2017): 125–46. See also n. 43 in
this chapter.

50 I employ Bourdieu's definition of cultural capital to explore the various advantages
participants claimed came from pageant participation. Cultural capital refers to
"forms of cultural knowledge, competencies or dispositions." This knowledge "equips
the social agent with empathy towards, appreciation for or competence in decipher-
ing cultural relations and cultural artefacts." Randal Johnson, "Editor's Introduction:
Pierre Bourdieu on Art, Literature, and Culture," in *The Field of Cultural Production:
Essays on Art and Literature*, by Pierre Bourdieu (New York: Columbia University
Press, 1993), 7. See also Naomi Wolf's discussion of beauty as currency in *The Beauty
Myth: How Images of Beauty Are Used against Women* (New York: HarperCollins
Perennial, 2002), 12.

51 The cultural upheaval of the sixties seems axiomatic, and the literature is voluminous, but see Arthur Marwick's magisterial tome *The Sixties* (Oxford: Oxford University Press, 1998) for the broad Zeitgeist of the age. For a work more focused on the American context, see Maurice Isserman and Michael Kazin, *America Divided: The Civil War of the 1960s*, 5th ed. (New York: Oxford University Press, 2015). On the women's movement in particular, see Alice Echols, *Daring to Be Bad: Radical Feminism in America, 1967–1975* (Minneapolis: University of Minnesota Press, 1989).

52 Bivans, *In Pursuit of the Crown*, 25–28; Deford, *There She Is*, 255–56; Dow, "Feminism, Miss America"; Virginia Lee Warren, "Beauty, She Insists, Isn't Skin Deep," *New York Times*, September 8, 1969. In 1970, Albert Marks, chairman and executive producer of the Miss America Pageant, incorrectly predicted that the swimsuit pageant would be eliminated in three years. "We are getting anti-bathing suit pressure. Most of it comes from contestants who find it uncomfortable to walk 140 feet of runway in a bathing suit under 450,000 watts of lighting. This is just not a natural surrounding for a bathing suit." He also noted, "The Miss America Pageant is not a skin show." Judy Klemesrud, "A Tradition on Way out at Contest?" *New York Times*, September 10, 1970. By 1974, Marks' rhetoric had changed. Speaking of the swimsuit competition in 1974, he said, "It is not our favorite operation. We are not a cheesecake competition, but to have a contestant who is not a professional walk 140 feet down the runway and back—under those blazing lights and before a television audience of 100 million people—is a great test of poise." Carol M. Sardella, "Miss America Faces Ms.," *New York Times*, September 1, 1974. When asked about the "brief shouting incident by a small group of young women protesters," Judith Ford, newly crowned Miss America 1969, replied, "It was just too bad, I'm sorry it happened." "Illinois Girl Named Miss America," *New York Times*, September 8, 1968. In an interview with NPR in 2008, Debra Barnes Snodgrass, Miss America 1968, expressed the frustration she felt toward the protesters, offering a defense of the pageant. Nell Greenfieldboyce, "Pageant Protest Sparked Bra-Burning Myth," *Morning Edition: Echoes of 1968*, National Public Radio, September 5, 2008, npr.org.

53 Much has been written about the 1968 feminist protest of the Miss America Pageant, including several pieces in 2018 on the fiftieth anniversary of the protest. See, for example, Bonnie J. Dow, "The Movement Meets the Press: The 1968 Miss America Pageant Protest," in *Watching Women's Liberation, 1970: Feminism's Pivotal Year on the Network News* (Champaign: University of Illinois Press, 2014), 29–51; Georgia Paige Welch, "'Up against the Wall Miss America': Women's Liberation and Miss Black America in Atlantic City, 1968," *Feminist Formations* 27, no. 2 (2015): 70–97; and Roberts, *Pageants, Parlors*, 257–62. For reflections on the fiftieth anniversary of the protest, see Karina Bland, "Miss America Protest Propelled Women's Movement into National Spotlight," *USA Today*, October 12, 2018; Roxane Gay, "Fifty Years Ago, Protestors Took on the Miss America Pageant and Electrified the Feminist Movement," *Smithsonian Magazine*, January 2018; Karen Heller, "The Bra-Burning Feminist Trope Started at Miss America. Except, That's Not What Really Happened," *The Washington Post*, September 7, 2018; and Laura Tanenbaum and

Mark Engler, "No More Miss America: A Collective Memory of Liberatory Action," *Dissent Magazine*, September 7, 2018. The protest is also featured in the documentary, *Miss America: A Documentary Film*, DVD, directed by Lisa Ades (Brooklyn: Clio and Orchard Films, 2001).

54 "No More Miss America!" in *Sisterhood Is Powerful: An Anthology of Writings from the Women's Liberation Movement*, ed. Robin Morgan (New York: Random House, 1970): 584–88; "No More Miss America!" *Time Magazine*, September 13, 1968, 36; Greenfieldboyce, "Pageant Protest"; Deford, *There She Is*, 257; "Protest Songs for the Miss America Protest," n.d., box S17, "Demonstrations: Miss America 1968" folder.

55 Carol Hanisch, "What Can Be Learned: A Critique of the Miss America Protest," November 27, 1968, box S17, "Demonstrations: Miss America 1968" folder, in Robin Morgan Papers, David M. Rubenstein Rare Book and Manuscript Library, Duke University, Durham, North Carolina.

56 Bivans, *In Pursuit of the Crown*, 25.

57 Bivans, *In Pursuit of the Crown*, 25.

58 Bivans, *In Pursuit of the Crown*, 25–26; Charlotte Curtis, "Miss America Pageant Is Picketed by 100 Women," *New York Times*, September 8, 1968; Deford, *There She Is*, 255–62; Dow, "Feminism, Miss America"; and Roberts, *Pageants, Parlors*, 257–62.

59 The protestors also succeeded in gaining national attention for the women's liberation movement. The 1968 protest of the Miss America Pageant is often credited with launching second-wave feminism into the spotlight. See Dow, "Movement Meets"; Hanisch, "What Can Be Learned"; Robin Morgan as told to Allison McNearney, "I Was There: The 1968 Miss America Pageant Protest," *History*, September 7, 2018, history.com; and Laura Tanenbaum and Mark Engler, "How 'No More Miss America' Announced a Feminist Upheaval," *The Nation*, September 7, 2018.

60 "The Unbeatable Madonna-Whore Combination" is one of the ten stated points of protest on the August 22, 1968, press release, "No More Miss America!" The protestors elaborated: "Miss America and Playboy's centerfold are sisters over the skin. To win approval, we must be both sexy and wholesome, delicate but able to cope, demure yet titillatingly bitchy. Deviation of any sort brings, we are told, disaster: 'You won't get a man!!'" In a separate point, titled "The degrading Mindless-Boob-Girlie Symbol," they lamented, "The Pageant contestants epitomize the roles we are all forced to play as women. The parade down the runway blares the metaphor of the 4-H Club county fair, where the best 'specimen' gets the blue ribbon. So are women in our society forced daily to compete for male approval, enslaved by ludicrous 'beauty' standards we ourselves are conditioned to take seriously."

61 Freedman, *Beauty Bound*, 42.

62 Hanisch, "What Can Be Learned."

63 The fact that women did not feel oppressed by the pageant and its corresponding beauty requirements did not necessarily mean they were not oppressed. As many scholars have noted, women often participate in systems that are oppressive. See Sandra Lee Bartky, *Femininity and Domination: Studies in the Phenomenology of Oppression* (New York: Routledge, 1990); Rachel M. Calogero, Stacey Tantleff-Dunn, and

J. Kevin Thompson, eds., *Self-Objectification in Women: Causes, Consequences, and Counteractions* (Washington, D.C.: American Psychological Association, 2011); Freedman, *Beauty Bound*; Jeffreys, *Beauty and Misogyny*; Peiss, *Hope in a Jar*; Rhode, *Beauty Bias*; Wolf, *The Beauty Myth*. Peiss notes, "Unattainable standards of beauty had an effect at once intense and narcotic: Women were driven into an absorption with appearances, into making themselves the objects of men's visual pleasure. Thus beauty practices simultaneously diverted and excluded women from intellectual work, meaningful social participation, and politics" (261). Another study by Barbara L. Fredrickson, Tomi-Ann Roberts, Stephanie M. Noll, Diane M. Quinn, and Jean M. Twenge is also worth quoting. In "That Swimsuit Becomes You: Sex Differences in Self-Objectification, Restrained Eating, and Math Performance," *Journal of Personality and Social Psychology* 75, no. 1 (1998): 269–84, the authors concluded, "Like any survival tactic, self-objectification has its benefits, as evidenced by the superior life outcomes experienced by women deemed attractive. Yet it also has its costs. We have demonstrated that experimentally induced self-objectification causes women (but not men) to (a) experience shame about their bodies, which in turn predicts restrained eating; and (b) perform more poorly on an advanced math test. These emotional and behavioral repercussions of self-objectification begin to document the psychological costs of raising girls in a culture that persistently objectifies the female body" (281). See also nn. 12 and 25 in this chapter.

64 Judy Klemesrud, "For Miss America '75, the Questions Get Tougher," *New York Times*, September 9, 1974.

65 Greenfieldboyce, "Pageant Protest."

66 Lichtenstein, "Miss New York."

67 Judy Klemesrud, "Miss America: She's Always on the Road," *New York Times*, July 4, 1974. Despite King's claim that the Miss America Pageant was not a "body-beautiful contest," the appearance of an article titled, "'Overweight' Beauty Queen" in the November 15, 1974 *New York Times* calls that into question. The short piece recounts the resignation of Miss Washington, Kathleen Beth Moore, "after pageant officials decided that she was overweight." She had lost eight of the ten pounds gained, but was disappointed that "the highest emphasis is on the figure. I had been led to believe the Miss Washington contest was not just another beauty pageant and the young woman should be a composite of talent, personality and beauty, with the emphasis on talent."

68 Melinda Beck et al., "A Controversial 'Spectator Sport,'" *Newsweek*, September 17, 1984, 60.

69 Bivans, *In Pursuit of the Crown*, 26.

70 Two examples will suffice. In "Miss New York," Lichtenstein notes that both Elizabeth Condon, Miss New York, and Mel Cunningham, the pageant's executive director, claim "sex . . . has nothing to do with it." "Yet when Miss Condon was asked about the fact that she appears as a beauty queen at every commercial function she attends, she says that 'the first attraction is mainly physical, sure.'" This emphasis on women as beauty objects remained in 1977. In a *New York Times* piece written by Miss America's

master of ceremonies, Bert Parks, he mused, "So I hope all Americans will join with me tonight in viewing a non-event, a beautiful piece of fluff . . . two hours of going back in time . . . a time for pure, unadulterated girl-watching, and appreciating, and for all of the values that connect with that marvelous pastime." Bert Parks, "And Now, a Few Words From the Emcee . . . ," *New York Times*, September 10, 1977.

71 Banet-Weiser, *Most Beautiful Girl*, 59; Katelyn Beaty, "Miss America and the Bikini Question," *Christianity Today*, January 20, 2011; John Curran, "The Public Wants Swimsuits: Poll Dominates 75th Anniversary Show," *Associated Press*, September 17, 1995. The reported number in favor of keeping the swimsuit competition varied from 73 percent (Banet-Weiser) to 80 percent (Beaty). I chose to report the number cited by Curran in the Associated Press article (79 percent).

72 "Viewers to Vote Yes or No on Miss America Swimsuits," *Baltimore Sun*, August 22, 1995.

73 "Viewers to Vote." Miss Montana, Amanda Granrude, was one of the few to express a negative view of the swimsuit competition.

74 Curran, "Public Wants Swimsuits."

75 Banet-Weiser, *Most Beautiful Girl*, 59–60. "The pageant commission's unusual decision to allow viewers to determine the fate of the event made the pageant and its legitimacy as a national cultural form vulnerable. But it also managed to market or to commodify the ambivalence structuring the swimsuit competition, a move that generated increased publicity and further legitimized the pageant as an event that celebrates the minds, not bodies, of the contestants. The Miss America pageant became 'our' event in a much more profound sense than ever before, and the call-in vote implied that the audience is the 'real' judge of the pageant. In other words, the contradictory presence of the swimsuit competition within a larger spectacle whose self-described true aim is to give college scholarships to smart, talented women was acknowledged by the pageant commission, who asked the public: Do we need it? This reliance on the legitimacy of consumer sovereignty pre-empted suggestions that the pageant was sexist and close-minded, and the American public answered: Yes, we do need it."

76 Miss America Pageant, Boardwalk Hall, Atlantic City, September 6–10, 2017, on-site visit.

77 Bivans, *101 Secrets*, esp. ch. 3, "The Winning Package," and ch. 5, "The Winning Swimsuit." Sayles, *How to Win Pageants*, esp. ch. 5, "Enhancing Your Image," and ch. 7, "Swimsuit Competition—Your Body's Language." Some contestants took more drastic measures. In her book *The Beauty Myth*, Naomi Wolf recounts, "Fifty million Americans watch the Miss America pageant; in 1989 five contestants, including Miss Florida, Miss Alaska, and Miss Oregon, were surgically reconstructed by a single Arkansas plastic surgeon" (267). Clearly these pageant winners were in need of Sayles' "Bosom Builders" advice: "If you choose to have breast augmentation, remember, don't discuss it with anyone—especially not the press" (239). Sayles also wrote, "I have given it a lot of thought and I find that plastic surgery should be treated no differently as a form of self-improvement than getting a tan, going on a

diet, exercising, or applying makeup or hair coloring" (189). Bivans also addresses the surge in cosmetic surgery in her book, concluding, "I cannot advise a contestant whether or not she should have cosmetic surgery, because there's no way to predict the personal tastes and insight of the people who will judge her. Each girl and her parents need to evaluate the pros and cons of cosmetic surgery and decide what is best for that young woman's health and lifelong goals." See also Banet-Weiser, *Most Beautiful Girl*, 71–74.

78 Cheryl Prewitt with Kathryn Slattery, *A Bright-Shining Place: The Story of a Miracle* (Garden City, N.Y.: Doubleday, 1981), 236–38.

79 See nn. 5, 9, and 77 in this chapter. A glance at pageant advice books suggests that the Miss America Pageant might not have evolved as much as it claims in its almost one-hundred-year history. While a contestant no longer garners a score based on a "100-point body breakdown," which awarded points for construction of head, eyes, hair, nose, mouth, facial expression, torso, legs, arms, hands, and grace of bearing (Deford, *There She Is*, 59), and her measurements are no longer printed in the paper, contestants still focus attention on perfecting individual parts of the body, maybe more so than ever before. For example, in a section titled "Guide to Swimsuit Figure Camouflage," in Bivans' *101 Secrets*, the reader is directed to find her figure in the list and use the advice accordingly. For a potential candidate with a "large buttocks," Bivans offers suggestions like, "Cover derriere fully! Avoid cheek exposure" and "try bare-back styles or pretty straps on upper back." Likewise, a contestant with a "slender torso/heavy legs" should "avoid dark colors, which cause legs to stand out first." Following the list of specific figure flaws is a section labeled, "Average Body with Minor Figure Flaws." She concludes, "Contestants with multiple figure flaws should 'correct' their problems in order of importance, tackling the most obvious and potentially point-losing flaw, then the next, and so on" (138–41). Quite literally, the body is a project to be perfected bit by bit.

80 Wolf, *Beauty Myth*, 21.

81 Wolf, *Beauty Myth*, 27–30.

82 Brumberg, *Body Project*, 123–24; Catherine G. Valentine, "Female Bodily Perfection and the Divided Self," in *Ideals of Feminine Beauty: Philosophical, Social, and Cultural Dimensions*, ed. Karen A. Callaghan (Westport, Conn.: Greenwood Press, 1994), 122. "My analysis of women's journals suggests that mediated images and standards of female bodily perfection, which fuse the surface of women's bodies with women's deepest feelings of self-worth, are a primary means of societal control of women . . . What better way to keep women in their place than with selves divided against themselves, awash in negative emotionality and engaged in self-surveillance. The inevitable failure of the female body to conform to images of perfection is experienced as moral stigma, producing a confluence of negative feelings that locks women into an unrelenting and unforgiving focus on the embodied self, a focus that ensures the continued social control of women by women as well as men and through self-policing."

83 Rhode, *Beauty Bias*, 61–63.

84 Rhode, *Beauty Bias*, 79. "Of the sixteen female United States senators between ages forty-six and seventy-four, not one has visible gray hair; nor do 90 percent of the women in the House of Representatives."

85 Rhode, *Beauty Bias*, 44.

86 Rhode, *Beauty Bias*, 26. "Parents and teachers give less attention to less attractive children, and they are less likely to be viewed as good, smart, cheerful, likeable, and socially skilled than their more attractive counterparts."

87 Rhode, *Beauty Bias*, 77.

88 Deford, *There She Is*, 70. This name change had been proposed as early as 1971 when Frank Deford's book on Miss America was published. Deford recalls that Ken Gaughran, the director of the Miss Westchester County Pageant in New York, said, "All you have to do is stop calling it 'swimsuit.' You call it 'Physical Fitness.' It's the same thing as always, but all of a sudden, it's health, not sex. Nobody can be against physical fitness."

89 Bivans, *In Pursuit of the Crown*, 73–75. The percentage of a contestant's score tied to the swimsuit competition has changed over time as has how judges assessed the contestants. The last year the lifestyle and fitness portion was held at the national pageant was the Miss America 2018 Pageant held in Atlantic City in September 2017. The 2018 Miss America Competition Magazine cited "maintain[ing] a healthy lifestyle of nutrition and physical fitness while displaying composure, energy, and confidence" as the criteria for scoring the lifestyle and fitness portion of the competition (71). By contrast, the 2011 Miss America Competition Magazine listed "overall 'first impression,' physical fitness, attractiveness, confidence & presence, and energy, charisma, a marketable presence" as the criteria.

90 Miss America's Outstanding Teen website, maoteen.org.

91 Miss America's Outstanding Teen website, maoteen.org.

92 Miss America television broadcast, 2011, 2014.

93 Miss Texas Pageant, Charles W. Eisemann Center, Richardson, Texas, June 30–July 2, 2016, on-site visit.

94 Will Henderson, "Top 10 Gowns of 2013," thepageantguy.com. Henderson ranked Rogers' gown seventh. He reported her thoughts about her gown as well as a quote from Angela Hardin, "veteran pageant judge in the USA system": "I love white, always, and the sheer cut outs just were so sexy. I loved just how daring her gown was I literally gasped when she walked out . . . it fit her perfectly!"

95 *Miss Alabama Pageant Program*. Contestants were taught that part of Miss America's job was playing a variety of roles with a kind of effortless perfection. Bivans, in her book *101 Secrets*, uses the language of "image." "Know the Image of the Pageant You Enter," and how to adjust your image depending on the setting, she counsels. She used Leanza Cornett, Miss America 1993, as an example of someone who did this well (44–49). Banet-Weiser, *Most Beautiful Girl*, offers helpful analysis of Miss America as "role model" (101–3).

96 Bernie Wayne, Miss America theme song, 1955.

97 Rhode, *Beauty Bias*, 46. Rhode also notes that height in men has proven a desirable trait across time and culture.

98 Sam Haskell with David Rensin, foreword by Ray Romano, *Promises I Made My Mother* (New York: Ballantine Books, 2009).

99 Miss America Pageant, Boardwalk Hall, Atlantic City, September 8, 2017, on-site visit.

100 Yashar Ali, "The Miss America Emails: How the Pageant's CEO Really Talks about the Winners," *Huffington Post*, December 22, 2017.

101 Ali, "Miss America Emails." Haskell drove potential clients away from Mallory Hagan's pageant coaching business and routinely was known for ostracizing people who challenged him. The patriarchy and sexism of American culture proved so rampant that it invaded even female spaces. Even there women could not be expected to govern themselves without a father figure. Trouble is, such heavy-handed and unquestionable authority is a breeding ground for abuse. Although the analogy is imperfect and one should be cautious, a similar dynamic may be seen in the (many) clergy sex abuse scandals. See Michael D'Antonio, *Mortal Sins: Sex, Crime, and the Era of Catholic Scandal* (New York: Thomas Dunne, 2013); and Curtis Freeman, "All-Male Clergy Deserves Scrutiny in Southern Baptist Abuse Scandal," *Houston Chronicle*, February 15, 2019.

102 Yashar Ali, "CEO Suspended after 49 Former Miss Americas Call on the Organizations Leaders to Resign," *Huffington Post*, December 27, 2017.

103 As Gretchen Carlson, Miss America Board Chair, noted, "We're experiencing a cultural revolution in our country with women finding the courage to stand up and have their voices heard on many issues. Miss America is proud to evolve as an organization and join this empowerment movement." Eun Kyung Kim, "Miss America Gets Rid of Swimsuit Competition: 'We are no longer a pageant,'" *Today*, June 5, 2018, today.com.

104 Kim, "Miss America Gets Rid."

105 Jessica Bennett, "Goodbye, Swimsuit Competition. Hello, 'Miss America 2.0,'" *New York Times*, June 5, 2018; Amanda Coyne, "Everything to Know about This Year's Miss America Pageant," *Cosmopolitan*, September 4, 2018.

106 Dow, "Feminism, Miss America."

107 Banet-Weiser, *Most Beautiful Girl*, ch. 4, "Bodies of Difference: Race, Nation, and the Troubled Reign of Vanessa Williams," 123–52; Bivans, *In Pursuit of the Crown*, 28; Craig, *Ain't I a Beauty Queen*, 75–76; and Dawn Perlmutter, "Miss America: Whose Ideal?" in *Beauty Matters*, ed. Peg Zeglin Brand (Indianapolis: Indiana University Press, 2000), 155–68. To be sure, Miss America still portrayed a very "white" style of beauty, so some African Americans criticized black women who chose to downplay their ethnic qualities to participate in this white arena. Nevertheless, this marked a crucial turning point in the pageant. While there is not room to discuss its significance fully, it should be noted that Sam Haskell formally apologized to Vanessa Williams at the 2016 Miss America Pageant. Williams served as one of the

celebrity judges for the final evening of competition. Holly Yan, "Vanessa Williams Gets Miss America Apology—32 Years Later," *CNN*, September 14, 2015, cnn.com.

108 See n. 47 in this chapter.

109 Alan Duke, "Miss Universe Pageant Ends Ban on Transgender Contestants," *CNN*, April 10, 2012, cnn.com.

110 Diana Tourjée, "Miss America Used to Ban Abortion—And Still Bans Moms, Wives, and Divorcées," *Vice*, September 13, 2017, vice.com.

111 A western state pageant official, quoted in Deford, *There She Is*, 70.

Chapter 2: Miss America as Entertainment

1 Tom Ryan, a vice president at Gillette, a longtime Miss America sponsor, quoted in Melinda Beck et al., "A Controversial 'Spectator Sport,'" *Newsweek*, September 17, 1984.

2 For a history of Miss America's relationship with television through the 1980s, see A. R. Riverol, *Live from Atlantic City: A History of the Miss America Pageant before, after and in spite of Television* (Bowling Green, Ohio: Bowling Green State University Popular Press, 1992).

3 Riverol, *Live from Atlantic City*. See also Frank Deford, "Live, from NBC," in Frank Deford, *There She Is: The Life and Times of Miss America* (New York: Viking Press), 190–208; and Angela Saulino Osborne, "Television," in Angela Saulino Osborne, *Miss America: The Dream Lives On: A 75 Year Celebration* (Dallas: Taylor, 1995), 104–15.

4 For example, 27 million people watched the pageant the first year it aired on television compared to only 4.3 million people who tuned in for the 2019 pageant held in September 2018. See Riverol, *Live from Atlantic City*, 56; and Toni Fitzgerald, "Miss America 2019 Ratings: Viewership Falls Again for Revamped Pageant," *Forbes*, September 10, 2018. According to Deford, the pageant reached peak viewership in 1970 when Nielsen computed that 80 million people watched the contest. Deford, *There She Is*, 195. According to Watson and Martin, Nielsen ratings dropped from the high 30s in the 60s to 13.1 in 1996 (119 and 124). Television ratings certainly tell a portion of the story, though that story can be interpreted in multiple ways. For example, Watson and Martin conclude, "If television ratings reflect societal beliefs, then the consistently declining ratings support the contention that the pageant is a thing of the past." Elwood Watson and Darcy Martin, "The Miss America Pageant: Pluralism, Femininity, and Cinderella All in One," *Journal of Popular Culture* 34, no. 1 (2000): 105–26, here 122. Journalist Joal Ryan suggested a compatible, though alternate, idea in 2015 that "the world got bigger." Miss America no longer "had the monopoly on girlhood dreams" and had been forced to share the stage with other entertainers, athletes, and ever growing opportunities for women to seek pleasure and accomplishment. Still, she maintains, "yes, some women will aspire to be Miss America. In a bigger world, after all, there's room for everybody. Everybody who survives. And Miss America is nothing if not a survivor." "So what ever happened to Miss America?" she mused. "Nothing and everything." Joal Ryan, "How Miss America Stopped Being Our Biggest Celebrity," *Yahoo! Entertainment*, September 13,

2015, yahoo.com. I contend that part of Miss America's ability to survive depended on the program's ability to continue marketing itself as entertainment beyond television even as it tried to maintain its primetime slot.

5 See, for example, pageantjunkies.com and pageantplanet.com.

6 Other movies about pageants include: *Smile* (1975), *Beautiful* (2000), *Miss Congeniality 2* (2005), *Little Miss Sunshine* (2006), and *Dumplin'* (2018). For a fascinating discussion of what movies about pageants teach us about female beauty, see Sophie Gilbert, "What *Dumplin'* and *Queen America* Say about Female Beauty," *Atlantic*, December 13, 2018.

7 In the early years of the pageant, the Miss America contest offered space to women formerly confined to the private sphere. "Respectable" women could seek pleasure and participate in public performance in ways formerly considered out of bounds. As Banet-Weiser noted, "The Miss America pageant rapidly became unlike any other beauty pageant or contest in the country in its relentless policing of femininity and behavior. This was precisely the effect that Lenora Slaughter sought in her crusade to construct the pageant as a rare entertainment venue for 'respectable' girls." See Sarah Banet-Weiser, *The Most Beautiful Girl in the World: Beauty Pageants and National Identity* (Los Angeles: University of California Press, 1999), 39. Women still cite a love of performing and having fun as reasons for participating in the pageant.

8 Evidence of Americans' obsession with entertainment and leisure are easily spotted. Consider, for example, the number of concerts and theater performances conducted around the nation each year. From community theater to Broadway, Americans routinely paid money to be entertained. For a basic overview of America's acceptance of sound movies, radio, and television, see Edward D. Berkowitz, *Mass Appeal: The Formative Age of the Movies, Radio, and TV* (New York: Cambridge University Press, 2010).

9 For an insightful overview of burlesque in American culture, see Robert Clyde Allen, *Horrible Prettiness: Burlesque and American Culture* (Chapel Hill: University of North Carolina Press, 1991). For a look at "lower-class" women and leisure in the early twentieth century, see Kathy Peiss, *Cheap Amusements: Working Women and Leisure in Turn-of-the-Century New York* (Philadelphia: Temple University Press, 1986).

10 Of course "women in the entertainment industry" can also refer to women who worked as prostitutes or were involved in the pornography industry where the line between consumer and producer becomes even more blurred. In the pageant, women were entertained even as they were entertaining.

11 Christie Anne Farnham, *The Education of the Southern Belle: Higher Education and Student Socialization in the Antebellum South* (New York: New York University Press, 1994), 168–69. For more on the image of the southern "lady," see Anne Firor Scott, *The Southern Lady: From Pedestal to Politics, 1830–1930*, 25th Anniversary Edition (Charlottesville: University Press of Virginia, 1995).

12 Judson College yearbook, *Conversationalist*, 1920, n.p.

13 Farnham, *Southern Belle*, 168–69.

14 Farnham, *Southern Belle*, 169–70.

15 Here, as in the pageant, women both embodied and reinscribed gender through their performance of femininity. See Judith Butler, preface to *Gender Trouble: Feminism and the Subversion of Identity* (New York: Routledge, 1999).

16 Lois W. Banner, *American Beauty* (Chicago: University of Chicago Press, 1983), 255–56; and Timothy J. Lukes, *Politics and Beauty in America: The Liberal Aesthetics of P. T. Barnum, John Muir, and Harley Earl* (New York: Palgrave Macmillan, 2016), 118.

17 Banner, *American Beauty*, 255–56; and Lukes, *Politics and Beauty*, 118.

18 Allen, *Horrible Prettiness*, 64–65. "At mid-century Barnum and Kimball lured this class to the theater through the back door of the museum and under the cloak of moral education. The key to their success was removing the impediments to middle-class women attending plays. All this required was transforming the theater as a social institution. The markers of gender and class solidarity were expunged: alcohol, prostitution, boisterous behavior, and audience control."

19 "People and Events: Origins of the Beauty Pageant," PBS, shoppbs.pbs.org; and Banner, *American Beauty*, 255–56. As Banner reports, Barnum "sold his museum before the photographs arrived," so he never implemented his "Congress of Beauty" (255). Still "the last report of the contest in *Humphrey's Journal* indicated that the new owners attempted to carry out his plan." And clearly Barnum was on to something. "Critic Alexander Woollcott remembered that during the Trilby craze all the dime museums in New York City held contests in which patrons voted among a number of women for the perfect Trilby" (258).

20 Banner, *American Beauty*, 258; "People and Events." See also Banner's discussion of newspaper contests in *American Beauty*, 256–58.

21 Banner, *American Beauty*, 265; and Deford, *There She Is*, 108–10.

22 Banner, *American Beauty*, 259–61.

23 William Morris, "In an Editorial Way," *Ladies' Home Journal* 24, no. 5 (April 1907), 5–6; and "The Loveliest Girls in America," *Ladies' Home Journal* 28, no. 5 (March 1, 1911), 3. Deborah G. Felder, *A Century of Women: The Most Influential Events in Twentieth-Century Women's History* (New York: Citadel Press Books, 1999), 111.

24 According to Allen in *Horrible Prettiness*, "burlesque is one of several nineteenth-century entertainment forms that is grounded in the aesthetics of transgression, inversion, and the grotesque. The burlesque performer represents a construction of what Peter Stallybrass and Allon White call the 'low other': something that is reviled by and excluded from the dominant social order as debased, dirty, and unworthy, but that is simultaneously the object of desire and/or fascination" (26). Thus burlesque had "transgressive potential" and "only when we come to see burlesque as a monstrosity 'out of all keeping,' as White called it, can we begin to sense the imperative to tame burlesque or at least to keep it out of sight" (156). As Allen demonstrates, burlesque does get integrated "into the American show business system" through its "marginalization and social reorientation toward a working-class male audience" (160). Like the Miss America Pageant, "burlesque is emblematic of the way that popular entertainment becomes an arena for 'acting out' cultural contradictions and even contestations and is exemplary of the complexities and ambiguities of this process" (27).

25 As Allen notes, "From *Ixion* on, burlesque in America was inextricably tied to the issue of the spectacular female performer, and from then on burlesque implicitly raised troubling questions about how a woman should be 'allowed' to act on stage, about how femininity should and could be represented, and about the relationship of women onstage to women in the outside, 'real' world." Allen, *Horrible Prettiness*, 21. See also 155–56.

26 Allen, *Horrible Prettiness*.

27 As Kate Shindle, Miss America 1998, noted, "Speaking for myself, when I competed 20 years ago, I found the swimsuit competition oddly empowering, because once I could walk across the stage in a two-piece swimsuit and high heels I could do just about anything. But I also don't think I processed everything at the time. It's strange—it gives strangers a kind of ownership over your body that you don't quite anticipate." Jessica Bennett, "Miss America Scraps Swimsuits, Making Strides to Reshape Image," *New York Times*, June 8, 2018.

28 In *American Beauty*, Banner claims that the Miss America Pageant "successfully combined the features of lower-class carnivals with upper-class festivals" (260–61). As noted in ch. 1, this freedom was not an unequivocal move toward progress. Again, these words from Banner are instructive: "As the beauty queen left her throne in the tournament and festival, stepped out of the photograph, and shed her clothes, donning a bathing suit so that more of her body could be seen, women also shed their association with morality, masked their professional skills, and became sex objects, competing in an arena where men were the judges and the promoters. The rise to eminence of the model opened a new career for women and dignified for them many sensual associations previously seen as suspect. On the other hand, the model brought with her an emphasis on the body that was not liberating, but rather confining, and that locked women into stereotypes in many ways more destructive than the old ones" (264). Banner, like many other scholars, resists the implication that the pageant was about anything other than beauty (269–70).

29 Banner, *American Beauty*, 268. See also Ann-Marie Bivans, *Miss America: In Pursuit of the Crown* (New York: MasterMedia Limited, 1991), 8–11; and Deford, *There She Is*, 110–16.

30 This sentiment, of course, extended beyond women "entertaining" or "performing" to include all of women's engagement in the public sphere. In 1905, former United States president Grover Cleveland argued against women's suffrage using this logic, claiming, "It is sane intelligence, and not sentimental delusion, that discovers between the relative duties and responsibilities of man and woman, as factors in the growth of civilization, a natural equilibrium, so nicely adjusted to the attributes and limitations of both that it cannot be disturbed without social confusion and peril." Thus, he notes later, "It is its [women's suffrage's] dangerous undermining effect on the characters of the wives and mothers of our land that we fear." In the same article, Cleveland lamented, "None of us can deny that we have unhappily fallen upon a time when doctrines are taught by women, and to women, which tend with more or less directness to the subversion of sane and wholesome ideas of the work and mission of womanhood,

and lead to a fanciful insistence upon sharing in the stern, rugged and unwomanly duties and responsibilities allotted to man." Women might think they would improve the world with the vote, but, Cleveland argued, women's suffrage would have little, if any, benefit on the outcome of elections. And, in the process, they would put their womanhood at stake. "Women change politics less than politics change women." Grover Cleveland, "Would Woman Suffrage Be Unwise?" *Ladies' Home Journal* 22, no. 11 (October 1905), 22. I am indebted to R. Marie Griffith for making me aware of this piece by Grover Cleveland. She quoted from the article in her lecture, "The Culture Wars in the Early 20th Century: Suffrage, Birth Control, and Censorship," given at Baylor University on September 17, 2018. Griffith also quotes Cleveland in her book, *Moral Combat: How Sex Divided American Christians and Fractured American Politics* (New York: Basic Books, 2017), xv.

31 Riverol, *Live from Atlantic City*, 46, 49–50, and 54–56. Pageant organizers were not wrong to anticipate how television would impact ticket sales. The 1954 pageant, held in September 1953, sold out all 25,000 tickets. In comparison, Miss America 1955, held in September 1954 and the first to be televised, sold only 18,000 tickets to the final night's competition. See also Deford, *There She Is*, 193–94.

32 At some point, the final night of competition changed to Sunday night.

33 Riverol, *Live from Atlantic City*, 55–56; and Deford, *There She Is*, 193–94.

34 Deford, *There She Is*, 204; and Riverol, *Live from Atlantic City*, 55. In later years, Miss Americas would regain some of their voice, speaking at various points during pageant week and often having a voiceover thank you speech during their final walks as Miss America before crowning their successors.

35 Riverol, *Live from Atlantic City*, 90–91 and 115–21. Riverol discusses some of these changes and adaptations through the decades in his book. He concludes, "Television had, has and will leave its mark on the basic structure of the pageant as experienced live and in person in Convention Hall. These changes were not abrupt but rather gradual" (115).

36 Riverol, *Live from Atlantic City*, 90.

37 Miss America 2019, held in September 2018, aired on ABC on Sunday, September 9, 2018 from 9:00 p.m. to 11:00 p.m. Eastern Standard Time. Jim Donnelly, "Watch the 2019 Miss America Competition Live SUNDAY, September 9 on ABC," *ABC*, August 29, 2018, abc.go.com/news/insider. To be sure, the preliminary competitions leading up to the televised finals went beyond this two-hour time frame.

38 See Banet-Weiser, *Most Beautiful Girl*, esp. 171–75. "More specifically," she writes, "mass-mediated entertainment culture—the culture of the Miss America pageant— provides the venue for a national identification with the Miss America contestant, as she simultaneously embodies national desire." "It's the biggest Cinderella story in America," Bert Parks wrote, "It's everyone's dream of what America should be like: The purity, the beauty, the great America Dream can all be vicariously realized, watching the beauty of this pageant unfold in its two hours on television." Bert Parks, "And Now, a Few Words from the Emcee . . . ," *New York Times*, September

10, 1977. The pageant contributed to American understandings of themselves in a manner designed to please, not provoke.

39 Deford, *There She Is*, 8–9. "The critics who attack Miss America for being irresponsible and escapist miss the whole point. Of course it is. Miss America is escapist, and so are Disneyland and the Baltimore Colts, so is a skinny dip and so is Johnny Carson . . . Bert Parks, Miss America emcee since 1955 . . . says, 'It's corny. Let's face it. It's corny and it's basic and it's American. But in this sick, sad world a little fairyland is welcome and refreshing. Apparently, from the figures, we are right. About the only thing I agree with Mr. Nixon on is that, yes, there are a lot of nice people out there beyond the big, slick areas—and these are good, straight people for the most part. Perhaps they are narrow, but they have a great longing for normalcy, as so many of us do, and Miss America buys them a piece of that dream. For two marvelous hours, you have it all. For two hours out of 365 days.'"

40 Miss America 2005, held in September 2004 and broadcast on ABC, got a record low (at that time) of 9.8 million viewers. This led to ABC discontinuing their contract with Miss America. Lisa de Moraes, "No More Miss America Pageantry for ABC," *Washington Post*, October 21, 2004.

41 Tanner Stransky, "Who Killed Miss America?" *Entertainment Weekly*, January 30, 2010, ew.com. Sarah Banet-Weiser and Laura Portwood-Stacer, "'I just want to be me again!' Beauty Pageants, Reality Television and Post-feminism," *Feminist Theory* 7, no. 2 (2006): 255–72; and Shindle, *Being Miss America*, 182–87.

42 Iver Peterson, "'Fear Factor' Era Poses a Challenge for Miss America," *New York Times*, April 9, 2005.

43 Peterson, "'Fear Factor' Era."

44 Associated Press, "Miss America Ratings Drop, Despite Gimmicks," *Today*, September 21, 2004, today.com.

45 The pageant aired on Country Music Television (CMT) in 2006 and 2007. When Miss America left network television, ratings dropped even lower, bottoming out at 2.4 million in 2007 on Country Music Television (CMT). Kimberly Nordyke, "CMT Drops Miss America Pageant," *Reuters*, March 30, 2007, reuters.com.

46 Jacques Steinberg, "Miss America as She Used to Be: Relocated Pageant Returns to Basics," *New York Times*, December 22, 2005.

47 Steinberg, "As She Used to Be."

48 CMT changed its tune a bit the next year. They added a two-hour special, "Pageant School," to help get the television audience primed for the main event. In other words, they saw some potential in adding back a few elements of reality television to increase audience buy-in. "Miss America 2007 Contestants Enroll in Pre-Pageant Training for CMT's 'Pageant School: Becoming Miss America,'" *CMT Press*, December 12, 2006, cmtpress.com.

49 Nordyke, "CMT Drops."

50 Stephanie Sadre-Orafai, "The Figure of the Model and Reality TV," in *Fashioning Models: Image, Text and Industry*, ed. Joanne Entwistle and Elizabeth Wissinger, 123–24; and Kate Shindle, *Being Miss America: Behind the Rhinestone Curtain* (Austin:

University of Texas Press, 2014), 182–83. See also I. A., "The Missed Potential of Miss America Reality Check," *MTV News*, January 24, 2008, mtv.com/news; Kathleen Hennessey, "Pageant Makes Miss America Butt of the Joke," *Today*, January 24, 2008, today.com; Dave Walker, "Show Injects a Little 'Survivor' into Miss America," *Seattle Times*, January 4, 2008; "Miss Michigan Wins Miss America 2008 Title," *Today*, January 26, 2008, today.com.

51 Sadre-Orafai, "Figure of the Model and Reality TV," 123–24.

52 Stransky, "Who Killed Miss America?" For a collection of interdisciplinary essays that consider "the ways in which reality is reflected by and refracted through television programming as well as the ways in which television serves to frame and fuel discussions about events in the world," see James Friedman, ed., *Reality Squared: Televisual Discourse on the Real* (New Brunswick, N.J.: Rutgers University Press, 2002), here p. 2.

53 Lesley Young, "Beauty Queen with Autism Makes Miss America History," *Disability Scoop*, January 15, 2013, disabilityscoop.com.

54 Jennifer Jones, "The Beauty Queen as Deified Sacrificial Victim," *Theatre History Studies* 18 (June 1998): 99.

55 See, for example, Deford, *There She Is*, 155–58; and Jane Jayroe with Bob Burke, *More Grace than Glamour: My Life as Miss America and Beyond* (Oklahoma City: Oklahoma Heritage Association, 2006), 93.

56 Miss Americas routinely write of their speaking engagements and other appearances in their autobiographies. For example, in *Being Miss America*, Kate Shindle discussed her experience speaking in schools "across every demographic group and age group and location" about HIV and AIDS. The school visits, she declared, were her "favorite of all" (101–7).

57 The most obvious example is that of local, state, and national pageants inviting previous titleholders back to perform at, or emcee for, the current year's pageant. As Jane Jayroe recounted of her year as Miss America 1967, "I attended a lot of pageants and fashion shows in the United States, Canada, and Europe and rode in many parades. I threw out the first baseball to open the season for the Kansas City Athletics and conducted symphony orchestras." Her experience reflected that of many others who wore the crown before and after. Jayroe, *More Grace than Glamour*, 108.

58 Frank Deford, writing in 1971, noted, "Miss America is a well-paid product. She has no transportation or other expenses on the road, nor is she required to pay an agent's or booking fee to Atlantic City. The bonanza is neatly spread over two tax years, too. Besides a free wardrobe and the $10,000 scholarship, any Miss America makes upward of $50,000 in her year." Deford, *There She Is*, 274. In 2018, Miss America's scholarship was $50,000, and she earned a six-figure salary during her year of service. Jordan Lauf, "What Does Miss America 2019 Win? The Prize May Be Similar to Last Year's, But the Pageant Is Radically Different," *Bustle*, September 9, 2018, bustle .com. For a discussion of the "salary structure, implemented around the time of the move from Atlantic City," see Shindle, *Being Miss America*, 200.

59   While numerous examples exist, five non-autobiographies written by Miss Americas prove the point. Vonda Kay Van Dyke, *Dear Vonda Kay: Former Miss America Vonda Kay Van Dyke Answers Questions Teen-agers Ask* (Westwood, N.J.: Fleming H. Revell Company, 1967); Heather Whitestone McCallum with Carolyn Curtis, *Believing the Promise: Daily Devotions for Following Your Dreams* (New York: Doubleday, 1999); Sharlene Hawkes, *Kissing a Frog: Four Steps to Finding Comfort Outside Your Comfort Zone* (Salt Lake City: Shadow Mountain, 2002); Katie Harman with the 2001 Miss America Contestants, *Under the Crown: 51 Stories of Courage, Determination and the American Spirit* (Seattle: Milestone Books, 2002); and Robin Marsh and Lauren Nelson, *God, Girls, and Getting Connected: Spiritual Apps for a Teen's Life* (Eugene, Ore.: Harvest House Publishers, 2012).

60   The Miss America Organization had a separate Twitter feed with over 54,000 followers.

61   Miss Alabama, for example, had over 5,000 Twitter followers and over 15,000 followers on Facebook. Miss Montana had roughly 2,400 followers on Twitter and 3,000 on Facebook. Not only did the number of followers vary drastically by state, so, too, did the frequency with which the social media profiles and pages were updated.

62   A plethora of news outlets covered this controversy. For two samples, see Lauren Carroll, "Miss America 2018 Cara Mund Pens Letter on Being 'Silenced,'" *Press of Atlantic City*, August 17, 2018; and Amy Argetsinger, "'No Miss America Should Be Humiliated': Before Giving Up Crown, Cara Mund Blasts Pageant Leadership," *Washington Post*, August 17, 2018.

63   See the Miss America website, missamerica.org.

64   For example, Nicole Johnson, Miss America 1999; Kirsten Haglund, Miss America 2008; and Nina Davuluri, Miss America 2014, all maintain a website. See nicolejohnson.com, kirstenhaglund.com, and ninadavuluri.com.

65   Chris Saltalamacchio, better known as Pageant Chris to his Twitter followers (@ pageantchris), is one such coach and pageant expert. Pageant Chris boasted almost 9,000 Twitter followers including past and present pageant contestants, clients, and fans. His company, Pageantry by Chris, offered a variety of services (in person, Skype video, and phone) to pageant hopefuls including interview coaching, wardrobe selection, and platform development. I became acquainted with Chris via his live-tweeting of pageants. See pageantrybychris.com.

66   Kate Shindle discusses the "unpleasant surprise of finding out what seemingly everybody thinks of me" in ch. 11 of her book, *Being Miss America*, here p. 127.

67   *Pageant Junkies*, pageantjunkies.com.

68   Some of the winners hosted by Lakey on her podcast included Teresa Scanlan, Miss America 2011; Ali Rogers, Miss South Carolina 2012; Katie Stam Irk, Miss America 2009; Ashton Campbell, Miss Arkansas 2014; and Taylor Wiebers, Miss Iowa 2015. Interviews with each of these women are filed under "Top 12 Podcasts of All Time."

69   For more on the presence, and potential dangers, of princess culture and the sexualization of girls in America, see Rebecca C. Hains, *The Princess Problem: Guiding our Girls through the Princess-Obsessed Years* (Naperville, Ill.: Sourcebooks, 2014); Peggy

Orenstein, *Cinderella Ate My Daughter: Dispatches from the Front Lines of the New Girlie-Girl Culture* (New York: HarperCollins, 2011); and Patrice A. Oppliger, *Girls Gone Skank: The Sexualization of Girls in American Culture* (Jefferson, N.C.: McFarland & Company, 2008).

70 The pervasiveness of this phenomenon is evidenced by the existence of a Huffington Post article about hosting a Miss America party. "Because after all, philosophical objections aside, everyone love [*sic*] a good party, and everyone wants a chance to be Queen." See Laura Hanby Hudgens, "Make Miss America Great Again! Host a Miss America Party," *Huffington Post*, July 22, 2016.

71 To be sure, not all viewers watched to be entertained. Some had far more complicated relationships to the pageant. Carol Hanisch, one of the organizers of the 1968 feminist protest of Miss America, recounted the reflections of the New York Radical Women regarding the influence of the pageant in their lives. "We discovered that many of us who had always put down the contest still watched it. Others, like myself, had consciously identified with it, and had cried with the winner." Carol Hanisch, "What Can Be Learned: A Critique of the Miss America Protest," November 27, 1968, box S17, "Demonstrations: Miss America 1968" folder, in Robin Morgan Papers, David M. Rubenstein Rare Book and Manuscript Library, Duke University, Durham, North Carolina. This feeling of uneasiness, or embarrassment, over watching the pageant remains for some viewers. See, for example, Jennifer Weiner, "Miss America, My Guilty Pleasure," *New York Times*, September 12, 2015.

Chapter 3: Miss America as Competition

1 Kate Shindle, *Being Miss America: Behind the Rhinestone Curtain* (Austin: University of Texas Press, 2014), 11.

2 Miss America Pageant, Planet Hollywood Resort & Casino, Las Vegas, January 15, 2011, on-site visit.

3 In 2018, the pageant shifted its internal language, choosing to refer to the event in Atlantic City as the Miss America Competition rather than the Miss America Pageant. Candidates, not contestants, competed for the job of Miss America. Certainly, the contest functioned as a competition long before this shift in nomenclature. Despite talk of personal bests and camaraderie between contestants, competitors wanted to win. And only one of them walked away with the crown. For an overview of how competition functions in beauty pageants, see Rebecca L. Shaiber, Laura L. Johnsen, and Glenn Geher, "Intrasexual Competition among Beauty Pageant Contestants," in *The Oxford Handbook of Women and Competition*, ed. Maryanne L. Fisher (New York: Oxford University Press, 2017). "While beauty pageants are novel and entirely modern, the traits that allow one to compete against rivals have a long, evolved history that match those that allow one to be successful in competing for mates." Shaiber, Johnsen, and Geher argued that "beauty competitions elicit similar intrasexually competitive behaviors observed in a mating context, such as self-promotion, competitor manipulation, and competitor derogation." These three

tactics were observed in my own research about how women compete in pageants and will be incorporated into the discussion in this chapter when useful.

4 Some studies have shown "gender differences in competitiveness" with men tending to be more competitive than women. "Although the phenomenon has been quite robustly established, more work is needed to assess the importance of gender differences in competitiveness in accounting for gender differences in educational and career outcomes." See Muriel Niederle and Lise Vesterlund, "Gender and Competition," *Annual Review of Economics* 3 (2001): 601–30, here 625; and Muriel Niederle and Lise Vesterlund, "Do Women Shy Away from Competition? Do Men Compete Too Much?" *Quarterly Journal of Economics* 122, no. 3 (2007): 1067–1101. These studies, of course, examine competition between men and women. Other scholars suggest that the conclusion that men are more competitive is too simple and that it is important to study and consider intrasexual competition to get a fuller picture. It may be the case, at least in part, that women merely compete differently than men and are motivated by different things.

The most comprehensive overview of women's competition is *The Oxford Handbook of Women and Competition*, ed. Maryanne Fisher (New York: Oxford University Press, 2017). From the introduction: "Researchers need to determine the spheres in which women compete, rather than simply examine hierarchies and dominance, as women compete in many arenas and these traditional schemas may not be relevant. Turning one's research focus to these previously unexplored areas was critical, given that women's intrasexual competition rarely involves escalating contests, and that women suppress it when men are present in order to avoid seeming undesirable. The chapters in this book indicate there have been sufficient advances in methodologies and research design that have enabled empirical examination of women's notoriously subtle and covert intrasexual competition."

Pageants represent just one space among many in which women compete "to gain access to males, status, dominance, or resources" (Fisher). See also Bobbi S. Low, "Competition throughout Women's Lives," in *The Oxford Handbook of Women and Competition*, ed. Maryanne L. Fisher (New York: Oxford University Press, 2017).

5 See L. Kocum, D. Courvoisier, and S. Vernon, "The Buzz on the Queen Bee and Other Characterizations of Women's Intrasexual Competition at Work," in *The Oxford Handbook of Women and Competition*, ed. Maryanne L. Fisher (New York: Oxford University Press, 2017); and Evelyn Fox Keller and Helene Moglen, "Competition and Feminism: Conflicts for Academic Women," *Signs* 12, no. 3 (1987): 493–511.

6 Deborah L. Rhode, *The Beauty Bias: The Injustice of Appearance in Life and Law* (New York: Oxford University Press, 2010), 46. See also Lois W. Banner, *American Beauty* (Chicago: University of Chicago Press, 1983); and Nancy Etcoff, *Survival of the Prettiest: The Science of Beauty* (New York: Doubleday, 1999).

7 "It's a totally contradictory model. She should be strong but weak, aggressive but submissive, totally committed to her career and her family, have touches of the social worker, and basically walk on water in high-heeled shoes and make it look easy."

Richard Wilk, quoted in Jill Neimark, "Why We Need Miss America," *Psychology Today* 31, no. 5 (1998). Pageant contenders, like many American women outside the pageant bubble, chased perfection in a desire to prove they could "have it all."

8   A quick Google search for "pageant coaches" turns up a number of resources. See, for example, prpageantcoaches.com, valeriehayes.com, and thepageantcoach.com. Pageant Planet, whose stated goal is "to connect and expand the pageant industry" (pageantplanet.com), ran a feature story on "Best Pageant Coaches: 2019 Edition" (with links to the 2016, 2017, and 2018 editions). The pageant-industrial complex in America was deep and wide.

9   At the national pageant, for example, it was common for state delegations to farm out letters to their fans that spelled the name of their respective state. These signs could be quite elaborate; some even contained blinking lights. As a participant observer, I often participated in the act of cheering for the competitors, gladly accepting props, signs, or buttons from proud family members or state delegations that adopted me. For example, I waved a light-up baton in support of Stephanie Yasechko's bid for Miss Ohio 2015. At the 2016 Miss America Pageant, held in September 2015, I helped hold up the sign for Miss Montana 2015, Danielle Wineman. And, at the 2019 Miss America Pageant, held in September 2018, I received a Texas state flag from the Texas delegation so that I could join them in their support of Miss Texas 2018, Madison Fuller. Being a pageant fan involved more than polite clapping after a talent number.

10 The final night of the national competition (televised) had "celebrity" judges and was scored differently. For the 2018 Miss America Pageant (held in September 2017), scores used to determine the winner were: composite score (25 percent), swimsuit (10 percent), evening wear (15 percent), talent (30 percent), question 1 (5 percent), and question 2 (15 percent).

11 Shirley Monty, *Terry* (Waco, Tex.: Word Books, 1982), 33.

12 Shindle, *Being Miss America*, 131–32.

13 Michelle Leifer, "She Lost 110 Lbs.—and Won Beauty Queen Crown," *Today*, July 8, 2011, today.com.

14 The Miss Alabama Local Judging Application noted, "Each Miss Alabama local preliminary pageant competition must have three judges from the official Miss Alabama Judges List. You may apply to be on the Miss Alabama Judges List by completing the attached forms and submitting them and all required attachments as noted at the bottom of the Miss Alabama Preliminary Judge Information Sheet." These items included the completed and signed sheet, a signed Miss Alabama Pageant Local Judges Agreement, a completed and signed Judges Disclaimer and Verification Form, a recent photo, and three letters of recommendation. The application to judge in the Miss North Carolina Pageant system was less extensive. It did not, for example, require recommendation letters. In 2007, I participated in Work Weekend for the Miss North Carolina Pageant in Raleigh, North Carolina. As part of that event, I attended the training session for individuals seeking to be certified as preliminary pageant judges in the Miss NC pageant system. That year, they combined the

seminar with one final preliminary pageant, Miss Raleigh. The packet of information stated, "The purpose of having a program during the seminar is to introduce judges to the actual processes, documents, and routine of judging." Panelists spoke on the mechanics of judges and adjudicating various elements of the competition throughout the pageant, and potential judges were encouraged to take notes and keep score. Potential judges also learned about one of the most controversial practices in pageant judging, "Final Ballot." See the following note for a discussion of Final Ballot.

15 For an example of the Miss America judges affidavit, see misskentuckypageant.com/sitebuildercontent/sitebuilderfiles/2016judgesaffidavit.pdf. Final Ballot involved ranking the top five contestants based on scores "in the order in which you believe each should finish in the pageant." Judges were to "think about the job description as well as the qualities and attributes necessary to perform the job of Miss Local/State. Consider all phases of competition and determine the order in which the contestants could best perform the job responsibilities of Miss America/Miss State/Miss Local and serve as the 'face' and the 'voice' of this Organization." Each ranking had a point value attached to it from ten points for a first-place ranking to one point for a fifth-place ranking. These points were then added up and the contestant with the most points won. In other words, "The outcome of the pageant is based solely on the scores from the final ballot. These points will NOT be added to the scores from the previous competitions" (Miss North Carolina Judging Seminar 2017 handouts). Individuals within the pageant community often had very strong feelings about the use of Final Ballot. At times, pageants were not required to use it, at times they were forbidden from using it, and at times it was left up to the local or state pageant. Even within the same pageant season, the rules could change. Finally, the national pageant did not always utilize Final Ballot either. But it remained a part of pageant parlance, loved by some, hated by others.

16 Frank Deford, *There She Is: The Life and Times of Miss America* (New York: Viking Press, 1971), 59. The points were awarded as follows: construction of head (15), eyes (10), hair (5), nose (5), mouth (5), facial expression (10), torso (10), legs (10), arms (10), hands (10), and grace of bearing (10).

17 "Named in honor of Miss America 1943, the Jean Bartel Quality of Life Award recognizes the countless community service hours that Miss America candidates contribute to charitable and humanitarian causes around the world. Recipients are chosen from qualified applicants who excel in their commitment to enhance the quality of life for others through volunteerism and community service, with emphasis on the depth of service, the creativity of the project, and the significant effects on the lives of others. In 1989, Miss America 1988 Kaye Lani Rae Rafko's community service efforts became the catalyst of the national platform for all candidates, as well as the inspiration for creating the Quality of Life Award." *Miss America 2.0 2019 Program*, 27.

18 Athletes who invested in outside practice, drills, and camps proved themselves willing to work hard and accept correction. They had not only their own interests, but also the interests of their team. Likewise, a proven record of service demonstrated a

contestant's willingness to work hard on behalf of a particular cause or organization. This signaled that they would also be a good goodwill ambassador for the pageant.

19 Pageant VoyForums became a popular site for discussing recent pageants, but fans could be found on practically every social media outlet commenting on pageant news. These discussions could turn ugly. See Shaiber, Johnsen, and Geher, "Intrasexual Competition."

20 Nicole Leonard, "Miss America Contestants Talk Strategy in Placement Lottery," *Press of Atlantic City*, July 14, 2015. "Current and former contestants said the lottery and placement selection requires research and patience to secure a spot that plays well to each contestant's strengths."

21 See debbyeturner.com.

22 Alec Harvey, "'War Eagle!': Miss America Mallory Hagan Talks Football and Growing Up in Opelika," al.com, January 14, 2013. Hagan spoke of her southern heritage in the article: "I've lived in like six different Brooklyn neighborhoods, so I definitely consider myself a New Yorker. I'm as New York as they come. I'm just wrapped in a more delicate Southern charm."

23 Adam Nougourney, "Mrs. Clinton Prepares for Residency and Campaign," *New York Times*, November 4, 1999.

24 In 1971, Deford noted in *There She Is* that Miss America "is strongest in the South and the western United States" (5). This claim holds true in 2019. In the history of the pageant, the South has produced thirty-four winners, the Midwest twenty-eight, the West sixteen, and the Northeast fifteen. The South's Miss America count increases to thirty-eight if you include the four Miss Americas from the South who won the national title while competing in a non-southern state (Nia Franklin, Miss America 2019, competed in Miss North Carolina before moving to New York to compete there. Miss America 2013, Mallory Hagan, competed in Miss Alabama before winning the title of Miss New York. Miss America 1990, Debbye Turner, competed in the Miss Arkansas pageant before capturing the Miss Missouri crown. And Miss America 1983, Debra Maffett, moved to California after failing to win the Miss Texas crown.) Of course, it should be noted that the South has seventeen contestants in the pageant each year compared to thirteen from the West, twelve from the Midwest, and nine from New England. Comparing divisions still highlights the success of southern and western states, but the East North Central division in the Midwest takes first place with nineteen Miss Americas from its five states of Illinois, Indiana, Michigan, Ohio, and Wisconsin. The South Atlantic and West South Central divisions tied for second with twelve Miss Americas each. New England has had only one Miss America, Marian Bergeron in 1933. Indeed, the idea that pageants are a southern phenomenon is so pervasive that it has been commented upon repeatedly by contestants, commentators, and scholars. For example, Kate Shindle, Miss America 1998, noted of the Miss America winners, "By and large, they are capital-L Ladies. Most are either Southern or have taken on a Southern-type identity of what it means to be feminine—a product, no doubt, of the fact that Miss America has always been more deeply in demand in the Bible Belt than anywhere else, and a girl's

got to learn how to walk softly and keep the big stick hidden." Shindle, *Being Miss America*, 11–12. See also n. 30 in this book's introduction.

25 For example, in the Miss America 2018 pageant, several of the finalists gave what would be considered liberal or progressive answers. See Sara M. Moniuszko, "Miss Texas Slammed Trump's Charlottesville Comments, More Miss America Political Moments," *USA Today*, September 11, 2017. In addition, the Northeast has produced only nine Miss Americas since 1921, with four of those wins occurring since 2013. Miss New York captured the crown to become Miss America 2013, 2014, 2015, and 2019. Of course, it should also be noted that two of those Miss New Yorks hailed from the South (2013, Alabama and 2019, North Carolina). One could also argue that more progressive women in traditionally conservative states found it easier to win in a non-southern state.

26 For one coach's opinion of how the three-point shot has fundamentally changed the game of basketball, see Michael Kaskey-Blomain, "Popovich Thinks 3-Point Shooting Has Made Basketball 'Boring,'" *24-7 Sports*, November 29, 2008, 247sports.com.

27 See "Four Points of the Crown and Four Winning Tips," *Four Points: Scholarship, Success, Style, Service*, April 30, 2013, fourpointsmagazine.com.

28 Miss America 1985, Sharlene Wells; Miss America 1990, Debbye Turner; and Miss America 2005, Deidre Downs, were among the many Miss Americas and Miss America hopefuls who participated with scholarships in mind. Sharlene Wells Hawkes, *Living in but Not of the World* (Salt Lake City: Deseret Book Company, 1997), 14–15; Lynn Norment, "Here She Is! Miss America Black, Beautiful, Brainy and Born-Again," *Ebony*, December 1989, 132; and Kristin Collins, "Miss America Exhorts Science Educators to Keep Teaching," National Science Teachers Association, December 12, 2007, nsta.org. See also Penny Pearlman, *Pretty Smart: Lessons from Our Miss Americas* (Bloomington, Ind.: AuthorHouse, 2009), 40, 53–54.

29 Even in states that awarded relatively low cash scholarship amounts, winners might gain access to in-kind scholarships. For example, in addition to her $5,000 scholarship, the 2015 Miss Rhode Island won full graduate-school tuition to Salve Regina University, half-tuition for an undergraduate tuition scholarship to Salve Regina University, and a $10,000 (renewable for four years) scholarship to Bryant University (*2015 Miss Rhode Island Scholarship Program*). Miss Ohio 2015 won a $10,000 scholarship as well as a $15,000 scholarship to Bluffton University, a $15,000 (renewable for four years) scholarship to Kenyon College, $1,000 (renewable for four years) to Muskingum University, and $2,500 (renewable for four years) scholarship to Malone University (*Miss Ohio 2015 Program*). Obviously, a state winner could not take advantage of all the awards available, which has led to some criticism about how the pageant counts the amount of scholarships it makes available. See ch. 1, n. 44 in this volume.

30 Some have questioned the benefit of travel baseball over Little League. See, for example, Eric Mann, "Academy's Chair of Sports Coaching Says 'Travel Ball' Model Is 'Misguided,'" *Sport Digest*, June 30, 2017, thesportdigest.com; and David Mendell,

"Stealing Home: How Travel Teams Are Eroding Community Baseball," *Washington Post*, May 23, 2014. Likewise, pageant critics note the high costs of competing. See Lucia Peters, "The Cost of Competing in Beauty Pageants Is Going to Blow Your Mind," *Bustle*, June 13, 2014, bustle.com; and Brenda Salina, "Beauty Pageant Economics: The Sash Isn't Cheap," NPR, *All Things Considered*, December 1, 2012, npr .org/programs/all-things-considered/.

31 For example, in addition to the $20,000 scholarship, Miss North Carolina 2018 won numerous "fashion awards," custom clothing, and gift certificates for clothes and shoes. She also received one year of fitness and nutritional services, a set of luggage, and a fashion watch—just to name a few of the bonus benefits. Indeed, the list of prizes was a page long. See missnc.org. Such awards from local sponsors were not unusual.

32 See ch. 2, n. 58 in this volume.

33 See missarkansas.org/news.htm.

34 For one example, see Trudi Gilfillian, "Designer to Make Dresses for All 53 Miss America contestants," *Press of Atlantic City*, August 3, 2014.

35 Pierre Bourdieu's theory of practice provided some helpful terminology for exploring the "capital" many pageant participants described. Bourdieu noted that much of his work focused on "the idea that struggles for recognition are a fundamental dimension of social life and that what is at stake in them is the accumulation of a particular form of capital." Pierre Bourdieu, *In Other Words: Essays Towards a Reflexive Sociology*, trans. Matthew Adamson (Stanford: Stanford University Press, 1990), 22. As Randal Johnson explained in an introduction to some of Bourdieu's work, "Authority based on consecration or prestige is purely symbolic and may or may not imply possession of increased economic capital. Bourdieu thus developed, as an integral part of his theory of practice, the concept of *symbolic power* based on diverse forms of capital which are not reducible to economic capital." Randal Johnson, "Editor's Introduction: Pierre Bourdieu on Art, Literature, and Culture," in *The Field of Cultural Production: Essays on Art and Literature*, by Pierre Bourdieu (New York: Columbia University Press, 1993), 7 (emphasis in original).

36 Johnson, "Editor's Introduction," 7.

37 Here I'm employing Bourdieu's description of symbolic capital "as capital founded on cognition [connaissance] and recognition [reconnaissance]." Bourdieu, *In Other Words*, 22.

38 Shaiber, Johnsen, and Geher, "Intrasexual Competition." "Likewise, winners of beauty pageants gain access to numerous resources (e.g., scholarship money, endorsements, and gifts) and high-status positions. While their reign as a beauty queen lasts for only one year, winners are able to make connections for future high-status and lucrative careers in entertainment, politics, literature, and finance. In other words, winning a beauty pageant solidifies a beauty queen's social standing for years to come."

39 Take, for example, Marilyn Van Derbur, Miss America 1958. An incest survivor, Van Derbur wrote, "I could never have imagined that, by using my story as the

scaffolding, it would be my mission to educate judges, doctors, nurses, lawyers, teachers, therapists and especially, parents. The titles of 'Miss America' and 'Outstanding Woman Speaker in America' gave me entrée into being the keynote speaker for audiences as diverse as the National Association of Juvenile and Family Court Judges . . . and Children's Advocacy Center fundraisers." Marilyn Van Derbur, *Miss America by Day: Lessons Learned from Ultimate Betrayals and Unconditional Love* (Denver: Oak Hill Ridge Press, 2012), 7.

40   As A. R. Riverol noted, "All the girls have a crack at being discovered for stardom. She might become Wonder Woman (Linda Carter), a governor's wife (Phyllis George). She might make it on TV (Lee Meriwether), or in the movies (Mary Ann Mobley). She might be even a politician (Bess Myerson). Losers are winners. A loser might be able to sell orange juice and wage war on homosexuality (Anita Bryant), be a Golden Girl (Susan Anton), or one of the weather girls on many of the TV stations coast to coast. And yes, she might even be marooned on 'Gilligan's Island' for eternity (Dawn Wells)." A. R. Riverol, "Myth America and Other Misses: A Second Look at the American Beauty Contests," *ETC: A Review of General Semantics* 40, no. 2 (1983): 213. See also Ann-Marie Bivans, "Almost Miss America—Returning Home Without the Crown," in *Miss America: In Pursuit of the Crown* (New York: MasterMedia Limited, 1991), 157–61.

41   Jane Jayroe with Bob Burke, *More Grace than Glamour: My Life as Miss America and Beyond* (Oklahoma City: Oklahoma Heritage Association, 2006), 60–61; Vonda Kay Van Dyke, *That Girl in Your Mirror* (Westwood, N.J.: Fleming H. Revell Company, 1966), 111–12. Granted, such rhetoric about self-improvement and camaraderie was easier for those contestants who won. It was also evidence of "self-promotion," a competitive tactic employed by women in pageants. "Beauty pageant competition is indicative of dressing in an attractive and sexy way (appearance); showing off one's body (body and athleticism); displaying a pleasant, funny, smart, and outgoing personality, while being social and acting innocent (personality advertisement) . . . Even though beauty pageant contestants are there to compete, it reflects more positively on a contestant to claim she is working on improving herself rather than outright competing with others when she's striving to outshine her peers." Shaiber, Johnsen, and Geher, "Intrasexual Competition."

42   Two examples of Miss Americas who made no apologies for their focus and drive to win are Yolande Betbeze, Miss America 1951; and Nicole Johnson, Miss America 1999. Betbeze was an Alabamian looking "to escape the South. At eighteen, she hit on *Miss America* as 'my *via aperta.*'" She took Atlantic City by storm. "Realizing immediately that she was the girl to beat, the other contestants at Atlantic City viewed her with envy. For her part, Yolande showered the others with intellectual contempt and they responded next with suspicion, then malice." Betbeze did not lie about her age (adding three years to make herself almost twenty-two) in order to make friends. Deford, *There She Is*, 178–79. Johnson, who was diagnosed with diabetes at age nineteen, recalled, "I did not have a hunger for the title. I had a hunger for the cause. I was all about my cause of diabetes. I had a very sharp, direct, intense

focus on that. I didn't spend time at the Miss America competition engaging in relationships and becoming very chummy with other contestants. I was just very, very
focused on the fact that I wanted the job to shine a spotlight on the cause." Nicole
Johnson, quoted in Pearlman, *Pretty Smart*, 55. Such admissions were outside the
normative competitive behavior expressed by Miss America contenders. In general,
they were far more likely to downplay their accomplishments and their chance of
winning even if they desperately wanted to win.

43 See the Miss America website, missamerica.org; Mia Watkins, "From Miss Alabama
to the ER: Amanda Tapley Sees Post-crown Success as Doctor," al.com, June 3, 2015;
"Miss America, 2005: Deidre Downs," pageantrymagazine.com; Pearlman, *Pretty
Smart*, 78–79.

44 With the advent of Miss America's Outstanding Teen in 2005, a young woman
entering a Miss America preliminary having previously competed in pageants was
common.

45 For example, of the eighteen Miss Alabama contestants who responded to my 2006
survey, six (or one-third of those who responded) competed in four or more preliminary pageants to earn their spot in the state pageant, with one of those young women
participating in at least ten preliminaries before she won. It took tenacity and a drive
to win to succeed on the pageant circuit.

46 This was the case for Miss Alabama 2008, Amanda Tapley. Tapley, who competed
in the Miss Alabama Pageant as Miss Samford University, entered the pageant at the
urging of her grandfather. An accomplished pianist, Tapley captured the Miss Alabama crown on her first attempt and placed in the top fifteen at the Miss America
Pageant. She was also second runner-up in the Quality of Life Award for Community Service. "Music and Medicine Motivate Miss Alabama: Amanda Tapley Uses
Her Talents to Serve her Community," *Samford School of the Arts*, June 11, 2009,
samfordarts.blogspot.com. Jane Jayroe, Miss America 1967, also won her first preliminary pageant, her first state pageant, and, of course, the title of Miss America.
Jayroe, *More Grace than Glamour*, 62, 67, 79–80.

47 See, for example, Cheryl Prewitt's description of the help she received to prepare
for the Miss America Pageant after she won the title of Miss Mississippi, including
moving to Vicksburg to live with Pat Hopson, an Associate Hostess of the Miss Mississippi Pageant. "As demanding as such a schedule was, it occurred to me at some
point that never again would I have the opportunity to so single-mindedly indulge
in getting myself in near-perfect shape—not only physically, but also mentally and
spiritually, too." Cheryl Prewitt with Kathryn Slattery, *A Bright Shining Place: The
Story of a Miracle* (Garden City, N.Y.: Doubleday, 1981), 225–40, here 238.

48 Joanne Caruso, Miss Connecticut 1984, expressed her disappointment upon not
making top ten at the national pageant. "It was so final. There were no do-overs,
no opportunity to try it again or go back and do it over." Debra Deitering Maddox,
"The Miss America Pageant's Influence on the Self-Construction of Its 1985 Contestants" (master's thesis, University of Nebraska, 2001), 50.

49 "If every little boy can be president, the pageant sponsors promise that every little girl can be a beauty queen." Riverol, "Myth America," 214. In this sense, the rhetoric of Miss America contenders could resemble that of politicians, any number of whom claimed to be called for a purpose beyond themselves for running. Rebecca Trueblood, Miss Idaho 1989, reflected on this fact in her book. "As I got to know more of the girls, I found that many of them were Christians. Many of them, like myself, had felt called to enter the pageant. Many of them had people praying for them. Any one of these Christian girls would use the office of Miss America to witness for God." Becki Trueblood, as told to Rhonda Graham, *Best for Me* (Boise, Idaho: Pacific Press Publishing Association, 1991), 73.

50 In observing the Miss Alabama Pageant for eight out of ten years (2006, 2007, 2009, 2010, 2011, 2012, 2014, 2015), I saw the transformation of many pageant contestants from novice to expert. Some perfected their talent. Some lost weight. Some shed the one-piece bathing suit for a two-piece. Some had professional headshots done. Some adopted a new platform issue or dedicated more hours to it. In short, seasoned contestants had more polish. There was a certain pageant "look" and each element of competition required careful execution. Watching the development of Miss Alabama contenders over a ten-year period helped me see how much of pageant competition is learned behavior.

51 Pearlman, *Pretty Smart*, 97. "It wasn't until her sixth year of competing that Nicole Johnson (1999) won the national title. Jennifer Berry (2006) and Donna Axum (1964) each competed for five years; Shawntel Smith (1996) didn't stop trying for four years and took part in twenty pageants. Angie Baraquio (2001) tried three times at the state level, ten times overall. It took two years for Phyllis George (1971) to become Miss America." This list, of course, is representative, not exhaustive.

52 Debra Deitering Maddox (Miss Iowa 1984) wrote her master's thesis on how the contestants in the 1985 Miss America Pageant constructed and continued to construct their identities. She found that contestants felt a "post-pageant void" that they struggled to fill. Maddox, "Miss America Pageant's Influence."

53 Elaine Campanelli Santo, *From Glamour to Glory* (Maitland, Fla.: Xulon Press, 2010), 41.

54 Santo, *From Glamour to Glory*, 35.

55 Maddox, "Miss America Pageant's Influence," 49. Incidentally, Donna Cherry reportedly "existed for months on a 600-calorie-a-day diet, worked out on Nautilus machines and studied videotapes of past pageants." She poured her heart and soul into preparation. That she experienced disappointment when she did not win was not surprising. Melinda Beck et al., "A Controversial 'Spectator Sport,'" *Newsweek*, September 17, 1984, 60.

56 Maddox, "Miss America Pageant's Influence," 50.

57 Shaiber, Johnsen, and Geher, "Intrasexual Competition." "Contestants have reported that they have formed lifelong friendships with other contestants. While many contestants do form friendships with one another, there are also instances where relationships with other contestants can be used to a contestant's advantage."

58   The Miss America State Titleholders Association (MASTA) had a Facebook page "where @MissAmericaOrg state titleholders can find each other!" MASTA also helped raise money for the Miss America Foundation (missamericafoundation.org). For example, in September 2017, I attended the Miss America State Titleholders Association cocktail reception to benefit the Miss America Foundation. State winners from numerous years as well as volunteers associated with state pageants turned out for the event, which, among other things, featured a silent auction to raise money.

59   Shindle, *Being Miss America*, 12.

60   At the Miss Alabama Pageant, this group ensured that wardrobe changes went swiftly between phases of competition, offered support and encouragement, and, yes, some even had the job of spraying the butt glue and securing swimsuits just prior to the swimsuit competition. On the final night of competition, dressing-room moms ensured that all of the dresses, makeup, and accessories of the top ten competitors got moved to a separate, designated dressing area. Dressing-room moms also donated a scholarship that was awarded to one of the contestants. That amount was $1,500 in 2018 (*Miss Alabama Program*, 2018). This is merely one example of how volunteers in the organization functioned as community to the contestants.

61   In her five-page farewell letter printed in the Miss America 2018 program, Savvy Shields thanked numerous volunteers, pageant sponsors, friends, fellow contestants, and family for their support and encouragement. The warmth she felt for each of them was conveyed in the concrete examples given, obvious references to inside jokes, and genuine passion for her work as Miss America that they helped her accomplish. For example, she wrote, "Ashley Mowery, you taught me how to point my toes and encouraged me to reach higher than I thought possible . . . You are my dance teacher and my heart builder." She thanked her "Miss America sisters . . . for lifting me up every step of the way. From the daily messages of encouragement to taking me in whenever I was in your state, I am forever grateful." And the Miss Arkansas Board "for believing in me and letting me be authentically Savvy." Such praise was common from outgoing winners at the local, state, and national level.

62   Thousands of volunteers help staff the pageant; see the Miss America website, missamerica.org. See also "Family," in Angela Saulino Osborne, *Miss America: The Dream Lives On: A 75 Year Celebration* (Dallas: Taylor, 1995), 140–62.

63   One of the annual awards was the National Academy of Honor Award "presented annually to an individual who has dedicated more than 20 years of outstanding service to the Miss America Organization at the local or state level." The 2017 award recipient, Jane Alderson, had more than thirty-five years of work with the Miss Tennessee Scholarship Pageant (*Miss America 2018 Program*, 184).

64   Melodie King Bobbitt, correspondence with the author.

65   While I embarked on this research with some knowledge of the pageant world, I was by no means fluent in pageant lingo. My fluency increased quickly and drastically as I read pageant blogs, contestant autobiographies, and other scholarship on the pageant. Still, none of that was any substitute for what I learned by attending pageants and talking to people in the pageant world.

66 I collected a number of buttons, ribbons, signed headshots, and even a T-shirt during my years of pageant-going.

67 See, for example, Brittany L. Jackson, "Last Chance at the Crown: Miss Tennessee Contestant Follows in Mom's Footsteps," *Jackson Sun*, May 11, 2018; and Drew Taylor, "Callie Walker, Mother Took Different Paths to Miss Alabama," *Tuscaloosa News*, June 17, 2018.

68 Caitlin Guffin Eiland, correspondence with the author.

69 *Miss America 2018 Program*, 169.

70 For example, Kate Shindle's family was fully immersed as volunteers in the national pageant. Her mother was on the hostess committee and eventually helped with the Miss New Jersey Pageant as well. Her father volunteered in a number of roles. Shindle and her brother grew up helping too. When she won a local pageant in Illinois, her father was serving on the pageant's board of directors but stepped "aside to avoid the appearance of impropriety." Shindle, *Being Miss America*, 70–72. Certainly, she had her parents' full support as well as decades of knowledge of pageant history.

71 Prewitt, *Bright-Shining Place*, 157.

72 Prewitt struggled with the fact that her dad did not approve of her decision to compete in pageants and was thrilled when he eventually relented and came to watch her compete in the Miss Mississippi Pageant. Prewitt, *Bright-Shining Place*, 157–59, 163, 196–98, 201–4.

73 Mark Oppenheimer, "There Are Three Activities I Won't Let My Daughters Try. One Is Beauty Pageants," *Los Angeles Times*, January 4, 2018. Of arguments in favor of pageants, Oppenheimer wrote, "These arguments aren't wrong, but they are not good arguments, because they're true of pretty much all human endeavors. *Everything* that you work hard at builds your work ethic: entomology, origami, chanting Torah for your bat mitzvah, gardening, micro-brewing, Rubik's Cube, Minecraft. *Everything* that involves striving teaches that, with striving, you improve."

74 Devin Loring, "Family Experience with Pageants Helps Many Miss America Contestants," *Press of Atlantic City*, September 4, 2014.

75 *Miss Alabama Program*, 1999.

76 See the Miss Texas website, misstexas.org.

77 Conversation with Amanda Wineman, Miss America Pageant, Atlantic City, New Jersey, September 2015.

78 See the Miss America's Outstanding Teen website, maoteen.org.

79 See the Miss Alabama website, missalabama.com, for one overview of this program. Miss Texas had a similar program called "Lone Star Princess," misstexas.org.

80 See the Miss America's Outstanding Teen website, maoteen.org.

81 The language of female empowerment adopted by the pageant is just one example of this shift. See "Miss America Empowered me . . ." (*Miss America 2.0 2019 Program*, 54–55). Heather French, Miss America 2000, said that Miss America empowered her "to stand up for our military veterans who have sacrificed so much for the freedoms we enjoy today!" BeBe Shopp, Miss America 1948, claimed Miss America

empowered her "through scholarships to receive a musical education, to become an independent woman, obtain leadership skills, and broaden my worldview."

82   This was often done at local and state pageants too. The reigning queen was royalty and thus the audience stood to greet her and to honor her.

83   Some pageant coaches, directors, and fans live-tweeted from the pageants. I found that following @pageantchris on Twitter provided helpful insights into the pageant world. It also helped connect me to others talking about the Miss America Pageant system in the Twittersphere.

84   Reunions were held at the state and national levels. For example, Miss Alabama held an annual alumni luncheon (*Miss Alabama Program*, 2012).

85   Maddox's thesis, "Miss America Pageant's Influence," offers multiple reflections from her fellow competitors in the 1984 Miss America Pageant. Many reported struggling with body issues and self-esteem despite the many positives they gained from their pageant participation. Elaine Campanelli, Miss Delaware 1975, also found reentry to "normal" life challenging: "Unfortunately, after an enormous, exhilarating event like the Miss America Pageant, I had to return to the confines of a normal life. That transforming occurrence of going from the heights of fame to the lows of reality is quite a trip. The effects, nonetheless, were daunting for me and left me battling some depression." Santo, *From Glamour to Glory*, 41. Miss Americas also confessed struggling with depression and eating disorders. For example, Miss America 2011, Teresa Scanlan, dealt with depression during her year of service. See "Miss America Reveals Struggle with Depression, Suicide," *Good Morning America*, September 9, 2013, abcnews.com.go/GMA.

86   Maddox, "Miss America Pageant's Influence," 61.

87   Maddox, "Miss America Pageant's Influence," 61.

88   Maddox, "Miss America Pageant's Influence," 49. Self-doubt was also very common. When Maryline Blackburn, Miss Alaska 1984, did not make the top ten at Miss America, she "entered a cycle of questioning herself: What had she done wrong? What had not worked? She was very disappointed in herself and felt she had done something wrong to cause her not to make Top Ten."

89   Neimark, "Why We Need." "Superwoman is alive and well. This pageant tells us what women are supposed to be . . . Today, Miss Americas are asked to be beautiful, to achieve, and to serve . . . She has a platform, and it's inevitably for the social good."

90   Shaiber, Johnsen, and Geher, "Intrasexual Competition."

Chapter 4: Faith *of* the Pageant, Faith *and* the Pageant

1   Charles Reagan Wilson, *Judgment and Grace in Dixie: Southern Faiths from Faulkner to Elvis* (Athens: University of Georgia Press, 1995), 158. As Wilson notes, "The worldview seen in twentieth-century southern popular religion, however, has accepted the images and rituals of the beauty culture along with strictures for modest behavior for women. Any tensions between the two have somehow been bridged, and to understand this accommodation one must see the beauty queen in the South as an embodiment of the southern civil religion. She represents values long

associated with a South that saw special symbolic meanings in its women, meanings with moral-religious overtones" (144–45).

2 "Attacks Bathing Review: Preacher Says Atlantic City Event Endangers Youthful Morals," *New York Times*, September 11, 1923, 15; "Criticism Well Deserved," *New York Times*, April 21, 1924, 16; "Attack Beauty Pageant: Philadelphia Women Sign Protest to Atlantic City Authorities," *New York Times*, March 1, 1927, 3; "Women Open Fight on Beauty Pageant: Tell Atlantic City Officials that Contests Harm Entrants and Commercialize Shore," *New York Times*, November 18, 1927, 12; "Bishop Condemns Beauty Pageant," *New York Times*, November 20, 1927, 10. See also A. R. Riverol, *Live from Atlantic City: A History of the Miss America Pageant before, after and in spite of Television* (Bowling Green, Ohio: Bowling Green State University Popular Press, 1992), 23–25; Frank Deford, *There She Is: The Life and Times of Miss America* (New York: Viking Press, 1971), 129–30; and ch. 1, nn. 32 and 33 in this volume.

3 Terry Meeuwsen et al., "Happy Birthday Miss America," Christian Broadcasting Network, *The 700 Club*, 2011, cbn.com/700club.

4 Much has been written about Slaughter and her contributions to the pageant. See, for example, Deford, *There She Is*; Angela Saulino Osborne, *Miss America: The Dream Lives On: A 75 Year Celebration* (Dallas: Taylor, 1995), 82–90; Susan Dworkin, *Miss America, 1945: Bess Myerson and the Year that Changed Our Lives* (New York: New Market Press, 1999), 98–102; and Kate Shindle, *Being Miss America: Behind the Rhinestone Curtain* (Austin: University of Texas Press, 2014). She was also spoken of—at length—by BeBe Shopp, Miss America 1948, at one of the preliminary competitions for Miss America 2019. Shopp recounted many of the reforms instituted by Slaughter in her quest to make the pageant respectable. "She was outspoken, not favored by many, and not liked by quite a few. But one thing they agreed on: she did an outstanding job with this pageant." Miss America Pageant 2019, Boardwalk Hall, Atlantic City, preliminary competition, night 3, September 7, 2018, on-site visit.

5 This is not to suggest that Christians did not participate in the pageant in its earliest days. Given that the majority of the nation professed Christianity as their religion, it stands to reason that there have been and are Christians who compete in Miss America. Rather, I am suggesting that Christians' public relationship with the pageant shifted over time.

6 This raises the question: what are the limits of what will be celebrated? Christians are not known for backing down from things with which they disagree; think, for example, of the lottery, abortion, and homosexuality. What about pageants made them above critique?

7 That is, the pageant, in some ways, offered a safe alternative to feminism. Women could still be in public, and may even pursue an education, but she did so in ways that preserved her primary identification as female. That is, she continued to look and act in "feminine" ways. She also competed against other women, not against men. Miss America did not threaten male power.

8   My choice to employ the term "Christian" in this chapter rather than "evangelical,"
    "mainline," "Protestant," or "Catholic" is intentional. The faith *of* the pageant was
    broadly "Christian" and existed alongside the individual faith traditions represented
    by the contestants on stage. The pageant spoke generally of God (not Jesus), faith,
    and country, allowing the contestants—and viewers—to fill in the blanks. Thus the
    faith *of* Miss America presented as a kind of "public Protestantism" as detailed by
    Catherine Albanese in her book *America: Religions and Religion*: "Moralistic in code,
    revivalistic in cultus, and millennial in creed, the dominant and public religion of
    America acted as a solvent for the separate centers of the many religions. The dom-
    inant and public tradition worked to break down barriers and to confuse boundar-
    ies so that a religious culture of oneness could be formed." Catherine L. Albanese,
    America: Religions and Religion, (Belmont, Calif.: Wadsworth Publishing Company,
    1981), 280–81. The faith *of* the pageant also served as a sort of civil religion to
    unite the country by celebrating and promoting national ideals. While much has
    been written about civil religion in America, Robert N. Bellah's 1967 article remains
    a necessary starting point for understanding the term. Robert N. Bellah, "Civil
    Religion in America," *Daedalus* 96, no. 1 (1967): 1–21. See also Jason A. Edwards
    and Joseph M. Valenzano III, eds., *The Rhetoric of American Civil Religion: Symbols,
    Saints, and Sinners* (New York: Lexington Books, 2016); Donald G. Jones and Rus-
    sell E. Richey, eds., *American Civil Religion* (San Francisco: Mellen Research Univer-
    sity Press, 1990); and Andrew M. Manis, "Civil Religion and National Identity," in
    The Columbia Guide to Religion in America History, ed. Paul Harvey and Edward J.
    Blum (New York: Columbia University Press, 2012), 89–104.

    The section of this chapter on faith *and* the pageant traces the relationship
    between the pageant and a variety of religious traditions, almost entirely Christian.
    Because of the diversity of Christian denominations represented, I chose, for prac-
    tical reasons, to continue using the term Christian when discussing the churches
    or contestants as a whole. There are moments, however, that I reference particular
    denominations both to offer clarity and to demonstrate the widespread support of
    pageants by Christians in America.

9   Katie Harman with the 2001 Miss America Contestants, *Under the Crown: 51 Stories
    of Courage, Determination and the American Spirit* (Seattle: Milestone Books, 2002),
    xviii.

10 Again, Sarah Banet-Weiser's words in *The Most Beautiful Girl in the World: Beauty
    Pageants and National Identity* (Los Angeles: University of California Press, 1999)
    prove instructive: "the Miss America pageant is a place where cultural meanings
    about the local, the national, the typical, and the ideal are produced, negotiated, and
    circulated" (181).

11 Jane Jayroe with Bob Burke, *More Grace than Glamour: My Life as Miss America and
    Beyond* (Oklahoma City: Oklahoma Heritage Association, 2006), 111–18.

12 Banet-Weiser, *Most Beautiful Girl*, 43. Banet-Weiser notes that most platforms "can
    be characterized as 'women's issues,' or rather, issues that are relegated to the private
    sphere and that entail nurturing, emotionality, and morality." For more on women as

moral guardians in the nineteenth century, see Nancy A. Hardesty, *Women Called to Witness: Evangelical Feminism in the Nineteenth Century*, 2nd ed. (Knoxville: University of Tennessee Press, 1999); and Laceye Warner, *Saving Women: Retrieving Evangelistic Theology and Practice* (Waco, Tex.: Baylor University Press, 2007).

13   Barbara Welter, "The Cult of True Womanhood: 1820–1860," *American Quarterly* 18, no. 2, part 1 (1966): 151–74. "The attributes of True Womanhood, by which a woman judged herself and was judged by her husband, her neighbors and society[,] could be divided into four cardinal virtues—piety, purity, submissiveness and domesticity. Put them all together and they spelled mother, daughter, sister, wife— woman. Without them, no matter whether there was fame, achievement or wealth, all was ashes. With them she was promised happiness and power" (152).

14   Jones, "Beauty Queen," *Theatre History Studies* 18 (June 1998): 99–106. See also Banet-Weiser, *Most Beautiful Girl*; and Jill Neimark, "Why We Need Miss America," *Psychology Today* 31, no. 5 (1998): 40ff.

15   As noted by Manis, "Whatever name one chooses to give it, civil religion can best be understood as a cultural blending of religion and patriotism that interprets the nation as unique by virtue of its special relationship with that society's conception of the sacred. As such, in the American context civil religion could be accurately conceived as American exceptionalism in a religious mode. Civil religion is the system of mythic meanings, embedded and diffused throughout their culture, by which Americans interpret the ultimate meaning of their nation." Manis, "Civil Religion," 91.

While she does not employ the language of civil religion, Banet-Weiser's work, *Most Beautiful Girl*, captures this sense of national pride in, and civic duty of, Miss America. My work in this section is best read and understood in conversation with hers, particularly ch. 4, "Bodies of Difference: Race, Nation, and the Troubled Reign of Vanessa Williams"; and ch. 5, "The Representational Politics of Whiteness and the National Body: Bess Myerson, Miss America 1945, and Heather Whitestone, Miss America 1995." "The Miss America contestant's body—through her disciplined physique, her commitment to virtue, and her testimony to stability—'codes the tantalizing ideal' of a well-managed collective American body. Through the display of female bodies and the performance of a particular version of female subjectivity, the beauty pageant transforms a culture's anxiety about itself—its stability as a coherent nation—into a spectacular reenactment and overcoming of that very anxiety. It is through the performance of the local and the national, and navigating how these categories are mutually constitutive, that those women crowned Miss America also perform the abstract character of liberal political membership within a particular national imaginary. . . . all Miss Americas are produced and produce themselves as national bodies" (179–80).

16   "Even if traditional religions or denominations divide the loyalties of citizens, the civil or national religion can provide a belief system about the nation around which all or most citizens can rally. This creed of civil religion expresses Americans' conviction of their nation's exceptionalism by embodying what they believe to be America's

divine purpose. These beliefs are called to mind by the sacred symbols (the flag), sacred rituals (pledging allegiance), sacred objects (the Liberty Bell), sacred holidays (the Fourth of July), sacred spaces (the Lincoln Memorial), and sacred personages (Washington, Jefferson, Lincoln). By reference to these components, Americans celebrate their country's unique status and recommit themselves to its values and its task in the world." Manis, "Civil Religion," 92.

17 The Miss America Pageant as ritual deserves far more attention than the mere mention I give it here. Catherine Bell's work on ritual and performance offers a natural starting point, as do the reflections already done by Harvey Cox and Jennifer Jones. See Catherine Bell, *Ritual: Perspectives and Dimensions* (New York: Oxford University Press, 2009); Catherine Bell, "Performance," in *Critical Terms for Religious Studies*, ed. Mark C. Taylor (Chicago: University of Chicago Press, 1998); Harvey Cox, "Miss America and the Cult of The Girl," *Christianity and Crisis* 7 (August 1961): 143–46; and Jones, "Beauty Queen."

18 This was certainly the case for the first Jewish Miss America, Bess Myerson; the first African American Miss America, Vanessa Williams; and the first Miss America of Indian descent, Nina Davuluri. Indeed, I have suggested elsewhere that most Americans do not pay attention to Miss America unless someone wins that the collective "they" deem not "American" enough. Bess Myerson and Vanessa Williams will be discussed later in this chapter. For more on the controversy surrounding Nina Davuluri, see Alex Williams, "Beauty Pageants Draw Social Media Critics," *New York Times*, September 20, 2013; and "Is Nina Davuluri 'American Enough' to Be Miss America?" *Tell Me More*, npr.org. Davuluri, the daughter of Hindu parents, also has her own website, ninadavuluri.com.

19 Mary Anne Schofield, "Miss America, Rosie the Riveter, and World War II," in *The Politics of Sex, Beauty, and Race in America's Most Famous Pageant*, ed. Elwood Watson and Darcy Martin (New York: Palgrave Macmillan, 2004), 53–66.

20 Neimark, "Why We Need."

21 "Attacks Bathing Review"; "Criticism Well Deserved"; "Attack Beauty Pageant"; "Women Open Fight"; and "Bishop Condemns Beauty Pageant." See also Riverol, *Live from Atlantic City*, 23–25; Deford, *There She Is*, 129–30; and ch. 1, n. 33 in this volume.

22 Southern Baptist Convention, "Resolution passed at the Southern Baptist Convention, 1926," *SBC Resolutions*, May 1926, sbc.net.

23 "Bishop Condemns Beauty Pageant."

24 "Women Open Fight." See also Deford, *There She Is*, 270.

25 Riverol, *Live from Atlantic City*, 24. See also "Bishop Condemns Beauty Pageant"; and "Attacks Bathing Review."

26 Deford, *There She Is*, 129ff; Riverol, *Live from Atlantic City*, 23–24. As noted, no pageant took place from 1928 to 1932. It was revived in 1933 but canceled again in 1934. It returned for a makeover in 1935. To be sure, the reasons for the cancellation of the pageant were numerous. Accusations that the pageant was not a

respectable enterprise and loss of financial backing by Atlantic City businessmen were also among the factors that led to its brief hiatus.

27 Banet-Weiser, *Most Beautiful Girl*, 37.

28 "Atlantic City to Drop Its Outdoor Pageant: Only Roller Chair Parade to Be Retained—Beauties Will Wear Evening Gowns," *New York Times*, March 12, 1928.

29 Deford, *There She Is*, 129ff. The lives of early winners did not always fit the stereotypically harsh profile. To be sure, some of the winners throughout its history desired the glamour of Hollywood and stardom, but not all early Miss Americas fit this mold. Some eschewed makeup, taught Sunday school, and recited Bible verses. See "Most Beautiful Girl Avoids All Cosmetics: Mary Katharine Campbell Wins New Test in Fighting Off Effects of a Cold," *New York Times*, September 13, 1922; and Deford, *There She Is*, 121, 127–28.

30 Michelle Tauber et al., "American Beauties: 80 Years," *People*, October 16, 2000, 143.

31 Ann-Marie Bivans, *Miss America: In Pursuit of the Crown* (New York: MasterMedia Limited, 1991), 12–13. Slaughter worked with the Miss America Pageant in some capacity from 1935 to 1967.

32 Dworkin, *Miss America, 1945*, 90.

33 Deford, *There She Is*, 270–71. Slaughter's first Quaker board member, J. Haines Lippincott of the Chalfonte-Haddon Hall Hotels, was the one who contacted Mrs. Charles D. White for Slaughter. White accepted the position as head of the hostess committee, provided she was allowed complete control of it.

34 Banet-Weiser, *Most Beautiful Girl*, 39; Deford, *There She Is*, 270ff.

35 Dworkin, *Miss America, 1945*, 96.

36 Deford, *There She Is*, 154.

37 Though to be sure much could be said about the pageant's entanglements with big business and television. See Shindle, *Being Miss America*, 195–96.

38 Bivans, *In Pursuit of the Crown*, 13–14.

39 Banet-Weiser, *Most Beautiful Girl*, 37–40.

40 Banet-Weiser, *Most Beautiful Girl*, 37–42.

41 Dworkin, *Miss America, 1945*, 98–99.

42 Deford, *There She Is*, 157. "No matter how many times it happens, the press finds itself surprised every time a beauty pageant winner is something other than a classic dumb blonde. They wrote about and interviewed Jean endlessly. 'Oh God,' she says, 'they would just all always call me *wholesome*.' She was a hit everywhere she went, with everyone." That Bartel represented the epitome of Miss America as civil religion has already been discussed. The ideals of virtue, wholesomeness, and general morality remained expectations of Miss America into the twenty-first century.

43 Dworkin, *Miss America, 1945*, 98–99; Deford, *There She Is*, 157–58. Deford also argued that Bartel was the first Miss America that really won the hearts of women. Women bought over eighty percent of the war bonds Bartel sold.

44 Deford, *There She Is*, 275–76.

45 Deford, *There She Is*, 303, 158–59.

46 Deford, *There She Is*, 155.

47 Banet-Weiser, *Most Beautiful Girl*, 39.

48 Bess Myerson, quoted in Michael Yockel, "Lenora Slaughter Fropart, the Doyenne of the American Beauty Pageant," *New York Press*, January 31, 2001.

49 *Miss America: A Documentary Film*, DVD, directed by Lisa Ades (Brooklyn: Clio and Orchard Films, 2001).

50 Dworkin, *Miss America, 1945*, 92–94.

51 Dworkin, *Miss America, 1945*, 145–49.

52 According to historian Vicki Gold Levi, "Bess was the answer to every Jewish woman's dream. Her win was such a multilevel symbol. It was a symbol of a certain statement against anti-Semitism. It was a symbol of a victory against Hitler. It was a symbol for women, and when she won there was great celebration in our house. It was like when Roosevelt won or something." The previous quotation is from the documentary on the Miss America Pageant.

53 Narrator, *Miss America*, DVD. Transcript available at this link: www.shoppbs.pbs .org/wgbh/amex/missamerica/filmmore/pt.html.

54 Dworkin, *Miss America, 1945*, 180–81.

55 Banet-Weiser offers a thorough and convincing argument that Myerson's "white ethnicity did not threaten the nationalist hold that whiteness commands, and her Jewish identity justified and legitimated the presence of U.S. soldiers overseas" (163). Of importance here, however, is the impact that her difference exerted on her reign as Miss America. Myerson's Judaism marked her and threatened the pageant as some pageant sponsors pulled their support. I see her as the exception that proves the rule. For more, see ch. 5, "The Representational Politics of Whiteness and the National Body: Bess Myerson, Miss America 1945, and Heather Whitestone, Miss America 1995," in *Most Beautiful Girl in the World*. See also Dworkin, *Miss America, 1945*; and Jennifer Preston, *Queen Bess: The Unauthorized Biography of Bess Myerson* (New York: Contemporary Books, 1990).

56 C. E. Bryant, "Miss America to Sing on Convention Program," *Baptist Press*, February 12, 1948; "They're Not for Her: Miss America, Abroad, Gives Falsies a Frown," *Los Angeles Times*, August 3, 1949, 5.

57 John W. Kennedy, "Miss (Christian) America," *Christianity Today International*, 2003. Vonda Kay Van Dyke's public declaration of her faith is discussed in more detail in ch. 5, "Faith in the Pageant."

58 Deford, *There She Is*, 274.

59 Kennedy, "Miss (Christian) America."

60 While my discussion here focuses on the relationship between the pageant and churches and the pageant and Christian media, the relationship between the Miss America Pageant and religious communities extended to religious colleges as well. For example, Baptist-affiliated Samford University hosts the Miss Alabama Pageant each year in the Wright Center, missalabama.com. And, in 2018, Liberty University began hosting the Miss Virginia Pageant in their Center for Music and the Worship Arts Concert Hall. Jeff Moody, "Officials: Miss Virginia Pageant to Be Held

in Liberty's Concert Hall," *Roanoke Times*, August 25, 2017. Finally, Methodist-affiliated Oklahoma City University boasts a statue honoring its three alumnae who have worn the Miss America crown. "Miss America University," *Roadside America*, roadsideamerica.com.

61 *Miss Alabama Program*, 2010, n.p.

62 *Miss Alabama Program*, 1999, n.p.

63 It should be noted, however, that such religious ads were more prevalent in the southern pageant programs I viewed.

64 *Miss America Program*, 2011, n.p.

65 Dana Williamson, "Miss Oklahoma Wants to Spend Year Sharing Faith with Youth," *Baptist Press*, September 29, 1998, bpnews.net.

66 *Miss Alabama Program*, 2000, n.p.

67 *Miss Alabama Program*, 2003, ad for Layla Carter, Miss Leeds Area, n.p.

68 *Miss Alabama Program*, 2007, n.p.

69 Anna Swindle, "Roanoke Baptist Wins Miss Alabama Title," *Alabama Baptist*, June 28, 2007, 4.

70 Bob Allen, "Miss America Member of CBF Church," *Ethics Daily*, September 21, 2004, ethicsdaily.com.

71 Holly McCray, "God's Promises Guide Miss America," *The United Methodist Reporter*, February 22, 2007, umportal.org.

72 Ann Maloney, "Back to Work: McCreary Has a Year of Appearances to Come," *Times Daily*, September 16, 1996, 3A.

73 Jill Lovett, "McCreary's Faith Shines Bright Even without Top Beauty Crown," *Alabama Baptist*, October 3, 1996, 7.

74 A contestant kept her state crown and continued her year of service as Miss [State] if she did not win Miss America. If she won Miss America, the runner-up at the state pageant assumed the role of state representative with all the privileges and responsibilities it afforded.

75 Aimee Berg, "The Next Jewish Miss America?" *Jewish Daily Forward*, January 3, 2001, forward.com.

76 Rabbi Jason Miller, "Could There Be a Jewish Miss America?" *Community Next Blog*, January 5, 2001, communitynxt.com (site no longer available).

77 Loren Galler Rabinowitz also competed in the Miss USA pageant system, making the semifinals in 2009.

78 Jay Copp, "A Catholic Miss America: Angela Perez Baraquio," *St. Anthony Messenger*, September 2001, americancatholic.org/messenger (site no longer available). This is one of the more surprising connections between faith and the pageant that I found. I fully anticipated the large number of evangelicals who spoke of the pageant as a mission field; I was less prepared to discover this rhetoric of witness among Catholics. Indeed, this example and that of other non-evangelicals forced me to broaden my understanding of faith's role of, and in, the pageant. While certainly Catholics and evangelicals understand the term differently, it is clear that they share an emphasis on the importance of witness. Much could be speculated about why and how

this rhetoric typically associated with American evangelicals comes to be used by a Roman Catholic priest, but here it is important to reiterate that the focus on the Miss America Pageant as a mission field was not merely an evangelical, or even a Protestant, thing.

79 Copp, "Catholic Miss America."

80 See Christopher Heffron, "Miss America Maintains Priorities during Whirlwind Year," *American Catholic*, August 15, 2001, americancatholic.org (site no longer available); and Kathleen Bagg-Morgan, "She's Got Character," *St. Augustine Catholic*, June–July 2001, 16ff.

81 Beauty pageants were not the only "secular" enterprise to be coopted by Christians as a mission field. Evangelicals in particular grew quite skilled at making a "Christian" version of things. Indeed, if for Shakespeare "all the world's a stage," for evangelicals, all the world's a mission field. For one collection of essays that explores this reality, see Shirley R. Steinberg and Joe L. Kincheloe, eds., *Christotainment: Selling Jesus through Popular Culture* (Boulder, Colo.: Westview Press, 2009).

82 "Two-Piece Swimsuits Return to the Miss America Pageant," *Kingman Daily Miner*, September 14, 1997, 5A. In 1947, contestants wore identical two-piece swimsuits. With the exception of that year, participants wore one-piece swimsuits until 1997. As discussed in ch. 1, most competitors chose to wear a two-piece. Those who donned the more conservative one-pieces stood out.

83 Nikki Bohne, "Highland's Modest Miss America Hopeful Finishes in the Top 10," *Herald Extra*, February 4, 2007, heraldextra.com.

84 See, for example, Sharon Haddock and Amy Choate-Nielsen, "Miss Utah Not Afraid to Be Herself," *Deseret News*, February 15, 2007.

85 Mary O'Hayes, "Miss Utah: 'She Doesn't Have to Show a Lot of Skin,'" *Modestly Yours*, February 7, 2007, modestlyyours.net.

86 Sharon Haddock and Wade Jewkes, "Two Mormon Contestants Compete in Miss America," *Deseret News*, February 10, 2010. Nelson noted that there were some non-Mormon contestants in 2010 that chose one-piece swimsuits too, stating, "That was a nice little surprise, that it wasn't just us LDS girls."

87 See, for example, Tyler Hinton, "Wearing a Missionary Crown," *Universe*, March 8, 2007, newsnet.byu.edu; Katelyn Beaty, "Miss America and the Bikini Question," *Christianity Today*, January 20, 2011; and Julie Dockstader Heaps, "Standing Her Ground on the National Stage," *Church News: The Church of Jesus Christ of Latter Day Saints*, January 26, 2008, ldschurchnews.com.

88 This reality serves as a useful reminder that Christian beliefs did not always match the pageant's values. There were limits to the way Christians could live out their beliefs in the pageant and be "successful." For those Christians in pursuit of the top crown, they often made compromises or offered justifications for stepping outside their normal practice, often in the name of some larger call or greater good.

89 Jay Reynolds and Kylie Conway, "Miss Utah Contestants Choose Less Modest Swim-wear," *ABC4: Salt Lake City*, abc4.com. When I attended the Miss Utah 2016 pageant in June 2016, eight of the fifty-one contestants (15.7 percent) wore a one-piece

swimsuit for the preliminary competition, but none of them advanced to the finals. This is the highest percentage of contestants to choose one-piece swimwear in the state pageants that I attended. Often I saw only one or two contestants choose a one-piece swimsuit and on some occasions none of the contestants donned a one-piece. Still, the stark contrast in attire deemed appropriate for women (even LDS women) in the pageant compared to the attire worn by the LDS women at Temple Square was striking. This is not, of course, to suggest that all of the contestants in the Miss Utah pageant were members of the LDS church.

90 This tension existed for evangelical contestants as well. For example, in response to the question, "Do you feel or sense tensions between your religious tradition and the MAP? If so, what are some of them?" one Miss Alabama contestant, a Baptist, responded, "Some, in the swimsuit area of competition. Most church members don't 'approve' of the idea at all. And they certainly don't think I should wear a two-piece (but I do)." Miss Alabama survey response, 2009.

91 McCray, "God's Promises."

92 Lovett, "McCreary's Faith."

93 See Heather Whitestone with Angela Elwell Hunt, *Listening with My Heart* (New York: Doubleday, 1997); and "Katie Stam: More Than a Pretty Face," Christian Broadcasting Network, *The 700 Club*, July 9, 2009, cbn.com/700club.

94 For a discussion of how this new element of the competition developed, see Shindle, *Being Miss America*, 89–93.

95 John DeRosier, "Here They Are: 2018 Miss America Contestants Arrive in Atlantic City," *Press of Atlantic City*, August 31, 2017.

96 Cindy Townsend, "Deidre Downs: A Woman on Mission for Kids!" *Missions Mosaic: The Magazine for Women on Mission*, November 2007, 8–11.

97 Townsend, "Deidre Downs." Matthew 25:40 states, "The King will reply, 'Truly I tell you, whatever you did for one of the least of these brothers and sisters of mine, you did for me.'"

98 Townsend, "Deidre Downs," 11.

99 Sheri L. Dew, preface to *Sharlene Wells: Miss America* (Salt Lake City: Deseret Book Company, 1985).

100 Don L. Searle, "For Miss America, It's a Busy Life . . . and a Missionary Opportunity," *Ensign*, November 1984, lds.org/ensign.

101 Searle, "For Miss America."

102 See Lara Riscol, "Miss America's Stealth Virginity Campaign," *Salon*, October 28, 2002, for one overview of the controversy. Harold's official platform was "Preventing Youth Violence and Bullying: Protect Yourself, Respect Yourself." She advocated sexual abstinence in addition to abstinence from drugs and alcohol. The conflict between Harold and the Miss America Pageant demonstrates that there were limits to how much Miss America's personal beliefs could inform the religion of Miss America. It is also worth noting that the (relatively) minor squabbles between Christians and the pageant served the purposes of both. The pageant got to assert its agency as a national icon that must make space for all, and Christian participants and

winners got to demonstrate that there were some things they would not compromise for earthly glory.

103 See, for example, Richard Daigle, "Spirit Filled Miss America Stands Firm on Absti-nence Message," *Charisma*, December 31, 2002, charismamag.com; and "Miss America Resists Pressure to Silence Abstinence Message," *Baptist Press*, October 9, 2002, bpnews.net.

104 John W. Kennedy, "Erika Harold: Miss America for Such a Time as This," *Pentecostal Evangel*, February 23, 2003, pentecostalevangel.ag.org.

105 Kennedy, "Erika Harold."

106 "Survival and Adaptation in the Modern Era, 1960–1989," in Edith L. Blumhofer, *Restoring the Faith: The Assemblies of God, Pentecostalism, and American Culture* (Champaign: University of Illinois Press, 1993).

107 Kennedy, "Erika Harold."

108 Kennedy, "Erika Harold."

109 Meeuwsen et al., "Happy Birthday Miss America." Other Miss Americas hosted by Meeuwsen on *The 700 Club* include Katie Stam, Miss America 2009; Caressa Cameron, Miss America 2010; Teresa Scanlan, Miss America 2011; and Laura Kaeppeler, Miss America 2012.

110 Rebecca Grace, "Miss America Crowns Purity as Priceless Message," *American Family Association Journal*, February 2005; and Trueblood, *Best for Me*, 7ff.

111 Rabbi Yonason Goldson, "The Private Life of Miss America," *Torah Ideals*, n.d., torahideals.com.

112 Amy E. Nevala, "Miss America Praises Abstinence for Youths," *Chicago Tribune*, November 24, 2002.

113 Cover photo, *Jet* magazine, October 23, 1989.

114 It would be interesting for someone to study more deeply how the Christian media portrays a Christian Miss America compared to how she is portrayed in the secular media. While I have not kept a running tally, I know that Christian publications are far more likely to choose a picture of "their" Miss America wearing a business suit or even one of her being crowned in her evening gown than they are to feature one of her in a swimsuit. For example, the 1996 March/April edition of *The Saturday Evening Post* featured Assemblies of God member Shawntel Smith, Miss America 1996, with arms folded across her conservative blazer. By making this editorial deci-sion, they effectively hide the thorniest issue surrounding Christian participation in pageants. As a result, Miss America is presented just as any other role model worthy of emulation. Peter K. Johnson, "Assemblies: Reaching Out to People in Need," *The Saturday Evening Post*, March/April 1996, 44–45, 72–73.

115 "Alumna Crowned Miss America, 2005, Uses Platform to Fight Cancer," October 2004, samford.edu.

116 For two books that consider the importance of body, body shape, and beauty in evangelical culture in particular, see Griffith, *Born Again Bodies*; and Lynne Gerber, *Seeking the Straight and Narrow: Weight Loss and Sexual Reorientation in Evangelical America* (Chicago: University of Chicago Press, 2011).

117 For a fascinating article on whether Miss America really does value diversity and allow for every facet of American culture to compete for public presence, see Hilary Levey Friedman, "Is Miss America for Nice Jewish Girls?" *Forward*, September 23, 2013, forward.com. "But if Miss America is really about embracing diversity," Friedman writes, "why hold the Pageant during the High Holy Days?" "The fact that there hasn't been a backlash over the timing of Miss America over High Holy Days is telling," she continues, "But that doesn't mean we shouldn't care and that we shouldn't push organizers to embrace all forms of diversity in America."

118 For an overview of Christian teachings on the body and a thorough account of American Christian diet culture, see R. Marie Griffith, *Born Again Bodies: Flesh and Spirit in American Christianity* (Los Angeles: University of California Press, 2004).

119 For evidence of just how entrenched Christian support of pageants was in some religious communities, see Larry Tomczak, "3 Reasons the US Should Not Crown a Lesbian Miss America," *Charisma News*, September 6, 2016, charismanews.com. Tomczak does not question what Christian little girls learn from participating in, and winning, beauty pageants. That competing in beauty pageants was sanctioned by Christians was assumed. Rather, he focuses on how a lesbian winning Miss America could be damaging to Christian children who looked up to her, including: "A lesbian Miss American can become a symbol of ideal womanhood." "If a lesbian is presented for our daughters and granddaughters as an 'ideal,' 'dream,' and 'Queen,'" Tomczak goes on to ponder, "what does this say about the moral condition of our nation?"

120 Elizabeth H. Flowers, *Into the Pulpit: Southern Baptist Women and Power since World War II* (Chapel Hill: University of North Carolina Press, 2012), esp. 54–58 and 76–86. Flowers demonstrated that conservative Baptist publications as early as the 1970s were responding to the threat of feminism by marketing their own version of womanhood. I wonder if some viewed markers of traditional femininity such as the pageant as comforting in the wake of feminism as they struggled to respond. See also Ann Braude, "Faith, Feminism, and History," in *The Religious History of American Women: Reimagining the Past*, ed. Catherine A. Brekus (Chapel Hill: University of North Carolina Press, 2007), 243. Of course, the relationship between religion and feminism in the 1960s was not as fraught as sometimes portrayed. As historian Ann Braude demonstrated, "*The Feminine Mystique* was required reading for the 175 national leaders of Methodist women at their 1963 annual meeting, entitled 'Women in a New Age.'" Still, she noted that "polarized perspectives emerging in the 1980s" promoted the antagonistic view that remains dominant in public consciousness (234). Here it should be noted that most of the women participating in pageants in the 1960s–1970s held more traditional views of womanhood.

121 Charles H. Lippy, ch. 14, "Quests for Unity amid Diversity," in *Introducing American Religion* (New York: Routledge, 2009), esp. 205–7, 210–11. See also Molly Worthen, "How Billy Graham Became an American Icon," *CNN Belief Blog*, November 9, 2013, religion.blogs.cnn.com; Marissa Lowe Wallace, "Billy Graham's Cold War Rhetoric: Evangelical and Civil Religious Revival," in *The Rhetoric of American Civil Religion: Symbols, Sinners, and Saints*, ed. Jason A. Edwards and Joseph M.

Valenzano III (New York: Lexington Books, 2016), 77–94; and Grant Wacker, "Billy Graham's America," *Church History* 78, no. 3 (2009): 489–511. Of course, this was not true for Catholic Christians as evidenced by the treatment of John F. Kennedy during the 1960 presidential election. Similarly, non-Christian Miss Americas faced more public scrutiny.

122 Worthen, "How Billy Graham."

123 Thomas Aiello, "Constructing 'Godless Communism': Religion, Politics, and Popular Culture, 1954–1960," *Americana: The Journal of American Popular Culture* 4, no. 1 (2005), americanpopularculture.com. See also Worthen, "How Billy Graham"; and Wacker, "Billy Graham's America."

124 Will Herberg, *Protestant, Catholic, Jew: An Essay in American Religious Sociology* (Chicago: University of Chicago Press, 1983).

125 See n. 120 in this chapter and Seth Dowland, *Family Values and the Rise of the Christian Right* (Philadelphia: University of Pennsylvania Press, 2015). Dowland's book "examines how and why family values came to play such a prominent role in evangelical worldviews" (3). For a work that considers how evangelical women have negotiated faith and feminism, see R. Marie Griffith, *God's Daughters: Evangelical Women and the Power of Submission* (Los Angeles: University of California Press, 2000).

126 See ch. 5, "Faith in the Pageant," for further discussion of Van Dyke's influence on Christian youth culture in the 1960s–1970s.

127 Again Elizabeth Flowers' careful study of gender in the Southern Baptist Convention is useful here, esp. ch. 2 and ch. 3. Her work described the threat of feminism as experienced by one conservative Christian denomination and highlighted some crucial organizational responses to it. Though not a planned attack, I contend that pageants offered another way for conservative Christians to trumpet their values over and against the new womanhood being touted by feminists.

128 Lippy, *Introducing American Religion*, ch. 14.

129 For a brief overview of evangelicalism in America, see Randall Balmer, *Evangelicalism in America* (Waco, Tex.: Baylor University Press, 2016). See also David W. Bebbington, *The Dominance of Evangelicalism: The Age of Spurgeon and Moody* (Downers Grove, Ill.: InterVarsity, 2005); Nathan O. Hatch, *The Democratization of American Christianity* (New Haven: Yale University Press, 1989); George M. Marsden, *Fundamentalism and American Culture: The Shaping of Twentieth-Century Evangelicalism 1870–1925* (New York: Oxford University Press, 1980); and Mark A. Noll, *The Rise of Evangelicalism: The Age of Edwards, Whitefield, and the Wesleys* (Downers Grove, Ill.: InterVarsity, 2003). Evangelicalism is not a monolithic movement. For just a few of the works that consider the variety of ways that evangelicals have sought to engage and/or influence American culture, see Balmer, *Mine Eyes Have Seen the Glory*; Brantley W. Gasaway, *Progressive Evangelicals and the Pursuit of Social Justice* (Chapel Hill: University of North Carolina Press, 2014); Lynn Neal, *Romancing God: Evangelical Women and Inspirational Fiction* (Chapel Hill: University of North Carolina Press, 2006); and Jill Stevenson, *Sensational Devotion: Evangelical Performance in Twenty-First-Century America* (Ann Arbor: University of Michigan Press, 2015).

130 Other studies that consider the interaction between religion and popular culture include Timothy K. Beal, *Roadside Religion: In Search of the Sacred, the Strange, and the Substance of Faith* (Boston: Beacon Press, 2005); Gary Laderman, *Sacred Matters: Celebrity Worship, Sexual Ecstasies, the Living Dead, and Other Signs of Religious Life in the United States* (New York: The New Press, 2009); Kathryn Lofton, *Oprah: The Gospel of an Icon* (Los Angeles: University of California Press, 2011); and Steinberg and Kincheloe, *Christotainment*.

131 Carrie Prejean, *Still Standing: The Untold Story of My Fight against Gossip, Hate, and Political Attacks* (Washington, D.C.: Regnery, 2009), 2.

132 Prejean, *Still Standing*, 2. It is worth noting that Miss America 2010, Caressa Cameron, was asked almost an identical question when she competed (and won) Miss Virginia just two months after Prejean's answer cost her the crown. Cameron gave a very similar answer, communicating that "she believed marriage should be between a man and a woman because of her religious beliefs, but she didn't think there should be laws against gay marriage." See Oskar Garcia, "22-Year-Old Goes from Miss Va. to Miss America," *San-Diego Union Tribune*, January 31, 2010. That a similar answer resulted in Cameron winning the crown and Prejean losing it can be read in multiple ways. First, some might use this as evidence that Miss America is still the more traditional and conservative of the two pageants. Second, the fact that Cameron was competing for a state crown in a southern state might mean that her views were representative of those she was being elected to serve. Finally, and more simply, it might have been the result of a different panel of judges. Pageants are incredibly subjective exercises. Three sets of judges adjudicating the same pageant would not necessarily choose the same set of winners.

133 "Gay Marriage Row at Miss USA Show," *BBC News*, April 20, 2009, news.bbc.co .uk.

134 Bob Allen, "Conservatives Divided over Miss USA Controversy," *Baptist News Global*, May 12, 2009, baptistnews.com; and Brian Brown, "National Organization for Marriage and Carrie Prejean Launch New Ad Showing Intolerance of Gay Marriage Activists, Illustrating Threats to Religious Liberty," *National Organization for Marriage* blog, April 30, 2009, nomblog.com.

135 Kate Harding, "Carrie Prejean Threatens to Storm Off 'Larry King Live,'" *Salon*, November 12, 2009; Alan Duke, "Miss California USA Prejean Dethroned," *CNN*, June 10, 2009, cnn.com; and Melissa McEwan, "Miss Anti-Gay USA: Homophobia and Misogyny Collide in One Delightful Beauty Pageant Car-Crash, Starring Perez Hilton and Miss California," *Guardian*, April 21, 2009.

136 Katelyn Beaty, "The Other Miss California Controversy," *Christianity Today*, April 24, 2009, christianitytoday.com.

137 Warren Throckmorton, "Carrie Prejean to Appear in Traditional Marriage Ad; Gets Liberty U Scholarship Offer," *Patheos* blog, April 30, 2009, patheos.com.

138 See, for example, Sharon Hodde Miller, "Should Christians Participate in Beauty Pageants?" *She Worships* blog, July 11, 2009, sheworships.com; Melody Maxwell, "Christians and the Miss America Competition," *Baptist News Global*, January 20,

2011, baptistnews.com; Bob Allen, "Conservatives Divided over Miss California USA Controversy," *Baptist News Global*, May 12, 2009, baptistnews.com; and Dave Welch, "Is Carrie Prejean Really a Hero?" *WND Commentary*, April 29, 2009, wnd.com.

139 Marc W. Gibson, "Can a Christian Be Miss America?" *Truth* magazine, April 20, 2006, 225, 249.

140 Gibson, "Can a Christian?" 225.

141 Gibson, "Can a Christian?" 225.

142 Gibson, "Can a Christian?" 249.

143 Tom Minnery, "The Tarnished Crown of Miss America," *Focus on the Family*, September 7, 1984, 13.

144 Minnery, "Tarnished Crown," 13.

145 Minnery, "Tarnished Crown," 13. This comparison of a "fallen" woman to Eve pervaded evangelical culture. For a fascinating study of how the biblical story of Adam and Eve comes to hold such cultural power, including its widespread usage, see Linda S. Schearing and Valarie H. Ziegler, *Enticed by Eden: How Western Culture Uses, Confuses, (and Sometimes Abuses) Adam and Eve* (Waco, Tex.: Baylor University Press, 2013).

146 Cox, "Cult of The Girl," 145.

147 Cox, "Cult of The Girl," 146.

148 Cox, "Cult of The Girl," 146.

149 See also Maxwell, "Christians and the Miss America Competition"; Margaret O' Brien Steinfels, "Here She Is! Miss America!" *Christianity and Crisis*, September 17, 1984; and Miller, "Should Christians Participate?"

150 "For if you keep silence at such a time as this, relief and deliverance will rise for the Jews from another quarter, but you and your father's family will perish. Who knows? Perhaps you have come to royal dignity for just such a time as this" (Esther 4:14). At times, contestants and fans used this phrase to point to the participant's greater purpose in competing. On one occasion, I even witnessed the verse on the back of a T-shirt promoting one of the contestants at Miss America.

151 See, for example, Alex Koppelman, "Sarah Palin, Anointed by God," *Salon*, September 18, 2008. For more on evangelical use of this narrative for their own purposes, see Rachel Held Evans, "Esther and Vashti: The Real Story," January 9, 2012, rachelheldevans.com.

152 Esther 2:3-4.

Chapter 5: Faith in the Pageant

1 "Miss America 2010: Caressa Cameron," interview by Terry Meeuwsen, Christian Broadcasting Network, *The 700 Club*, cbn.com/700club.

2 Heather Whitestone with Angela Elwell Hunt, *Listening with My Heart* (New York: Doubleday, 1997).

3 Mandy E. McMichael, "Pageant Preachers," *Christianity Today*, June 17, 2009.

4 Most of the Christian pageant contestants that I encountered were evangelicals broadly conceived, or, at the least, they spoke the language of evangelicalism. With religious historian Randall Balmer, I understand American evangelicals as a diverse group that share "some generic characteristics: an embrace of the Holy Bible as inspired and God's revelation to humanity, a belief in the centrality of a conversion or 'born again' experience, and the impulse to evangelize or bring others to the faith." Randall Balmer, *The Making of Evangelicalism: From Revivalism to Politics and Beyond* (Waco, Tex.: Baylor University Press, 2010), 2. The language that pervades pageant testimonies is the language of evangelicalism. And it is the flexibility of evangelicalism, in part, that allows for Christian participation in the pageant. As Balmer wrote, "The genius of evangelicalism throughout American history is its malleability and the uncanny knack of evangelical leaders to speak the idiom of the culture, whether embodied in the open-air preaching of George Whitefield in the eighteenth century, the democratic populism of Peter Cartwright and Charles Finney on the frontier, or the suburban, corporate-style megachurches of the twentieth century. Evangelicalism is always changing, adapting to new surroundings and fresh circumstances" (3). Evangelical pageant contestants stand in this tradition of malleability, taking the message of the gospel to the people. They saw the Miss America Pageant, and the world the crown opened, as a mission field ripe for harvest. Equally important to evangelical pageant contestants was their own personal piety and faith formation and the sense that the pageant aided them in that. Finally, the Miss America Pageant gave young women ample opportunities to live lives of service alongside evangelism, to practice what David Bebbington refers to as "activism." See David W. Bebbington, *The Dominance of Evangelicalism: The Age of Spurgeon and Moody* (Downers Grove, Ill.: InterVarsity, 2005), 36–40. Consequently, faith in the pageant had a decidedly evangelical feel. Some of this familiarity with, and tendency to speak in, evangelical terms may be traced to the southernization of American religion. See Mark A. Shibley, "The Southernization of American Religion: Testing a Hypothesis," *Sociological Analysis* 52, no. 2 (1991): 159–74.

And yet evangelicals were not the only Christians represented in pageants. As noted in ch. 4, Catholics, Mormons, and mainline Protestants float in and out of the story. In addition, far more contestants identified as a particular denomination or as Christian than "evangelical." Thus I have chosen to continue identifying Christian pageant participants with the broad term "Christian" or by their particular denomination in order to honor religious self-identification. That said, I note connections between evangelicalism in the pageant and broader culture. I also consider the way evangelicalism appears to be functioning in the pageant, working with the pageant to shape contestants' identities. Evangelicalism in the pageant also influences—at certain points—the faith *of* the pageant and faith *and* the pageant.

5 Katie Harman with the 2001 Miss America Contestants, *Under the Crown: 51 Stories of Courage, Determination and the American Spirit* (Seattle: Milestone Books, 2002), xix.

6   In surveying the book, I looked for key words like "prayer," "God," "faith," "church," or "Christian." Some contestants mentioned the words almost as an aside, but faith featured prominently in pieces written by others. The percentage of "probably Christians" increases from 68.6 percent to 70.6 percent with the inclusion of Miss Alabama. Kelly Jones did not discuss her faith in her essay, but the essay by Miss Georgia indicated that Jones, too, professed Christianity.

7   Harman, *Under the Crown*, 163, 45, 70.

8   Harman, *Under the Crown*, 23, 77.

9   Vonda Kay Van Dyke, *That Girl in Your Mirror* (Westwood, N.J.: Fleming H. Revell Company, 1966), 118.

10   John W. Kennedy, "Miss (Christian) America," *Christianity Today International*, 2003.

11   Barbara Welter, "The Cult of True Womanhood: 1820–1860," *American Quarterly* 18, no. 2, part 1 (1966): 151–74.

12   For a classic account of these experiences, see Carol Gilligan, *In a Different Voice: Psychological Theory and Women's Development* (Cambridge, Mass.: Harvard University Press, 1982), 1–4, 64–106. This work has been criticized significantly since its publication for essentializing socially constructed gender roles, but it nevertheless serves as a useful starting point for many conversations regarding moral psychology. See Steven M. Jaffee and Janet Shibley Hyde, "Gender Differences in Moral Orientation: A Meta-analysis," *Psychological Bulletin* 132 (2000): 23–72; and Carol Gilligan, *Joining the Resistance* (Cambridge, U.K.: Polity, 2011).

13   Most semi-famous pageant participants do not serve in clergy roles, but Terry Meeuwsen, Miss America 1973; Vonda Kay Van Dyke, Miss America 1965; and others serve or have served nonprofit Christian institutions. In addition, Debra Barnes, Miss America 1968, has worked as a music director in a nondenominational church, and BeBe Shopp, Miss America 1948, served as a lay leader in the Episcopal Church. Three contestants in the 2004 Miss America Pageant made their way into ministry. In fact, two were in seminary at the time they competed in the Miss America Pageant. Miss Minnesota 2003, Megan Torgerson, ordained in the (mainline) Evangelical Lutheran Church in America (ELCA) tradition, ministered as an associate pastor. Miss California 2003, Nicole LaMarche, served as an ordained minister in the (mainline) United Church of Christ. Miss Michigan 2003, Erin Moss, worked as a pastor of adult ministries in a Church of God congregation. What is harder to discern are the numbers of lower-level participants who receive encouragement from their participation and thus seek leadership roles in church contexts.

14   For the significance of adolescence and young adulthood in human religious identity, see James W. Fowler, *Stages of Faith: The Psychology of Human Development and the Quest for Meaning* (New York: HarperOne, 1976), 69–86.

15   See ch. 3 on testimony in Grant Wacker, *Heaven Below: Early Pentecostals and America Culture* (Cambridge, Mass.: Harvard University Press, 2001), 58–69.

16   Scot McKnight and Hauna Ondrey, *Finding Faith, Losing Faith: Stories of Conversion and Apostasy* (Waco, Tex.: Baylor University Press, 2008), 1–2. McKnight and

Ondrey's three foundational claims apply here: "All conversions go through the same process. No conversions are identical. But many conversions fall into similar patterns." They noted, "Each person emerges from a *context* as a result of a *crisis* of some sort that leads them to a conversion. That crisis prompts a *quest* to find a solution to that crisis. Converts then *encounter* and interact with those who advocate a new faith, leading them to a *commitment* and to *consequences* for life. There are then six dimensions to all conversions: context, crisis, quest, encounter, commitment and consequences." While all six dimensions are discernable in pageant conversions, I chose to organize my analysis around Wacker's more simplified model of crisis, faith, and reward. See Wacker, *Heaven Below*, 58–59. Still, each of the six dimensions can be found within the narratives offered in the simplified structure.

17 Anna Carter Florence, *Preaching as Testimony* (Louisville: Westminster John Knox, 2007), xiii. Testimony acts "as both a narration of events and a confession of belief: we tell what we have seen and heard, and we confess what we believe about it."

18 Edwin S. Gaustad, ed., *Memoirs of the Spirit: American Religious Autobiography from Jonathan Edwards to Maya Angelou* (Grant Rapids: Eerdmans, 1999), xv.

19 Incidentally, this is not unlike Christianity's relationship to other popular culture phenomena. See, for example, Deann Alford, "Racing for Jesus: How God-Fearing Drivers and a National Ministry Bring Faith to NASCAR," *Christianity Today*, August 2008.

20 Other scholars cited Prewitt's story as evidence of a relationship between religion and pageantry. As historian Charles Reagan Wilson noted, "In Prewitt's persona, the beauty queen has become an icon of religious edification." Charles Reagan Wilson, *Judgment and Grace in Dixie: Southern Faiths from Faulkner to Elvis* (Athens: University of Georgia Press, 1995), 158. Karen W. Tice came to similar conclusions, arguing that Prewitt offered "another noteworthy example of a Miss America who has successfully merged pageants and preaching." Karen W. Tice, *Queens of Academe: Beauty Pageantry, Student Bodies, and College Life* (New York: Oxford University Press, 2012), 166. Tice quotes Wilson at length when writing about Prewitt (167). My work overlapped with Tice's study of beauty contests on college campuses. More specifically, her chapter "Flesh and Spirit: Bibles, Beauty, and Bikinis" explored similar trends in the relationship between Christianity and pageants. Beginning my research in the summer of 2006, sometimes I built on her work, sometimes we reached the same conclusions independently, sometimes we drew different interpretations from the same data, and sometimes we simply differed. Both Wilson and Tice, like *Christianity Today*'s Kennedy, saw a blossoming relationship between conservative Christian contestants and the pageant (and, in the case of Wilson, a relationship between beauty culture and the South). They observed that contestants testified to their faith in the midst of the secular pageant and showed how that language bore out in the public sphere. Neither, however, dissected the predictable and repeated pattern used by evangelical Miss Americas in pageant "testimonies" to discern the characteristics of evangelicalism that made this unlikely relationship possible. See also McMichael, "Pageant Preachers."

21 Cheryl Prewitt with Kathryn Slattery, *A Bright-Shining Place: The Story of a Miracle* (Garden City, N.Y.: Doubleday, 1981), 245.

22 Prewitt, *Bright-Shining Place*, 127.

23 Prewitt, *Bright-Shining Place*, 131.

24 Prewitt, *Bright-Shining Place*, 209–10.

25 Prewitt, *Bright-Shining Place*, 210.

26 Prewitt, *Bright-Shining Place*, 233ff.

27 Prewitt, *Bright-Shining Place*, 213.

28 Prewitt, *Bright-Shining Place*, 214.

29 Prewitt, *Bright-Shining Place*, 214–15.

30 Prewitt, *Bright-Shining Place*, 238–40.

31 Kate Bowler's work on the American Prosperity Gospel offers useful insights for understanding Prewitt's Pentecostalism. Prewitt's testimony bore out Bowler's argument that individuals in faith movement churches "preached a gospel of triumph," and her work to win Miss America mirrored the techniques of triumph Bowler described. Kate Bowler, *Blessed: A History of the American Prosperity Gospel* (New York: Oxford University Press, 2013), esp. ch. 5, "Victory."

32 Prewitt, *Bright-Shining Place*, 245.

33 Prewitt, *Bright-Shining Place*, 236.

34 Prewitt's body work mirrored that of other Protestants seeking to perfect their temples for Christ. See R. Marie Griffith, *Born Again Bodies: Flesh and Spirit in American Christianity* (Los Angeles: University of California Press, 2004), especially ch. 4, "Pray the Weight Away: Shaping Devotional Fitness Culture."

35 When Wilson published his essay in 1989, he focused on how the expectations for a beauty queen—such as purity—fit well with "evangelical morality" in the South. He concluded that "Prewitt's example [was], of course, an extreme case of southern religiosity validating the beauty culture." Wilson, *Judgment and Grace in Dixie*, 158. It appears true that religious justification for pageantry was less common in 1989 than it was in 2011. However, even if some of her religious claims were "extreme," Prewitt was not alone in her religious defenses of beauty competitions. Miss America 1965, Miss America 1973, and Miss America 1985 all spoke or wrote about God directing their pageant steps too. And as noted, the validation of pageantry became almost second nature among religious communities across the nation after Vonda Kay Van Dyke's onstage answer in 1965. Increasingly, evangelical contestants described their participation in starkly religious terms. Tice pushed Wilson's argument further, acknowledging that the once unthinkable relationship between religion and beauty pageants became normalized in the second half of the twentieth century. She stopped short, however, of exploring the shape of their narratives. This is not intended as a critique of Tice's important work. Her chapter "Flesh and Spirit: Bibles, Beauty, and Bikinis" was part of a larger project examining the relationship between beauty pageants and higher education. The religious lives of the contestants were secondary. Examining participants' words alongside those of their religious communities proves

crucial for understanding their motivations and, more important, how they represented their faith traditions.

36 Whitestone, *Listening with My Heart*, 90.

37 "Teresa Scanlan: Miss America 2011, A Groundbreaking Miss America," Christian Broadcasting Network, *The 700 Club*, cbn.com/700club. Scanlan noted that "pageantry helped her trust God because she couldn't control the outcome and she had to trust Him." "Focus on the Family Transcript," Tara Dawn Christensen website, http://www.taradawnchristensen.com/Focus_on_the_Family_Transcript.htm.

38 NASCAR offers another example with Christian drivers, crew members, and sponsors staking a claim in a culture where "liquor and raw language flow." It, too, is seen as an evangelistic field ripe unto harvest. Alford, "Racing for Jesus." Many scholars have made this point about the flexibility of evangelical culture. Like Randall Balmer, "I wanted to show variations within a subculture generally regarded as monolithic." Randall Balmer, *Mine Eyes Have Seen the Glory: A Journey into the Evangelical Subculture in America*, 3rd ed. (New York: Oxford University Press, 2000), 7. See also Brenda E. Brasher, *Godly Women: Fundamentalism and Female Power* (New Brunswick, N.J.: Rutgers University Press, 1998); Elizabeth H. Flowers, *Into the Pulpit: Southern Baptist Women and Power since World War II* (Chapel Hill: University of North Carolina Press, 2012); Charles H. Lippy, *Introducing American Religion* (New York: Routledge, 2009), 236ff.; and Tice, *Queens of Academe*, 180.

39 H. Richard Niebuhr, *Christ and Culture* (New York: Harper & Brothers, 1951), esp. ch. 6, "Christ the Transformer of Culture." Evangelicals, unlike fundamentalists, were happy to work in the world to change the world. For pageant contestants, that meant that they should take their faith with them to the stage. For a helpful discussion of evangelicals' engagement with Niebuhr's five types, see John G. Stackhouse Jr., "In the World, But . . ." *Christianity Today*, April 22, 2002.

40 Shirley Monty, *Terry* (Waco, Tex.: Word Books, 1982), 21.

41 Monty, *Terry*, 22.

42 Stephen Prothero, *American Jesus: How the Son of God Became a National Icon* (New York: Farrar, Straus, and Giroux, 2003). In ch. 4, "Superstar," Prothero discussed the spread of this movement in the 1960s and 1970s, arguing "they brought to the United States another evangelical revival, and another conception of Jesus tailor-made for its time" (126).

43 Kennedy, "Miss (Christian) America."

44 Sarah Banet-Weiser, ch. 5, "The Representational Politics of Whiteness and the National Body: Bess Myerson, Miss America 1945, and Heather Whitestone, Miss America 1995," in *The Most Beautiful Girl in the World: Beauty Pageants and National Identity* (Los Angeles: University of California Press, 1999). The signs of American beauty ideals were apparent to observers and to participants, and they served as key markers in the building up of a very distinct kind of community. For an important work along these lines, see Anthony P. Cohen, *The Symbolic Construction of Community* (New York: Routledge, 1985).

45 Whitestone, *Listening with My Heart*, 77.

46 Van Dyke, *That Girl in Your Mirror*, 111.

47 Van Dyke, *That Girl in Your Mirror*, 111–12.

48 Van Dyke, *That Girl in Your Mirror*, 112.

49 Van Dyke, *That Girl in Your Mirror*, 112.

50 Van Dyke, *That Girl in Your Mirror*, 113.

51 This idea of working with God was endemic in the Reformed/Wesleyan evangelical tradition, where many of the women came from. As far back as the Puritans, Christians saw their role as one that demonstrated God's goodness and worked for God's purpose. See Edmund S. Morgan, *The Puritan Dilemma: The Story of John Winthrop* (New York: Longman, 1999); and William R. Hutchison, *Religious Pluralism in America: The Contentious History of a Founding Ideal* (New Haven: Yale University Press, 2003), esp. ch. 3, "Marching to Zion: The Protestant Establishment as a Unifying Force."

52 The human ability to ascribe religious meaning to neutral events, people, or places is, of course, wide-ranging. One need only think of the football player pointing to the sky in gratitude to God after a winning drive or, somewhat more surprisingly, the attribution of business success to the divine. Religious accounts are magisterial and may thus envelop whole worlds within their frameworks of belief. For book-length treatments of sports theology, see William J. Baker, *Playing with God: Religion and Modern Sport* (Cambridge, Mass.: Harvard University Press, 2009); and Shirl James Hoffman, *Good Game: Christianity and the Culture of Sports* (Waco, Tex.: Baylor University Press, 2010). For an exploration of God and business, see Beth Kreydatus, "'Enriching Women's Lives': The Mary Kay Approach to Business, Beauty, and Feminism," *Business and Economic History Online* 3 (2005), www.thebhc.org.

53 Kennedy, "Miss (Christian) America."

54 Linda Nees, "Miss America 1990," *Pageantry*, Winter 2000, www.pageantrymagazine .com.

55 Becki Trueblood, as told to Rhonda Graham, *Best for Me* (Boise, Idaho: Pacific Press Publishing Association, 1991), 72.

56 Kennedy, "Miss (Christian) America." On at least one occasion, Turner was reprimanded for performing her Christian rap in a public school setting. The original press releases indicated that Turner agreed not to perform the Christian rap in those venues again. See "Christian Rap's Out, Pageant Decides," *Deseret News*, March 14, 1990. In contrast, Kennedy's piece noted, "Complaints to pageant officials and threats of lawsuits didn't stop her. 'I wasn't going to be ashamed of my beliefs,' she says. 'I told them I lived in a country where I could express my views freely.'" This revisionist history suggests a shaping of the story to better fit evangelical ideals regarding standing against cultural pressure.

57 Whitestone, *Listening with My Heart*, 64.

58 Whitestone, *Listening with My Heart*, 72.

59 Whitestone, *Listening with My Heart*, 73.

60 Whitestone, *Listening with My Heart*, 73 (emphasis in original). This contrasts with Prewitt's certainty. Prewitt believed that testifying to God's promises ahead of time

pointed to her trust in God's promise. Whitestone worried that knowing would result in human error. This is one place where you can see evidence of individual traditions. Prewitt's Pentecostalism mandated that she confess and believe that she would win while Whitestone's more general evangelical background belied such a certainty of outcome. Bowler's work on the American Prosperity Gospel offered help in understanding the "positive confession" idea embedded in Prewitt's thinking. See Bowler, *Blessed*, 21–22, 66–67, 151–52, 158–59.

61 Van Dyke, *That Girl in Your Mirror*, 114.

62 Van Dyke, *That Girl in Your Mirror*, esp. ch. 19, "Enjoy Yourself!" 115–19.

63 Van Dyke, *That Girl in Your Mirror*, 117–18.

64 Van Dyke, *That Girl in Your Mirror*, 118.

65 Van Dyke, *That Girl in Your Mirror*, 118.

66 The "persecution" necessary for true refinement also played a role in pageant preparation and success (at times limiting that success) and will be discussed in the next section.

67 More on how pageant testimonies served as inspiration to others will be discussed in the identity section below.

68 Nicole Johnson, *Living with Diabetes: Nicole Johnson, Miss America 1999* (Washington, D.C.: Lifeline Press, 2001), 121–22.

69 The community service platforms chosen by these four Christian winners were: Turner: 1990 Motivating Youth to Excellence; Holland: 1997 Literacy Advocacy and Tutoring; Harold: 2003 Preventing Youth Violence and Bullying and Sexual Abstinence; and Scanlan: 2011 Dangers of Eating Disorders.

70 Kennedy, "Miss (Christian) America."

71 Southern evangelicalism, which influenced many of the pageant contestants, placed a powerful emphasis on witness. See, for example, Samuel S. Hill, *Southern Churches in Crisis Revisited* (Tuscaloosa: University of Alabama Press, 1999), esp. ch. 5, "The Central Theme"; and Wayne Flynt and Gerald W. Berkley, *Taking Christianity to China: Alabama Missionaries in the Middle Kingdom, 1850–1950* (Tuscaloosa: University of Alabama Press, 1997).

72 Teresa Scanlan, "Miss America Is Here: Why Am I Competing?" January 4, 2011, teresastravelsandtidbits.blogspot.com.

73 Scanlan, "Miss America Is Here: Why Am I Competing?"

74 Dana Williamson, "Miss Oklahoma Wants to Spend Year Sharing Faith with Youth," *Baptist Press*, September 29, 1998, apnews.net.

75 Banet-Weiser, *The Most Beautiful Girl in the World*, 43. Banet-Weiser notes that most platforms "can be characterized as 'women's issues,' or rather, issues that are relegated to the private sphere and that entail nurturing, emotionality, and morality." For more on women as moral guardians in the nineteenth century, see Nancy A. Hardesty, *Women Called to Witness: Evangelical Feminism in the Nineteenth Century*, 2nd ed. (Knoxville: University of Tennessee Press, 1999); and Laceye Warner, *Saving Women: Retrieving Evangelistic Theology and Practice* (Waco, Tex.: Baylor University Press, 2007).

76 It was a reward because it allowed them to go into all the world, and it was rewarding because they could see they were making a difference (or feel as if they were).

77 Of course, the mission field existed both inside and outside the pageant. The pageant itself was a mission field because of unsaved, as they put it, participants. Christian contestants sometimes formed communities to pray throughout the pageant.

78 Jane Jayroe with Bob Burke, *More Grace than Glamour: My Life as Miss America and Beyond* (Oklahoma City: Oklahoma Heritage Association, 2006), 62.

79 Jayroe, *More Grace than Glamour*, 66.

80 Jayroe, *More Grace than Glamour*, 72.

81 Jayroe, *More Grace than Glamour*, 72, 74.

82 Jayroe, *More Grace than Glamour*, 75–80.

83 Jayroe, *More Grace than Glamour*, 79.

84 Jayroe, *More Grace than Glamour*, 80.

85 Jayroe, *More Grace than Glamour*, 83.

86 Jayroe, *More Grace than Glamour*, 84–85.

87 Christian contestants also possessed and earned "spiritual capital" that acted as cultural capital within particular spheres. In the case of evangelical pageant participants, they used the language of their tradition and their newly earned titles to gain access to pulpits and publications. As argued by sociologist Bradford Verter, "Personal piety may be viewed as a matter of taste . . . and thus as a marker of status within struggles for domination in a variety of contexts. Spiritual knowledge, competencies, and preferences may be understood as valuable assets in the economy of symbolic goods." Spiritual capital, he noted, "may be translated into other forms of capital" and "might bring social and economic advancement." Bradford Verter, "Spiritual Capital: Theorizing Religion with Bourdieu against Bourdieu," *Sociological Theory* 21, no. 2 (2003): 150–74, here 152 and 168.

88 Ali Rogers, Miss South Carolina 2012 and first runner-up to Miss America 2013, was a deeply committed Christian who only recognized the potential for missions and evangelism after receiving the crown. Like Jane Jayroe, Miss America 1967, she took full advantage of each opportunity, but she did not enter the contest with ministry in mind. Rogers had been involved in community service long before she began competing and wanted to continue serving children with disabilities far beyond her pageant career. She saw the opportunities to speak in churches, at Fellowship of Christian Athlete rallies, and in schools as added benefits. Rogers also mused that perhaps some individuals, especially in southern states like South Carolina, played the "God card" because they thought it gave them an advantage. She thought it suspicious when women claimed that God called them to compete. It might happen, but she doubted if it was ever the sole driving force. That she articulated one of the very things I had been afraid to say forced me to consider other connections and motivations. Interview and conversation with Ali Rogers, "Faith and Beauty in America: The Church's Ongoing Relationship with the Pageant," Park Road Baptist Church, Charlotte, North Carolina, August 11, 2013.

One other story makes the point about the deep connection between Christianity and the pageant and thus the perceived advantage of being a Christian when competing. "Outsiders" to both pageantry and conservative Christianity saw the relationship between the two as natural. When Michelle Anderson, Miss Santa Cruz 1988, decided to "draw attention to what she and many other feminists regard[ed] as the exploitive nature of beauty pageants" by participating in the contests herself, she took on a whole new persona. In addition to tanning bed visits, voice lessons, bleached hair, and weight loss plans, Anderson presented herself as a fundamentalist Christian. Michael Neil with Dirk Mathison, "Pageant Officials Are Calling Michelle Anderson Every Name in the Book Except Miss California," *People*, July 4, 1988.

89 Of course, the isolation of single or primary motives is exceedingly difficult, and is perhaps ill-advised in any event, but the narration of evangelism on the part of the actor in the midst of obviously mixed motives is itself an important piece of information. Evangelism is the acceptable and noble reason, whereas for whatever reason others are less so. Ethnography is of course deeply concerned with this issue, as in Dan McAdams, *The Stories We Live by: Personal Myths and the Making of the Self* (New York: Guilford, 1993); or H. L. Goodall Jr., *Writing the New Ethnography* (Lanham, Md.: AltaMira, 2000).

90 The pressure faced by individuals who lived their lives in the spotlight is immense. For a useful entrée into the psychology of fame and its myriad effects, see David Giles, *Illusions of Immortality: A Psychology of Fame and Celebrity* (New York: Palgrave Macmillan, 2000).

91 Mona Charen, "Pageant Tries, but Miss America Won't Be Silenced," *Baltimore Sun*, October 14, 2002.

92 For an example of negative press, see Lara Riscol, "Miss America's Stealth Virginity Campaign," *Salon*, October 28, 2002. For an example of positive press, see "Miss America Resists Pressure to Silence Abstinence Message," *Baptist Press*, October 2, 2002, bpnews.net.

93 Jim Bennett, "Miss America Unmuzzled," *WorldNetDaily (WND)*, October 5, 2003, wnd.com.

94 John W. Kennedy, "Erika Harold: Miss America for Such a Time as This," *Pentecostal Evangel*, February 23, 2003.

95 Sara Moslener, *Virgin Nation: Sexual Purity and American Adolescence* (New York: Oxford University Press, 2015). Incidentally the pageant espoused similar values. Miss America contestants needed to portray at least the appearance of being virginal and available, as discussed in ch. 1.

96 Whitestone, *Listening with My Heart*, 94.

97 Whitestone, *Listening with My Heart*, 95.

98 Whitestone, *Listening with My Heart*, 134.

99 For an intriguing look at private improvement and public humility, see Jonathon D. Brown and Frances M. Gallagher, "Coming to Terms with Failure: Private

Self-Enhancement and Public Self-Effacement," *Journal of Experimental Social Psychology* 28, no. 1 (1992): 3–22. See also Gilligan, *In a Different Voice*, 106–27.

100 Jayroe, *More Grace than Glamour*, 109–10.

101 Caressa Cameron, interview by Terry Meeuwsen, Christian Broadcasting Network, *The 700 Club*, April 2010, cbn.com/700club.

102 Jay Copp, "A Catholic Miss America: Angela Perez Baraquio," *St. Anthony Messenger*, September 2001, americancatholic.org/messenger (site no longer available).

103 Monty, *Terry*, 56. Johnson, *Living with Diabetes*, 106–9.

104 Sheri L. Dew, *Sharlene Wells: Miss America* (Salt Lake City: Deseret Books, 1985), 183.

105 Whitestone, *Listening with My Heart*, 154–55.

106 Jayroe, *More Grace than Glamour*, 116.

107 Johnson, *Living with Diabetes*, 156.

108 Prewitt, *Bright-Shining Place*, 219–20.

109 Prewitt, *Bright-Shining Place*, 257.

110 Katie Stam, interview by Terry Meeuwsen, Christian Broadcasting Network, *The 700 Club*, April 2010, cbn.com/700club.

111 The relatively quick road to disappointment and disillusionment in this public idealistic role parallels that among clergy, a well-documented phenomenon. See Elizabeth Ann Jackson-Jordan, "Clergy Burnout and Resilience: A Review of the Literature," *Journal of Pastoral Care and Counseling* 67, no. 1 (2013): 1–5. Although one should not make too much of the parallel, the similar trajectories are suggestive.

112 Sharlene Wells, epilogue in Sheri L. Dew, *Sharlene Wells: Miss America* (Salt Lake City: Deseret Books, 1985), 185–86.

113 Rebecca "Becki" Trueblood, Miss Idaho 1989, in Trueblood, *Best for Me*, 41.

114 Williamson, "Miss Oklahoma Wants."

115 Julie Dockstader Heaps, "Standing Her Ground on the National Stage," *Church News*, January 26, 2008, ldschurchnews.com.

116 Trueblood, *Best for Me*, 9.

117 Trueblood, *Best for Me*, 10.

118 Trueblood, *Best for Me*, 11.

119 Trueblood, *Best for Me*, 34.

120 Trueblood, *Best for Me*, 38.

121 Pageantry is not the only arena in which multiple individuals claim to be called by God to participate. Politics offers perhaps the most obvious example. Such claims stem from Christian understandings about how to interpret the will of God. For an overview and comparison of the three main views on God's will, see Douglas S. Huffman, ed., *How Then Should We Choose? Three Views on God's Will and Decision Making* (Grand Rapids: Kregel Publications, 2009). For a brief article that summarizes the views, see Dennis J. Horton, "Discerning Spiritual Discernment: Assessing Current Approaches for Understanding God's Will," *Journal of Youth Ministry* 7, no. 2 (2009): 7–31.

122 Trueblood, *Best for Me*, 73.

123 Trueblood, *Best for Me*, 73.

124 Trueblood, *Best for Me*, 111–12.

125 Trueblood, *Best for Me*, 117.

126 Trueblood, *Best for Me*, 121.

127 Prewitt, *Bright-Shining Place*, 247.

128 Women have a long history of testifying in the Christian tradition. Indeed, "many historical women preachers described their preaching as *testimony*." "Preaching in the testimony tradition provides us with a historical, biblical, theological, and homiletical memory of women's preaching: in short, a women's preaching tradition." Florence, *Preaching as Testimony*, xix and xxvi. Pageant contestants stand in this tradition of women who used the avenues open to them to share their faith stories.

129 Wacker, *Heaven Below*, 68–69.

130 Again, this harkens back to the nineteenth-century ideal that women should be "useful." See Hardesty, *Women Called to Witness*.

131 For example, Rebecca Trueblood, Miss Idaho 1989, heard Kellye Cash, Miss America 1987, speak, and Tara Dawn Holland, Miss America 1997, read the autobiography of Cheryl Prewitt, Miss America 1980.

132 I am struck by the similarities between pageant confessions and those by individuals running for public office. In politics, as with pageantry, Christians (particularly evangelicals) often felt compelled to describe their vocation in religious terms like calling. Christian politicians wanted to reform the world too.

133 A similar argument was made by some in the Christian NASCAR community. See Alford, "Racing for Jesus."

134 Mary Vespa, "Miss America, Tawny Godin, Puts a Ring on Her Finger and Steps on Some Toes," *People*, March 26, 1976.

135 Michelle Tauber et al., "American Beauties," *People*, October 16, 2000, 170.

136 Rick Hampson, "Vanessa Williams Gives Up Her Miss America Crown," *Gettysburg Times*, July 24, 1984, 4.

137 Frank Deford, *There She Is: The Life and Times of Miss America* (New York: Viking Press, 1971), 144. For the fuller story of Cooper's win, disappearance, and denial, see 139–46.

138 Tauber, "American Beauties," 144.

139 For one example, see Amanda Angelotti, "Confessions of a Beauty Pageant Drop-Out," *Generation Progress* (formerly *Campus Progress*), January 25, 2006, genprogress.org.

140 Shelli Yoder, "Pursuing a Crown of Perfection: A Journey from Atlantic City to Vanderbilt University Divinity School," *The Spire* 23, no. 2 (2002): 23.

141 Yoder, "Pursuing a Crown of Perfection," 23.

142 Yoder, "Pursuing a Crown of Perfection," 24. The pursuit of perfection in this context parallels the ideal in Christian theology embodied most famously by John Wesley, who held that "entire sanctification" was indeed possible for the Christian believer. See his work *A Plain Account of Christian Perfection*, ed. Randy Maddox and Paul W. Chilcote (Kansas City, Mo.: Beacon Hill, 2015 [1777]). As the Christian could become an ideal believer in holiness with respect to God, so also could women become perfected as women.

143 "Pursuing a Crown of Perfection," 23.
144 "Pursuing a Crown of Perfection," 23–24.

Conclusion: Born Again: Miss America 2.0

1 Dana Feldman, "Miss America 2019: Is The Pageant Still Relevant Today?" *Forbes*, September 7, 2018; Mary Elizabeth Williams, "Miss America's #MeToo Reboot: Can a Former Beauty Pageant Really Evolve?" *Salon*, June 5, 2018; and Andrea Pyser, "Why It's Not Worth It to Save Miss America," *New York Post*, June 13, 2018. As has been demonstrated, these feelings of ambivalence, distaste, and disinterest in the pageant are nothing new. Thus, the study of pageants has also been considered trivial and inconsequential. And yet pageants are rich, complex sites that are ripe for further study. To pretend we exist outside of popular culture and/or that popular culture demands no explanation or analysis is both dismissive and lazy. See Sarah Banet-Weiser, *The Most Beautiful Girl in the World: Beauty Pageants and National Identity* (Los Angeles: University of California Press, 1999), 4–6 and 212, n. 7. "In general," she writes, "beauty pageants are grouped with popular cultural forms that are regarded as either too 'low' to merit serious investigation or so obvious and opaque that vigorous interrogation would be both uninteresting and unnecessary" (4).

2 Jill Neimark, "Why We Need Miss America," *Psychology Today* 31, no. 5 (1998): 40ff. "The fact is, Miss America informs us about our culture's ideals and conflicts . . . The Miss America contest has always knit together in its middle-class queen the deep schisms in American society. Whether her contestants flaunt pierced belly buttons or Ph.Ds. in veterinary medicine, wear pants or ballgowns, Miss America is a mirror of America, even now." Neimark goes on to ask, "what is she really saying about us—and why do we need to know, anyway?" Neimark highlights ten things the Miss America Pageant reveals about America: "we're a big clubhouse, but we're not sure you should be a member"; "we're still a nation of Yankees and Southern belles"; "Cinderella ought to come from the middle class and go to college"; "we've got faith"; "we've got pluck"; "we're all equal, but we love royalty"; "we love gossip"; "we love glitz"; "superwoman is alive and well"; and "it's all for one and one for all." Miss America tells us what we value.

3 Yashar Ali, "The Miss America Emails: How the Pageant's CEO Really Talks about the Winners," *Huffington Post*, December 22, 2017; Yashar Ali, "CEO Suspended after 49 Former Miss Americas Call on the Organization's Leaders to Resign," *Huffington Post*, December 27, 2017; and Jessica Bennett, "Goodbye, Swimsuit Competition. Hello, 'Miss America 2.0,'" *New York Times*, June 5, 2018.

4 See n. 21 in this book's introduction and nn. 103 and 105 in ch. 1.

5 Lauren Carroll, "'So Fake' Gretchen Carlson Posters Appear in Atlantic City," *Press of Atlantic City*, September 6, 2018.

6 Robert Clyde Allen, *Horrible Prettiness: Burlesque and American Culture* (Chapel Hill: University of North Carolina Press, 1991), 244. "The completely revealed female form was twentieth-century burlesque's only trump card. When it was finally played, authorities in New York City moved to close down the game. Even where

strip-oriented burlesque evaded closure, it merely briefly forestalled rather than pre-
vented the form's institutional demise."

7 Amanda Auble, "Will Miss America Stay in Atlantic City?" *Press of Atlantic City*,
April 5, 2019.

8 Ann-Marie Bivans, *Miss America: In Pursuit of the Crown* (New York: MasterMedia
Limited, 1991), 7.

9 Rebecca L. Shaiber, Laura L. Johnsen, and Glenn Geher, "Intrasexual Competition
among Beauty Pageant Contestants," in *The Oxford Handbook of Women and Competition*, ed. Maryanne L. Fisher (New York: Oxford University Press, 2017).

10 To be sure, most Europeans came for financial gain rather than religious freedom.
Still, Spanish, French, and English settlers all brought their religions with them to
the "New World," a land already inhabited by Native Americans with their own
diversity of religious traditions. Questions of who could be converted and how as
well as what counted as the true religion have occupied Americans' imagination
from some of the earliest encounters between Native Americans and Europeans. And
those Pilgrims that settled in Massachusetts to be "a city on a hill" spilled plenty of
ink over matters of religion. Religion has been a formidable force in America.

11 "Despite predictions regarding secularization, religion has grown in importance at
the beginning of the postmodern twenty-first century. Positivism notwithstanding,
religion is not going away as a factor in societies around the world. Still less likely is it
to wither away in the United States, which is by all accounts the most institutionally
religious nation among all modern Western democracies. Religion in general, and
civil religion in particular, is unlikely to disappear from American politics, American international relations, or American efforts to define who and what we are as a
people." Andrew M. Manis, "Civil Religion and National Identity," in *The Columbia
Guide to Religion in American History*, ed. Paul Harvey and Edward J. Blum (New
York: Columbia University Press, 2012), 89–104, here 102.

12 Mark Noll, *America's God: From Jonathan Edwards to Abraham Lincoln* (New York:
Oxford University Press, 2002); and Catherine L. Albanese, *America: Religions
and Religion* (Belmont, Calif.: Wadsworth Publishing Company, 1981). As Albanese argued in chs. 10 and 11, all Americans share in a public Protestantism and
a civil religion in addition to whatever specific faiths they claim. One quotation
from ch. 10 will suffice: "To sum up, public Protestantism was and is the dominant
religion of the United States. Present from colonial times in Calvinistic Christianity,
sheer numbers, political and social prestige, economic power, and an early educational monopoly all contributed to the ascendancy of public Protestantism in the
'one religion.' The many who were not Protestant also contributed to its ascendancy
by their acceptance of its influence and their imitation of its ways. Hence, as both
extraordinary and ordinary religion, public Protestantism shaped America" (80).

13 For another account of Miss America as sacrifice, see Jennifer Jones, "The Beauty
Queen as Deified Sacrificial Victim," *Theatre History Studies* 18 (June 1998): 99–106.

Appendix: Miss Alabama, Contestant Survey

1 This survey was mailed to Miss Alabama contestants along with a letter introducing myself and my research and an informed consent form for four consecutive
   years (2006, 2007, 2008, and 2009). Contestants who chose to participate mailed
   the surveys and consent forms back to me. A self-addressed, stamped envelope was
   included for their convenience. Since some women participated in Miss Alabama for
   multiple years during this time, I have two or more surveys from some contestants.
   This allowed me to see some evolution of thought and relationship to the pageant by
   some participants that informed my observations and analysis.

Bibliography

Aiello, Thomas. "Constructing 'Godless Communism': Religion, Politics, and Popular Culture, 1954–1960." *Americana: The Journal of American Popular Culture* 4, no. 1 (2005).

Albanese, Catherine L. *America: Religions and Religion.* Belmont, Calif.: Wadsworth Publishing Company, 1981.

Allen, Robert Clyde. *Horrible Prettiness: Burlesque and American Culture.* Chapel Hill: University of North Carolina Press, 1991.

Bailey, Michael, and Guy Redden, eds. *Mediating Faiths: Religion and Socio-Cultural Change in the Twenty-First Century.* Burlington, Vt.: Ashgate, 2011.

Baker, William J. *Playing with God: Religion and Modern Sport.* Cambridge, Mass.: Harvard University Press, 2009.

Baldwin, Cecelia. *How the Media Shape Young Women's Perceptions of Self-Efficacy, Social Power and Class: Marketing Sexuality.* Lewiston, N.Y.: Edwin Mellen Press, 2006.

Balmer, Randall. *Evangelicalism in America.* Waco, Tex.: Baylor University Press, 2016.

———. *The Making of Evangelicalism: From Revivalism to Politics and Beyond.* Waco, Tex.: Baylor University Press, 2010.

———. *Mine Eyes Have Seen the Glory: A Journey into the Evangelical Subculture in America.* 3rd ed. New York: Oxford University Press, 2000.

Banet-Weiser, Sarah. *The Most Beautiful Girl in the World: Beauty Pageants and National Identity.* Los Angeles: University of California Press, 1999.

Banet-Weiser, Sarah, and Laura Portwood-Stacer. "'I just want to be me again!' Beauty Pageants, Reality Television and Post-feminism." *Feminist Theory* 7, no. 2 (2006): 255–72.

Banner, Lois W. *American Beauty*. Chicago: University of Chicago Press, 1983.

Bartky, Sandra Lee. *Femininity and Domination: Studies in the Phenomenology of Oppression*. New York: Routledge, 1990.

Beal, Timothy K. *Roadside Religion: In Search of the Sacred, the Strange, and the Substance of Faith*. Boston: Beacon Press, 2005.

Bean, Jennifer M., and Diane Negra, eds. *A Feminist Reader in Early Cinema*. Durham, N.C.: Duke University Press, 2002.

Bebbington, David W. *The Dominance of Evangelicalism: The Age of Spurgeon and Moody*. Downers Grove, Ill.: InterVarsity, 2005.

———. *Evangelicalism in Modern Britain: A History from the 1730s to the 1980s*. London: Unwin Hyman, 1989.

Behar, Ruth. *The Vulnerable Observer: Anthropology That Breaks Your Heart*. Boston: Beacon Press, 1996.

Bellah, Robert N. "Civil Religion in America." *Daedalus* 96, no. 1 (1967): 1–21.

Berkowitz, Edward D. *Mass Appeal: The Formative Age of the Movies, Radio, and TV*. New York: Cambridge University Press, 2010.

Bivans, Ann-Marie. *101 Secrets to Winning Beauty Pageants*. New York: Carol Publishing Group, 1995.

———. *Miss America: In Pursuit of the Crown*. New York: MasterMedia Limited, 1991.

Blumhofer, Edith L. *Restoring the Faith: The Assemblies of God, Pentecostalism, and American Culture*. Champaign: University of Illinois Press, 1993.

Bordo, Susan. *Unbearable Weight: Feminism, Western Culture, and the Body*. Los Angeles: University of California Press, 1993.

Bourdieu, Pierre. *The Field of Cultural Production: Essays on Art and Literature*. New York: Columbia University Press, 1993.

———. *In Other Words: Essays Towards a Reflexive Sociology*. Translated by Matthew Adamson. Stanford: Stanford University Press, 1990.

Bowler, Kate. *Blessed: A History of the American Prosperity Gospel*. New York: Oxford University Press, 2013.

Brand, Peg Zeglin, ed. *Beauty Matters*. Indianapolis: Indiana University Press, 2000.

Brasher, Brenda E. *Godly Women: Fundamentalism and Female Power*. New Brunswick, N.J.: Rutgers University Press, 1998.

Brekus, Catherine A., ed. *The Religious History of American Women: Reimagining the Past*. Chapel Hill: University of North Carolina Press, 2007.

Brown, Jonathon D., and Frances M, Gallagher. "Coming to Terms with Failure: Private Self-Enhancement and Public Self-Effacement." *Journal of Experimental Social Psychology* 28, no. 1 (1992): 3–22.

Brumberg, Joan Jacobs. *The Body Project: An Intimate History of American Girls*. New York: Vintage Books, 1998.

Butler, Judith. *Gender Trouble: Feminism and the Subversion of Identity*. New York: Routledge, 1999.

Butler, Judith, and Joan W. Scott, eds. *Feminists Theorize the Political*. New York: Routledge, 1992.

Byrne, Julie. *O God of Players: The Story of the Immaculata Mighty Macs*. New York: Columbia University Press, 2003.

Callaghan, Karen A., ed. *Ideals of Feminine Beauty: Philosophical, Social, and Cultural Dimensions*. Westport, Conn.: Greenwood Press, 1994.

Calogero, Rachel M., Stacey Tantleff-Dunn, and J. Kevin Thompson, eds. *Self-Objectification in Women: Causes, Consequences, and Counteractions*. Washington, D.C.: American Psychological Association, 2011.

Cartwright, Martina M. "Princess by Proxy: What Child Beauty Pageants Teach Girls about Self-Worth and What We Can Do about It." *Journal of the American Academy of Child and Adolescent Psychiatry* 51, no. 11 (2012): 1105–7.

Chaves, Mark. "Rain Dances in the Dry Season: Overcoming the Religious Congruence Fallacy." *Journal for the Scientific Study of Religion* 49, no. 1 (2010): 1–14.

Chinoy, Helen Krich, and Linda Walsh Jenkins, eds. *Women in American Theatre*. New York: Theatre Communications Groups, 1981.

Cohan, John Alan. "Towards a New Paradigm in the Ethics of Women's Advertising." *Journal of Business Ethics* 33, no. 4 (2001): 323–37.

Cohen, Anthony P. *The Symbolic Construction of Community*. New York: Routledge, 1985.

Cohen, Colleen Ballerino, Richard Wilk, and Beverly Stoeltje, eds. *Beauty Queens on the Global Stage: Gender, Contests, and Power*. New York: Routledge, 1996.

Conley, Terry D., and Laura R. Ramsey. "Killing Us Softly? Investigating Portrayals of Women and Men in Contemporary Magazine Advertisements." *Psychology of Women Quarterly* 35, no. 3 (2011): 469–78.

Cox, Harvey. "Miss America and the Cult of The Girl." *Christianity and Crisis* 7 (August 1961): 143–46.

Craig, Maxine Leeds. *Ain't I a Beauty Queen? Black Women, Beauty, and the Politics of Race*. New York: Oxford University Press, 2002.

D'Antonio, Michael. *Mortal Sins: Sex, Crime, and the Era of Catholic Scandal*. New York: Thomas Dunne, 2013.

Deford, Frank. *There She Is: The Life and Times of Miss America*. New York: Viking Press, 1971.

Dew, Sheri L. *Sharlene Wells: Miss America*. Salt Lake City: Deseret Book Company, 1985.

Dow, Bonnie J. "Feminism, Miss America, and Media Mythology." *Rhetoric and Public Affairs* 6, no. 1 (2003): 127–49.

———. *Watching Women's Liberation, 1970: Feminism's Pivotal Year on the Network News*. Champaign: University of Illinois Press, 2014.

Dowland, Seth. *Family Values and the Rise of the Christian Right*. Philadelphia: University of Pennsylvania Press, 2015.

Dworkin, Susan, and Bess Myerson. *Miss America, 1945: Bess Myerson and the Year that Changed our Lives*. New York: Newmarket Press, 2000.

Echols, Alice. *Daring to Be Bad: Radical Feminism in America, 1967–1975*. Minneapolis: University of Minnesota Press, 1989.

Edwards, Jason A., and Joseph M. Valenzano III, eds. *The Rhetoric of American Civil Religion: Symbols, Saints, and Sinners*. New York: Lexington Books, 2016.

Entwistle, Joanne, and Elizabeth Wissinger, eds. *Fashioning Models: Image, Text and Industry*. New York: Berg, 2012.

Etcoff, Nancy. *Survival of the Prettiest: The Science of Beauty*. New York: Doubleday, 1999.

Farnham, Christie Anne. *The Education of the Southern Belle: Higher Education and Student Socialization in the Antebellum South*. New York: New York University Press, 1994.

Felder, Deborah G. *A Century of Women: The Most Influential Events in Twentieth-Century Women's History*. New York: Citadel Press Books, 1999.

Fisher, Maryanne L., ed. *The Oxford Handbook of Women and Competition*. New York: Oxford University Press, 2017.

Florence, Anna Carter. *Preaching as Testimony*. Louisville: Westminster John Knox, 2007.

Flowers, Elizabeth H. *Into the Pulpit: Southern Baptist Women and Power since World War II*. Chapel Hill: University of North Carolina Press, 2012.

Flynt, Wayne, and Gerald W. Berkley. *Taking Christianity to China: Alabama Missionaries in the Middle Kingdom, 1850–1950*. Tuscaloosa: University of Alabama Press, 1997.

Fowler, James W. *Stages of Faith: The Psychology of Human Development and the Quest for Meaning*. New York: HarperOne, 1981.

Fredrickson, Barbara L., Tomi-Ann Roberts, Stephanie M. Noll, Diane M. Quinn, and Jean M. Twenge. "That Swimsuit Becomes You: Sex Differences in Self-Objectification, Restrained Eating, and Math Performance." *Journal of Personality and Social Psychology* 75, no. 1 (1998): 269–84.

Freedman, Rita. *Beauty Bound*. Lexington, Mass.: Lexington Books, 1986.

Freese, Jeremy, and Sheri Meland. "Seven Tenths Incorrect: Heterogeneity and Change in the Waist-to-Hip Ratios of Playboy Centerfold Models and Miss America Pageant Winners." *Journal of Sex Research* 39, no. 2 (May 2002): 133–38.

Friedman, James, ed. *Reality Squared: Televisual Discourse on the Real*. New Brunswick, N.J.: Rutgers University Press, 2002.

Gasaway, Brantley W. *Progressive Evangelicals and the Pursuit of Social Justice*. Chapel Hill: University of North Carolina Press, 2014.

Gaustad, Edwin S., ed. *Memoirs of the Spirit: American Religious Autobiography from Jonathan Edwards to Maya Angelou*. Grand Rapids: Eerdmans, 1999.

George, Phyllis. *Never Say Never: Ten Lessons to Turn You Can't into Yes I Can*. New York: McGraw-Hill, 2003.

Gerber, Lynne. *Seeking the Straight and Narrow: Weight Loss and Sexual Reorientation in Evangelical America*. Chicago: University of Chicago Press, 2011.

Giles, David. *Illusions of Immortality: A Psychology of Fame and Celebrity*. New York: Palgrave Macmillan, 2000.

Gilligan, Carol. *In a Different Voice: Psychological Theory and Women's Development*. Cambridge, Mass.: Harvard University Press, 1993.

———. *Joining the Resistance*. Malden, Mass.: Polity Press, 2011.

Gimlin, Debra L. *Body Work: Beauty and Self-Image in American Culture*. Los Angeles: University of California Press, 2002.

Glassberg, David. *American Historical Pageantry: The Uses of Tradition in the Early Twentieth Century*. Chapel Hill: University of North Carolina Press, 1990.

Goodall, H. L., Jr. *Writing the New Ethnography*. Lanham, Md.: AltaMira, 2000.

Griffith, R. Marie. *Born Again Bodies: Flesh and Spirit in American Christianity*. Los Angeles, University of California Press, 2004.

———. *God's Daughters: Evangelical Women and the Power of Submission*. Los Angeles: University of California Press, 2000.

———. *Moral Combat: How Sex Divided American Christians and Fractured American Politics*. New York: Basic Books, 2017.

Hains, Rebecca C. *The Princess Problem: Guiding our Girls through the Princess-Obsessed Years*. Naperville, Ill.: Sourcebooks, 2014.

Hall, David S., ed. *Lived Religion in America: Toward a History of Practice*. Princeton, N.J.: Princeton University Press, 1997.

Hamilton, Michael S. "Women, Public Ministry, and American Fundamentalism, 1920–1950." *Religion and American Culture: A Journal of Interpretation* 3, no. 2 (1993): 171–96.

Hardesty, Nancy A. *Women Called to Witness: Evangelical Feminism in the Nineteenth Century*. 2nd ed. Knoxville: University of Tennessee Press, 1999.

Harman, Katie. *Under the Crown: 51 Stories of Courage, Determination and the American Spirit*. Seattle: Milestone Books, 2002.

Harvey, Paul, and Edward J. Blum, eds. *The Columbia Guide to Religion in American History*. New York: Columbia University Press, 2012.

Haskell, Sam, with David Rensin. Foreword by Ray Romano. *Promises I Made My Mother*. New York: Ballantine Books, 2009.

Hatch, Nathan O. *The Democratization of American Christianity*. New Haven: Yale University Press, 1989.

Hawkes, Sharlene. *Kissing a Frog: Four Steps to Finding Comfort Outside Your Comfort Zone*. Salt Lake City: Shadow Mountain, 2002.

———. *Living in but Not of the World*. Salt Lake City: Deseret Book Company, 1997.

Herberg, Will. *Protestant, Catholic, Jew: An Essay in American Religious Sociology*. Chicago: University of Chicago Press, 1983.

Hill, Samuel S. *Southern Churches in Crisis Revisited*. Tuscaloosa: University of Alabama Press, 1999.

Hoffman, Shirl James. *Good Game: Christianity and the Culture of Sports*. Waco, Tex.: Baylor University Press, 2010.

Horton, Dennis J. "Discerning Spiritual Discernment: Assessing Current Approaches for Understanding God's Will." *Journal of Youth Ministry* 7, no. 2 (2009): 7–31.

Huffman, Douglas S., ed. *How Then Should We Choose? Three Views on God's Will and Decision Making*. Grand Rapids: Kregel Publications, 2009.

Hutchison, William R. *Religious Pluralism in America: The Contentious History of a Founding Ideal*. New Haven: Yale University Press, 2003.

Isserman, Maurice, and Michael Kazin. *America Divided: The Civil War of the 1960s*. 5th ed. New York: Oxford University Press, 2015.

Jackson-Jordan, Elizabeth Ann. "Clergy Burnout and Resilience: A Review of the Literature." *Journal of Pastoral Care and Counseling* 67, no. 1 (2013): 1–5.

Jaffee, Steven M., and Janet Shibley Hyde. "Gender Differences in Moral Orientation: A Meta-analysis." *Psychological Bulletin* 132 (2000): 23–72.

Jayroe, Jane, and Bob Burke. *More Grace than Glamour: My Life as Miss America and Beyond*. Oklahoma City: Oklahoma Heritage Association, 2006.

Jeffreys, Sheila. *Beauty and Misogyny: Harmful Cultural Practices in the West*. New York: Routledge, 2005.

Johnson, Nicole. *Living with Diabetes: Nicole Johnson, Miss America 1999*. Washington, D.C.: Lifeline Press, 2001.

Jones, Donald G., and Russell E. Richey, eds. *American Civil Religion*. San Francisco: Mellen Research University Press, 1990.

Jones, Jennifer. "The Beauty Queen as Deified Sacrificial Victim." *Theatre History Studies* 18 (June 1998): 99–106.

Keller, Evelyn Fox, and Helene Moglen. "Competition and Feminism: Conflicts for Academic Women." *Signs* 12, no. 3 (1987): 493–511.

King-O'Riain, Rebecca Chiyoko. "Making the Perfect Queen: The Cultural Production of Identities in Beauty Pageants." *Sociology Compass* 21, no. 1 (2008): 74–83.

———. *Pure Beauty: Judging Race in Japanese American Beauty Pageants*. Minneapolis: University of Minnesota Press, 2006.

Kreydatus, Beth. "'Enriching Women's Lives': The Mary Kay Approach to Business, Beauty, and Feminism." *Business and Economic History Online* 3 (2005).

Laderman, Gary. *Sacred Matters: Celebrity Worship, Sexual Ecstasies, the Living Dead, and Other Signs of Religious Life in the United States*. New York: The New Press, 2009.

Latham, Angela J. "Packaging Woman: The Concurrent Rise of Beauty Pageants, Public Bathing, and Other Performances of Female 'Nudity.'" *Journal of Popular Culture* 29, no. 3 (1995): 149–67.

———. *Posing a Threat: Flappers, Chorus Girls, and Other Brazen Performers of the American 1920s*. Hanover, Mass.: Wesleyan University Press, 2000.

Lassiter, Luke Eric. *The Chicago Guide to Collaborative Ethnography*. Chicago: University of Chicago Press, 2005.

Lippy, Charles H. *Introducing American Religion*. New York: Routledge, 2009.

Lofton, Kathryn. *Oprah: The Gospel of an Icon*. Los Angeles: University of California Press, 2011.

Lukes, Timothy J. *Politics and Beauty in America: The Liberal Aesthetics of P. T. Barnum, John Muir, and Harley Earl*. New York: Palgrave Macmillan, 2016.

Lumsden, Linda J. *Rampant Women: Suffragists and the Right of Assembly*. Knoxville: University of Tennessee Press, 1997.

Maddox, Debra Deitering. "The Miss America Pageant's Influence on the Self-Construction of Its 1985 Contestants." Master's thesis, University of Nebraska, 2001.

Maffly-Kipp, Laurie F., Leigh Eric Schmidt, Mark R. Valeri, eds. *Practicing Protestants: Histories of Christian Life in America: 1630–1965*. Baltimore: Johns Hopkins University Press, 2006.

Marsden, George M. *Fundamentalism and American Culture: The Shaping of Twentieth-Century Evangelicalism, 1870–1925*. New York: Oxford University Press, 1980.

Marsh, Robin, and Lauren Nelson. *God, Girls, and Getting Connected: Spiritual Apps for a Teen's Life*. Eugene, Ore.: Harvest House Publishers, 2012.

Martin, Nancie E. *Miss America through the Looking Glass: The Story behind the Scenes*. New York: Little Simon, 1985.

Marwick, Arthur. *The Sixties: Cultural Revolution in Britain, France, Italy, and the United States, c. 1958–c. 1974*. Oxford: Oxford University Press, 1998.

McAdams, Dan. *The Stories We Live by: Personal Myths and the Making of the Self*. New York: Guilford, 1993.

McCallum, Heather Whitestone, and Angela Hunt. *Let God Surprise You: Trust God with Your Dreams*. Grand Rapids: Zondervan, 2003.

McKnight, Scot, and Hauna Ondrey. *Finding Faith, Losing Faith: Stories of Conversion and Apostasy*. Waco, Tex.: Baylor University Press, 2008.

Miss America: A Documentary Film. DVD. Directed by Lisa Ades. Brooklyn: Clio and Orchard Films, 2001.

Monty, Shirlee. *Terry*. Waco, Tex.: Word Books, 1982.

Morgan, Edmund S. *The Puritan Dilemma: The Story of John Winthrop*. New York: Longman, 1999.

Morgan, Robin, ed. *Sisterhood Is Powerful: An Anthology of Writings from the Women's Liberation Movement*. New York: Random House, 1970.

Moslener, Sara. *Virgin Nation: Sexual Purity and American Adolescence*. New York: Oxford University Press, 2015.

Neal, Lynn. *Romancing God: Evangelical Women and Inspirational Fiction*. Chapel Hill: University of North Carolina Press, 2006.

Neimark, Jill. "Why We Need Miss America." *Psychology Today* 31, no. 5 (1998).

Niebuhr, H. Richard. *Christ and Culture*. New York: Harper & Brothers, 1951.

Niederle, Muriel, and Lise Vesterlund. "Do Women Shy Away from Competition? Do Men Compete Too Much?" *Quarterly Journal of Economics* 122, no. 3 (2007): 1067–1101.

———. "Gender and Competition." *Annual Review of Economics* 3 (2001): 601–30.

Noll, Mark A. *America's God: From Jonathan Edwards to Abraham Lincoln*. New York: Oxford University Press, 2002.

———. *The Rise of Evangelicalism: The Age of Edwards, Whitefield, and the Wesleys*. Downers Grove, Ill.: InterVarsity, 2003.

Oliver, M. Cynthia. *Queen of the Virgins: Pageantry and Black Womanhood in the Caribbean*. Jackson: University of Mississippi Press, 2009.

Oppliger, Patrice A. *Girls Gone Skank: The Sexualization of Girls in American Culture*. Jefferson, N.C.: McFarland & Company, 2008.

Orenstein, Peggy. *Cinderella Ate My Daughter: Dispatches from the Front Lines of the New Girlie-Girl Culture*. New York: HarperCollins, 2011.

Osborne, Angela Saulino. *Miss America: The Dream Lives On: A 75 Year Celebration*. Dallas: Taylor, 1995.

Pearlman, Peggy. *Pretty Smart: Lessons from Our Miss Americas*. Bloomington, Ind.: AuthorHouse, 2009.

Peiss, Kathy. *Cheap Amusements: Working Women and Leisure in Turn-of-the-Century New York*. Philadelphia: Temple University Press, 1986.

———. *Hope in a Jar: The Making of America's Beauty Culture*. New York: Metropolitan Books, 1998.

Penaloza, Lisa, Nil Toulose, and Luca Massimiliano Visconti, eds. *Marketing Management: A Cultural Perspective*. New York: Routledge, 2012.

Platek, Steven M., and Devendra Singh. "Optimal Waist-to-Hip Ratios in Women Activate Neural Reward Centers in Men." *PLoS ONE* 5 no. 2 (2010): pe9042.

Prejean, Carrie. *Still Standing: The Untold Story of My Fight against Gossip, Hate, and Political Attacks*. Washington, D.C.: Regnery, 2009.

Preston, Jennifer. *Queen Bess: An Unauthorized Biography of Bess Myerson*. Chicago: Contemporary Books, 1990.

Prewitt, Cheryl, with Kathryn Slattery. *A Bright-Shining Place: The Story of a Miracle*. Garden City, N.Y.: Doubleday, 1981.

Prothero, Stephen. *American Jesus: How the Son of God Became a National Icon*. New York: Farrar, Straus and Giroux, 2003.

Rajagopal, Indhu, and Jennifer Gales. "It's the Image That Is Imperfect: Advertising and Its Impact on Women." *Economic and Political Weekly* 37, no. 32 (2002): 3333–37.

Rhode, Deborah L. *The Beauty Bias: The Injustice of Appearance in Life and Law*. New York: Oxford University Press, 2010.

Riverol, A. R. *Live from Atlantic City: A History of the Miss America Pageant before, after and in spite of Television*. Bowling Green, Ohio: Bowling Green State University Popular Press, 1992.

———. "Myth America and Other Misses: A Second Look at the American Beauty Contests." *ETC: A Review of General Semantics* 40, no. 2 (1983): 207–17.

Roberts, Blain. *Pageants, Parlors, and Pretty Women: Race and Beauty in the Twentieth-Century South.* Chapel Hill: University of North Carolina Press, 2014.

Roberts, Mary Louise. "Gender, Consumption, and Commodity Culture." *American Historical Review* 103, no. 3 (1998): 817–44.

Rowe, Rochelle. *Imagining Caribbean Womanhood: Race, Nation, and Beauty Contests, 1929–1970.* Manchester: Manchester University Press, 2013.

Santo, Elaine Campanelli. *From Glamour to Glory.* Maitland, Fla.: Xulon Press, 2010.

Sayles, Ginie Polo. *How to Win Pageants.* Plano, Tex.: Wordware, 1990.

Scott, Anne Firor. *The Southern Lady: From Pedestal to Politics 1830–1930.* 25th Anniversary Edition. Charlottesville: University Press of Virginia, 1995.

Scott, Joan W. "Gender: A Useful Category of Historical Analysis." *The American Historical Review* 91, no. 5 (1986): 1053–75.

Schearing, Linda S., and Valarie H. Ziegler. *Enticed by Eden: How Western Culture Uses, Confuses, (and Sometimes Abuses) Adam and Eve.* Waco, Tex.: Baylor University Press, 2013.

Shibley, Mark A. "The Southernization of American Religion: Testing a Hypothesis." *Sociological Analysis* 52, no. 2 (1991): 159–74.

Shindle, Kate. *Being Miss America: Behind the Rhinestone Curtain.* Austin: University of Texas Press, 2014.

Singh, Devendra. "Adaptive Significance of Female Physical Attractiveness: Role of Waist-to-Hip Ratio." *Journal of Personality and Social Pyschology* 65, no. 2 (1993): 293–307.

Singh, Devendra, and Patrick K. Randall. "Beauty Is in the Eye of the Plastic Surgeon: Waist-Hip Ratio (WHR) and Women's Attractiveness." *Personality and Individual Differences* 42 (2007): 329–40.

Steinberg, Shirley R., and Joe L. Kincheloe, eds. *Christotainment: Selling Jesus through Popular Culture.* Boulder, Colo.: Westview Press, 2009.

Stevenson, Jill. *Sensational Devotion: Evangelical Performance in Twenty-First-Century America.* Ann Arbor: University of Michigan Press, 2015.

Tice, Karen W. *Queens of Academe: Beauty Pageantry, Student Bodies, and College Life.* New York: Oxford University Press, 2012.

Trueblood, Becki, as told to Rhonda Graham. *Best for Me.* Boise, Idaho: Pacific Press Publishing Association, 1991.

Tweed, Thomas A., ed. *Retelling U.S. Religious History.* Los Angeles: University of California Press, 1997.

Van Derbur, Marilyn. *Miss America by Day: Lessons Learned from Ultimate Betrayals and Unconditional Love.* Denver: Oak Hill Ridge Press, 2012.

Van Dyke, Vonda Kay. *Dear Vonda Kay: Former Miss American Vonda Kay Van Dyke Answers Questions Teen-agers Ask.* Westwood, N.J.: Fleming H. Revell Company, 1967.

————. *That Girl in Your Mirror*. Westwood, N.J.: Fleming H. Revell Company, 1966.

Verter, Bradford. "Spiritual Capital: Theorizing Religion with Bourdieu against Bourdieu." *Sociological Theory* 21, no. 2 (2003): 150–74.

Wacker, Grant. "Billy Graham's America." *Church History* 78, no. 3 (2009): 489–511.

————. *Heaven Below: Early Pentecostals and America Culture*. Cambridge, Mass.: Harvard University Press, 2001.

Warner, Laceye. *Saving Women: Retrieving Evangelistic Theology and Practice*. Waco, Tex.: Baylor University Press, 2007.

Watson, Elwood, and Darcy Martin, eds. *The Politics of Sex, Beauty, and Race in America's Most Famous Pageant*. New York: Palgrave Macmillan, 2004.

————. "The Miss America Pageant: Pluralism, Femininity, and Cinderella All in One." *Journal of Popular Culture* 34, no. 1 (2000): 105–26.

Welch, Georgia Paige. "'Up against the Wall Miss America': Women's Liberation and Miss Black America in Atlantic City, 1968." *Feminist Formations* 27, no. 2 (2015): 70–97.

Welter, Barbara. "The Cult of True Womanhood: 1820–1860." *American Quarterly* 18, no. 2, part 1 (1966): 151–74.

Wesley, John. *A Plain Account of Christian Perfection*. Edited and annotated by Randy Maddox and Paul W. Chilcote. Kansas City, Mo.: Beacon Hill, 2015.

Whitestone, Heather, with Angela Elwell Hunt. *Listening with My Heart*. New York: Doubleday, 1997.

Wilson, Charles Reagan. "Beauty, Cult of." In *The New Encyclopedia of Southern Culture*, Volume 13: Gender, edited by Nancy Bercaw and Ted Ownby, 30–40. Chapel Hill: University of North Carolina Press, 2009.

————. *Judgment and Grace in Dixie: Southern Faiths from Faulkner to Elvis*. Athens: University of Georgia Press, 1995.

Wolf, Naomi. *The Beauty Myth: How Images of Beauty Are Used against Women*. New York: HarperCollins Perennial, 2002.

Wright, Kelsey. "Sexual Objectification of Female Bodies in Beauty Pageants, Pornography, and Media." *Dissenting Voices* 6, no. 1 (2017): 125–46.

Yano, Christine R. *Crowning the Nice Girl: Gender, Ethnicity, and Culture in Hawai'i's Cherry Blossom Festival*. Honolulu: University of Hawai'i' Press, 2006.

Index

perfection: effortless, 179n95; inability to achieve, 149, 178n82; promoted by pageants, 29, 59, 77, 140, 147; pursuit of, 13, 124, 139, 191n7, 226n142

Phillips, Marti Sue, 136

photo contest, 13, 39–40, 183n19

physical fitness: pageant's emphasis on, 29, 57; swimsuit competition and, 25, 27, 179n88, 179n89; *see also* swimsuit competition

Pickford, Mary, 14, 166n18

platform, 2, 4, 52, 60, 67, 82, 84, 97, 99, 100, 111, 125–26, 129–30, 143, 147, 159n24, 192n17, 201n89, 203n12, 210n102, 222m69; *see also* charity work; community service

poise, 27, 73, 75, 119–120, 160n26, 174n52

pornography, 182n10; pageants as different from, 20, 31, 32, 33, 172n43

power, agency and, 169n25

prayers: at pageants, 86; for pageant contestants, 94, 95, 133; of pageant contestants, 70, 113, 115–17, 120, 124, 127, 130, 133, 135–37, 141, 223n77; in public sphere, 104

Prejean, Carrie, 105–6, 108, 214n132

Prewitt, Cheryl, 3, 26, 74, 82, 101, 111, 113, 114–17, 120, 124, 126, 132, 136, 197n47, 200n72, 218n20, 219n31, 219n34, 219n35, 221n60, 226n131

Princess Camp, 75

princess culture, 6, 188n68

prostitution, 20, 33, 183n18; compared to pageants, 23–24

Pure International Pageants, 160n25

Quality of Life Award, 60, 99, 192n17, 197n46

Rabinowitz, Loren Galler, 96, 208n77

Raffo, Claudia, 64

Rafko, Kaye Lani Rae, 192n17

reality television: featuring pageants, 51–52; impact on Miss America Pageant, 37, 45–47, 146, 186n48

Rising Stars, 75

ritual, pageant as, 7, 13, 86, 148, 205n17

Rogers, Ali, 9, 28, 179n94, 188n68, 223n88

Rosie the Riveter, 87

Saltalamacchio, Chris, 188n65

Samford University, 102, 197n46, 207n60

Sawyer, Diane, 97

Scanlan, Teresa, 13, 55–56, 117, 126, 188n68, 201n85, 211n109, 220n37, 222n69

scholarships: amount for Miss America winner, 187n58; disparity between states, 63, 194n29; Miss America Pageant's emphasis on, 4, 24, 29, 30, 31, 46, 78; establishment of, 19, 91–92; first Miss America to benefit from, 92–93; marketing women's bodies for, 19, 139, 177n75; reason for competing, 2–3, 24, 63, 122, 194n28; *see also* Oliver, John

Scott, Joan W., 159n20, 161n39

Sesame Street, 6, 161n35

sexualization of young girls, 6, 188n69

Shelton, Sarah, 96

Shelton, Stephanie, 94

Shields, Savvy, 74, 199n61

Shindle, Kate, 59, 70, 184n27, 187n56, 187n58, 188n66, 193n24, 200n70, 206n37, 210n94

Shopp, BeBe, 200n81, 202n4, 217n13

Show Me Your Shoes Parade, 8, 85